VICTORIAN CONTINGENCIES

Victorian Contingencies

Experiments in Literature, Science, and Play

TINA YOUNG CHOI

STANFORD UNIVERSITY PRESS
Stanford, California

STANFORD UNIVERSITY PRESS
Stanford, California

Printed in the United States of America on acid-free, archival-quality paper

Library of Congress Cataloging-in-Publication Data

Names: Choi, Tina Young, author.

Title: Victorian contingencies : experiments in literature, science, and play / Tina Young Choi.

Description: Stanford, California : Stanford University Press, [2022] | Includes bibliographical references and index.

Identifiers: LCCN 2021007876 (print) | LCCN 2021007877 (ebook) | ISBN 9781503629288 (cloth) | ISBN 9781503629769 (ebook)

Subjects: LCSH: English literature—19th century—History and criticism. | Science—Great Britain—History—19th century. | Amusements—Great Britain—History—19th century. | Great Britain—Civilization—19th century. | Great Britain—Social life and customs—19th century.

Classification: LCC DA533 .C545 2022 (print) | LCC DA533 (ebook) | DDC 941.081—dc23

LC record available at https://lccn.loc.gov/2021007876

LC ebook record available at https://lccn.loc.gov/2021007877

Cover illustration: Two views of Mt. Vesuvius, interleaved, from "Spooner's Protean Views" (London: W. Spooner, c. 1840).

Cover design: George Kirkpatrick

Text design: Kevin Barrett Kane

Typeset at Stanford University Press in 11/15 Arno Pro

Table of Contents

List of Illustrations

Acknowledgments

This book is the product of many years' worth of conversations, friendships, and events. At York University, much encouragement came from members of the Victorian Studies Network, especially Janet Friskney, Lesley Higgins, and David Latham, and from my colleagues in Science and Technology Studies, Katey Anderson and Bernie Lightman, who were exceptionally generous with their support and feedback. I feel privileged to have enjoyed long conversations about causality with Barbara Leckie and with Edward Jones-Imhotep; the experience of co-authoring essays with both of them contributed in meaningful ways to my thinking about contingency. They and Dennis Denisoff, Debra Gettelman, Tamara Ketabgian, Christine Lehleiter, and Simon Reader were friendly, thoughtful readers of portions of this work. Dan Bivona, Cathy Gallagher, Hao Li, and Andrew Miller offered advice and encouragement at crucial points, and Darren Gobert, Roslyn McKendry, and the late Nancy Abelmann enlivened periods of research and writing with their kindness, humor, and wisdom.

Various conferences—hosted by the Northeast Conference on British Studies, the International Society for the Study of Narrative, the Modern Language Association, and especially the North American Victorian Studies Association—effectively served as a series of workshops for this manuscript over the years. I'm also grateful to colleagues who invited me to give presentations at their institutions, where I received substantive feedback about portions of this work; these include Mark Knight, Christine Lehleiter, Terry Robinson, and Rebecca Woods at the University of Toronto; and Shelley King and Glenn Willmott at Queen's University.

Preliminary versions of my argument about Maxwell and *Daniel Deronda in Chapter 4* appeared in a workshop proceeding following an event organized by Mathias Grote, Laura Otis, and Max Stadler at the Max Planck Institute for the History of Science in 2011, and later as a chapter, "Physics Disarmed: Probabilistic Knowledge in the Works of James Clerk Maxwell and George Eliot," in *Fact and Fiction: Literary and Scientific Cultures in Germany and Britain*, edited by Christine Lehleiter (University of Toronto Press, 2016). A much earlier version of my argument about Darwin and *Adam Bede* appeared as "Natural History's Hypothetical Moments: Narratives of Contingency in Victorian Culture" in *Victorian Studies* 51 (2009): 275–297, and criticisms and suggestions from the special issue editor, Jonathan Smith, and two anonymous readers were invaluable in shaping not only that article but also what eventually became this book's second chapter.

York University provided much needed material support at key points, enabling me to employ Leslie Garratt and Olivia Holzapfel, graduate assistants whose excellent efforts at this project's earliest stages paid dividends for years afterwards, and Rachelle Stinson, a research assistant to whose careful eye I entrusted the final version. A Faculty of Arts Research Grant from the university allowed me to begin archival research on this project. I am also grateful for support from the Faculty of Liberal Arts & Professional Studies at York University as well as a Social Sciences and Humanities Research Council Exchange—Knowledge Mobilization Grant administered by York, both of which helped to bring this book to publication.

The research that went into these chapters depended on much invisible labor by librarians and archivists across North America and Britain, and I regret not being able to acknowledge them all properly here. Among those I came to know personally, I'd like to thank Lisa Sloniowski at York University Libraries and Catherine Howell at the Victoria and Albert Museum of Childhood. During the pandemic, the staff at several archives worked wonders to assist with requests in the final stages, including those at Harvard Business School's Baker Library, at Yale University's Beinecke Library and Center for British Art,

at the Bill Douglas Cinema Museum (especially Dr. Phil Wickham, the curator there), at the London Metropolitan Archives, and at the Lillian H. Smith
Branch of the Toronto Public Library.

I feel beyond fortunate that my manuscript landed in Faith Wilson Stein's
inbox at Stanford University Press. Her enthusiasm about the project from the
outset—and her prompt responses, candor, and wise counsel throughout—
made a potentially difficult process seem straightforward. Thanks to her, I had
two readers who engaged with my manuscript in truly thoughtful and perceptive ways. And she, Emily Smith, and Jennifer Gordon guided the manuscript
through its final stages at Stanford with exceptional professionalism and care.

This book also belongs in part to my mother, Elizabeth Choi, who has long
loved the contingencies of the stock market and of roller coaster rides, and to
my late father, Sung C. Choi, a statistician. And to Louis Suárez-Potts, who
shared in every stage of this project and was always happy to read another
draft—and is reading another right now, even as I write this—these pages
and I owe so much.

Victorian Contingencies

Experiments in Literature, Science, and Play

TINA YOUNG CHOI

STANFORD UNIVERSITY PRESS
Stanford, California

STANFORD UNIVERSITY PRESS
Stanford, California

Printed in the United States of America on acid-free, archival-quality paper

Library of Congress Cataloging-in-Publication Data

Names: Choi, Tina Young, author.

Title: Victorian contingencies : experiments in literature, science, and play / Tina Young Choi.

Description: Stanford, California : Stanford University Press, [2022] | Includes bibliographical references and index.

Identifiers: LCCN 2021007876 (print) | LCCN 2021007877 (ebook) | ISBN 9781503629288 (cloth) | ISBN 9781503629769 (ebook)

Subjects: LCSH: English literature—19th century—History and criticism. | Science—Great Britain—History—19th century. | Amusements—Great Britain—History—19th century. | Great Britain—Civilization—19th century. | Great Britain—Social life and customs—19th century.

Classification: LCC DA533 .C545 2022 (print) | LCC DA533 (ebook) | DDC 941.081—dc23

LC record available at https://lccn.loc.gov/2021007876

LC ebook record available at https://lccn.loc.gov/2021007877

Cover illustration: Two views of Mt. Vesuvius, interleaved, from "Spooner's Protean Views" (London: W. Spooner, c. 1840).

Cover design: George Kirkpatrick

Text design: Kevin Barrett Kane

Typeset at Stanford University Press in 11/15 Arno Pro

Table of Contents

List of Illustrations

Acknowledgments

This book is the product of many years' worth of conversations, friendships, and events. At York University, much encouragement came from members of the Victorian Studies Network, especially Janet Friskney, Lesley Higgins, and David Latham, and from my colleagues in Science and Technology Studies, Katey Anderson and Bernie Lightman, who were exceptionally generous with their support and feedback. I feel privileged to have enjoyed long conversations about causality with Barbara Leckie and with Edward Jones-Imhotep; the experience of co-authoring essays with both of them contributed in meaningful ways to my thinking about contingency. They and Dennis Denisoff, Debra Gettelman, Tamara Ketabgian, Christine Lehleiter, and Simon Reader were friendly, thoughtful readers of portions of this work. Dan Bivona, Cathy Gallagher, Hao Li, and Andrew Miller offered advice and encouragement at crucial points, and Darren Gobert, Roslyn McKendry, and the late Nancy Abelmann enlivened periods of research and writing with their kindness, humor, and wisdom.

Various conferences—hosted by the Northeast Conference on British Studies, the International Society for the Study of Narrative, the Modern Language Association, and especially the North American Victorian Studies Association—effectively served as a series of workshops for this manuscript over the years. I'm also grateful to colleagues who invited me to give presentations at their institutions, where I received substantive feedback about portions of this work; these include Mark Knight, Christine Lehleiter, Terry Robinson, and Rebecca Woods at the University of Toronto; and Shelley King and Glenn Willmott at Queen's University.

Preliminary versions of my argument about Maxwell and *Daniel Deronda in Chapter 4* appeared in a workshop proceeding following an event organized by Mathias Grote, Laura Otis, and Max Stadler at the Max Planck Institute for the History of Science in 2011, and later as a chapter, "Physics Disarmed: Probabilistic Knowledge in the Works of James Clerk Maxwell and George Eliot," in *Fact and Fiction: Literary and Scientific Cultures in Germany and Britain*, edited by Christine Lehleiter (University of Toronto Press, 2016). A much earlier version of my argument about Darwin and *Adam Bede* appeared as "Natural History's Hypothetical Moments: Narratives of Contingency in Victorian Culture" in *Victorian Studies* 51 (2009): 275–297, and criticisms and suggestions from the special issue editor, Jonathan Smith, and two anonymous readers were invaluable in shaping not only that article but also what eventually became this book's second chapter.

York University provided much needed material support at key points, enabling me to employ Leslie Garratt and Olivia Holzapfel, graduate assistants whose excellent efforts at this project's earliest stages paid dividends for years afterwards, and Rachelle Stinson, a research assistant to whose careful eye I entrusted the final version. A Faculty of Arts Research Grant from the university allowed me to begin archival research on this project. I am also grateful for support from the Faculty of Liberal Arts & Professional Studies at York University as well as a Social Sciences and Humanities Research Council Exchange—Knowledge Mobilization Grant administered by York, both of which helped to bring this book to publication.

The research that went into these chapters depended on much invisible labor by librarians and archivists across North America and Britain, and I regret not being able to acknowledge them all properly here. Among those I came to know personally, I'd like to thank Lisa Sloniowski at York University Libraries and Catherine Howell at the Victoria and Albert Museum of Childhood. During the pandemic, the staff at several archives worked wonders to assist with requests in the final stages, including those at Harvard Business School's Baker Library, at Yale University's Beinecke Library and Center for British Art, at the Bill Douglas Cinema Museum (especially Dr. Phil Wickham, the curator there), at the London Metropolitan Archives, and at the Lillian H. Smith Branch of the Toronto Public Library.

I feel beyond fortunate that my manuscript landed in Faith Wilson Stein's inbox at Stanford University Press. Her enthusiasm about the project from the outset—and her prompt responses, candor, and wise counsel throughout—made a potentially difficult process seem straightforward. Thanks to her, I had two readers who engaged with my manuscript in truly thoughtful and perceptive ways. And she, Emily Smith, and Jennifer Gordon guided the manuscript through its final stages at Stanford with exceptional professionalism and care.

This book also belongs in part to my mother, Elizabeth Choi, who has long loved the contingencies of the stock market and of roller coaster rides, and to my late father, Sung C. Choi, a statistician. And to Louis Suárez-Potts, who shared in every stage of this project and was always happy to read another draft—and is reading another right now, even as I write this—these pages and I owe so much.

VICTORIAN CONTINGENCIES

INTRODUCTION

IN A SERIES OF ARTICLES published between June and September of 1837, the *Saturday Magazine* introduced readers to a relatively new consumer product, life insurance, by way of an actuarial vocabulary of numbers and ratios, payments and premiums. Yet in approaching the subject of "probability," the *Magazine*'s language took a dramatic, ominous turn. "[E]very event in nature is open to the possibility of happening or failing," the unnamed author explained, before conjuring a set of apocalyptic scenarios for readers: "The commonest occurrences, such as the rising and setting of the sun, and the changes of the seasons, which from infancy we have been accustomed to look upon as morally certain, are only, therefore, mathematically probable in a very high degree."[1]

The universe, it announced, was a contingent place. Past experience, which might have lent occurrences like the rising of the sun a semblance of certainty, was no guarantee of future events—just as, the article would go on to emphasize in subsequent pages, middle-class readers might find the long-enjoyed comforts of a steady income suddenly disrupted by illness or death. The contingencies of life and death as experienced through childbirth, warfare, and old age would surely have been familiar to these readers, many of whom would recall the way they'd been tested during the 1831–32 cholera epidemic and, a bit further back, in the Napoleonic Wars. But by situating contingency in the most quotidian and otherwise unexceptional of circumstances, the *Saturday Magazine* sought to startle readers, even healthy ones, out of complacency. It presented the seemingly extraordinary not within an older framework of miracle or divine intervention but in a newer language of probabilities and the calculus of chance, and it transformed even the most prosaic and certain occurrences so that not just the most expected or desired outcome, but any number of futures, might be possible at any given moment. By actively undetermining what were once thought to be assured outcomes, thinking contingently encompassed the previously unimaginable, inviting speculation about the relationships between past and future, cause and effect, a predictable result and an exceptional one. When and how, the *Magazine*'s readers might well have asked, had the "commonest occurrences" come to be treated as contingent?

To focus on contingency, to open "every event" to a range of potential outcomes, I argue, became a way for nineteenth-century writers, readers, scientists, and artists of all stripes to analyze causal operations and question narrative teleologies, as it also encouraged the shaping of new representational practices, techniques, and technologies. Scholarly work by sociologists, historians, and literary critics, among others, has had much to say about contingency, often associating it with twentieth- and twenty-first-century epistemologies, with modernism's refusals of determinism, and more lately, with the experimental qualities of postmodern and digital narratives. From this perspective, the Victorians, concerned as they were with order and closure, were slow to admit contingency's play of possibility. The present book, however, shows that contingency performed an essential, productive function in nineteenth-century culture. If the period revealed its investments in order and structure, it did so in dialogue with the sometimes disruptive but also creative engagements contingency invited with the formal apparatus of nineteenth-century visual and narrative representations. Through contingency, historical writing embraced narrative and temporal plasticity, while established fictional and visual genres experimented with incompletion, divergence, and reversibility. At the same time, through the act of representing contingency, these works established new sets of formal rules and parameters to describe the limits of chance.

The *Saturday Magazine* articles encouraged readers to see contingency as a part of their everyday lives, and that suggestion was amply reflected across a range of mid-century historical, scientific, literary, and religious texts, where authors wielded contingency as an analytical and epistemological tool for studying the causalities at the center of novelistic and natural narratives, for rethinking the nature of providential oversight, and for querying the teleologies that governed systems. When, at the end of Dickens's 1852–53 *Bleak House*, Esther Summerson looks back on the illness that marked a turning point in her life, she enlists the language of contingency, "I thought it was impossible that you *could* have loved me any better, even if I had retained [my looks]," as does Darwin in his 1859 *On the Origin of Species*, when he refers repeatedly to the "many complex contingencies" shaping the natural world.[2] The spatial logic of mid-century board games, with their multiply diverging and intersecting paths, made confrontations with contingency central to play, and scientific accounts calibrated the higher faculties of thinking and feeling against an ability to accommodate contingency. Thus Darwin, tracing the growth of the human mind, writes that the "direct instinct" of the child would eventually lead to "enlarged powers to meet with contingency,"[3] and Charles Babbage, explaining how a chess-playing automaton might approximate cognitive processes, describes a sequence of computations (of a type still recognizable to programmers) based on an assessment of contingencies: "If not, can he win it at the next move? If so, make that move."[4]

To be sure, contingency has a longer history than the one sketched by these examples. Classical and biblical texts demonstrated a grasp of the concept in other times and places, just as it was also relevant to both gambling and legal practice in Britain throughout the eighteenth century. But as early nineteenth-century writings turned to questions about origins and processes—whether in the form of post-Napoleonic histories tracing the links between past and present or in scientific investigations into geological and natural history—the operations of causality and contingency came under greater scrutiny than ever before. Through contingency radical discontinuities between past and future became imaginable. If a middle-class wife could become a penurious widow, then contingency raised the stakes on foresight, which the rising middle classes, poised between the certainties of aristocratic privilege on the one hand and of working-class poverty on the other, championed as their defining virtue. At the same time, the languages that might be used to describe contingency, which in earlier periods had been associated with philosophical and theological inquiry, expanded in the early decades of the century to encompass the apocalyptic as well as the actuarial and entered a range of genres. The emerging statistical and probabilistic sciences, the new geo- and natural histories of the earth, and on a more quotidian level, the rhetoric of life insurance and of historical reenactment: All of these spoke the language of contingency—and invited the public to consider the dimensions and limits of possibility.

While the concerns that contingency brought to the fore—regarding the relationships between determinism and chance, providence and free will, structure and free play—might have been abstract ones, the present book is particularly interested in the material forms it took during this period. Publishers and writers used contingency to animate narrative and natural systems, where it served as a virtual hinge joining one condition to another in temporal or causal relation.[5] When, in *Bleak House*, Esther ends her narrative "sitting here thinking" about the contingencies that have shaped her life,[6] she does just what so many of her contemporaries did, playing and replaying contingencies in the imagination. The board games they enjoyed as children increasingly reflected the workings of chance on a thematic and spatial level, allowing them to take a railway journey or evade pirate ships, for example, and the protean views— those optical toys that offered before-and-after images—they purchased as adults allowed them to visualize a specific point of historical contingency, such as the moment when an avalanche buried a Swiss village, for instance, or flames consumed the Royal Exchange. Like the table of projected outcomes in a life insurance advertisement, these objects made contingency legible, and contributed to the emblematic form it assumed in many of these works, where the volcanic eruption, the figure of Napoleon, and the roll of the dice stood as shorthand for contingency and its range of outcomes.

In encouraging speculation and in testing the limits of possibility at any given moment, these engagements with contingency also functioned as a kind of experimental practice. The assessment of outcomes and of possible alternatives reproduced the logic (and indeed sometimes borrowed the language) of scientific hypothesis, where a posited "if" anticipated, whether explicitly or implicitly, an "if not" and an array of foreclosing "thens." Like experiments in the laboratory, these uses of contingency were structured operations, analytical explorations of causality and possibility often conducted under controlled conditions. But the link between contingency and experiment is more than a useful premise in the chapters that follow. For Darwin, thinking through contingencies served as a key tool in scientific inquiry, where it assumed a place alongside the laboratory and the natural world as a domain for empirical observation and experiment. Likewise for Babbage, Ada Lovelace, Charles Lyell, and James Clerk Maxwell, it became central to the thought experiments they mounted, as they altered conditions and envisioned outcomes on the printed page.

Although such engagements with contingency had a central role in scientific thought, the form they took was narrative. Whether as sequential arrangements of words, numbers, or images, they expressed a temporal, spatial, or causal relation,[7] even as, I suggest, they also called the conventions of narrative into question by disrupting established causalities and, through the use of speculative, often conditional language, arrested its teleologies and forward momentum. Narrative causality remains, according to Marina Grishakova and others, "one of the most neglected and undertheorized" in contemporary theory, where it's also been inconsistently historicized.[8] Still, narratological methods, with their close attention to sequence and temporality, structure and closure—not only in prose but also in non-prose-based genres like hypertext, graphic novels, and video games—offer one of the most fruitful analytical approaches to the transmedial, often experimental texts at the center of this book's inquiry. Indeed, through the exploration of possibility, multiplicity, and simultaneity, contingency often unsettled established generic conventions and encouraged innovative transpositions. Such exchanges were not uncommon in nineteenth-century Britain, where, as Gillian Beer explains, "*ideas* . . . metaphors, myths, and narrative patterns" slipped across fields of research and genres;[9] as natural historians borrowed from political economy and theology, so too, did poets reflect on findings in geology and physics. But by linking the methods of New Historicism and of historical epistemology, especially as advanced by Lorraine Daston and Mary Poovey, to Caroline Levine's new formalism, the chapters that follow are also interested in the sometimes unexpected ways in which (to borrow Levine's words) the "abstract organizing principles" of contingency were transmitted "to new contexts" and "across varied materials,"[10] where historical writing adopted elements of novelistic conventions, children's play drew on cartographic practices, and prose turned to image.

Still, as these explorations and experiments focused on and pressed up against existing representational practices, their performance always took shape within structured narrative or visual forms. Even when inviting readers to contemplate possibility, these works offered reminders that the contingent operated within a circumscribed field and through articulated statistical, narrative, and spatial channels. Rather than a kind of "resistance to system, to structure, to meaning,"[11]nineteenth-century treatments of contingency in fact asked readers to invest in a governing form or system. Contingency might admit the uncertainty of the future, but its representation in these works also pointed to a finite set of possible outcomes. It helped to transform a shapeless, unknowable future into an imaginable, knowable realm of expectation, if not of choice, and as a form of risk management, it helped to domesticate accidents and disasters, so that these assumed the quality of events that could be, if not predicted, then at least anticipated.[12] The language of contingency allowed Lyell to redirect the narrative and temporal foreclosure of biblical accounts and of natural theology, but through its use he also affirmed his adherence to the established causalities of modern geology; so, too, as Lewis Carroll's and Maxwell's experimental works would demonstrate, "possibility" was itself a foreclosed space, not so much an open-ended freedom as a range, a defined distribution, a finite system as structured as the metropolitan sewerage plan or the network of railways being constructed in those same decades.

A principle extending across contexts, genres, and time periods, contingency has an understandably variegated profile in recent scholarship, where it has been defined and historicized in different ways and by a range of disciplines. For social theorist Niklas Luhmann, contingency, that which is "neither necessary nor impossible," is "modern society's defining attribute."[13] Others from outside the literary and historical disciplines, though, have tended to regard thinking contingently as a practice without cultural or historical specificity, as a timeless feature of human existence. Philosopher Nicholas Rescher, for example, asserts that "*Homo sapien* is an amphibian who lives and functions in two very different realms—the domain of existing reality that we can investigate in observational inquiry, and the domain of suppositional projection that we can explore in creative imagination"; not only is the ability to contemplate an outcome and its unrealized alternative "commonplace" in the sciences, but such "[c]ontingency planning" also operates, he argues, "in everyday life."[14]And while social psychologists Neal J. Roese and James M. Olson acknowledge that, "[t]he current consensus" in their field is "that language and culture influence the content of counterfactuals and also their application in specific situations," they nonetheless agree with Rescher that the "ability to imagine alternative . . . versions of actual occurrences appears to be a pervasive, perhaps even essential, feature" of human existence.[15]

Stephen Jay Gould lamented that "contingency has been consistently underrated (or even unacknowledged) in stereotypical descriptions of scientific practice," but, he contended, it was a "perennial favorite among literary folk."[16] Yet even as contingency and causality have been and continue to be central to literary production—one can scarcely imagine plot without them—"literary folk," alongside their cousins in cultural history and media studies, have offered a limited and uneven account of its history. Even when associating contingency with twentieth-century writing, many have acknowledged the nineteenth-century roots of complex causal and contingent thinking. Investigating the genre of crime fiction, for example, Stephen Kern enumerates the factors, the "increasing specificity, multiplicity, complexity, probability, and uncertainty of causal knowledge," that reshaped representations of causality beginning in the nineteenth century.[17] Yet Kern still regards modernists as the true innovators in this regard and emphasizes the Victorians' reliance on less complex causal explanations, positing that "chance or coincidence was invariably a sign of some transcendent controlling destiny if not divine plan" in nineteenth-century writing, a point echoed in Brian Richardson's claim that nineteenth-century literature depended on a "providential teleology" that only gave way to "varieties of contingency" in the twentieth century.[18] For film studies scholar Mary Ann Doane, who recognizes the "centrality of chance" to Darwin's work and to nineteenth-century statistics, contingency nevertheless communicates most tellingly through cinematic media, in the interval before one frame has given way to the next.[19]

But, according to Kern, Doane, and others, the elements that characterize twentieth-century works—rejection of determinism, acknowledgment of causal complexity, temporal manipulations, and multiplication of possibility—were key aspects of nineteenth-century engagements with contingency and causality. Thinking about how the Victorians thought contingently, as the following chapters ask us to do, illuminates the ways in which they managed the complex, uneven terrain between religion and science, past and present, history and literature. It invites us to attend to the experimental qualities of their writing, evident in the ways they imagined the role of chance in a providential world order, for example, or their handling of temporal representation, or the mechanisms they devised—both material and imagined—to explore and contain the possibilities that contingency made available.

In developing this argument, I turn to those critics and historians who, like Doane and Gould, have considered how an awareness of contingency traversed disciplinary and generic divides. But my work also leans on the literary historians who have focused more consistent attention to the ways nineteenth-century writers questioned deterministic narratives and explanations and advanced a more complex understanding of the relationship between what Paul Fyfe, in his study of Victorian accident, calls "design and chance."[20] Catherine Gallagher, for example, shows how the use of counterfactuals in Napoleonic- and post-Napoleonic-era military guides became a way of training students and officers to evaluate the likely outcomes of different circumstances and strategies on the battlefield.[21] Looking to the period's natural sciences, George Levine sees Darwin's writings as central to a transformed understanding of teleology and chance; the "open-ended nature of his world," he writes, signaled a "resistance to closure" and "preoccupation with new possibilities," and likewise in the possibilities made available through the thermodynamic sciences, Michael Tondre identifies promising alternatives to the period's normalizing tendencies.[22] Others have examined how nineteenth-century novels engaged with chance by generating alternative, counterfictional narratives, which appeared both as elements of narration—as in William Thackeray's *Vanity Fair*, where the forecasting of alternatives transformed both history and fiction into stylized performance, or in George Eliot's *Middlemarch*, where projections into the future encouraged readerly imagination and engagement—and as features of character development, where the envisioning of such alternatives enabled a necessary consolidation of self.[23]

Nineteenth-century engagements with contingency were not limited to the realm of the secular, but scholars have varied in their accounts of contingency's relationship to theology. For both Gallagher and Luhmann, the late modern concern with contingency developed out of, but was also distinct in meaningful ways from, earlier investigations into questions about "God's nature" and its relationship to "human free will."[24] The present book, however, charts a less straightforward historical relationship between the theological and the secular than either of these scholars describes.

Although scientific writings occupy a central place in my analysis, I nonetheless suggest that nineteenth-century experiments with contingency do not neatly align with a story of increasing secularism and argue rather that the period's engagements with contingency frequently served as a means of negotiating a still-influential set of Christian narratives and beliefs. Thus, where philosopher and mathematician Leibniz, writing in 1710, described all things as "contingent" and claimed that God "must needs have had regard or reference to all these possible worlds in order to fix upon one of them," for "if there were not the best (*optimum*) of all possible worlds, God would not have produced any,"[25] a century later authors like William Paley and William Whewell adopted similar terms to describe the place of contingency in their own theories of natural history. Likewise, even as the *Saturday Magazine* instructed its readers to regard the sun's movements as only "mathematically probable," it did not, as the official journal for the Society for Promoting Christian Knowledge, encourage them to discard a providential understanding of nature's operations altogether.[26] In fact, attentive readers would have recalled that just two weeks earlier the *Magazine* had published a reassuring quotation from Whewell, advising that they need "no more fear that the moral than that the physical laws of God's creation should be forgotten in any particular case."[27] In asking its readers to consider how providence and contingency might govern natural operations in tandem, the journal—and, I suggest, the culture that produced it—promoted a more complex understanding of the relation between secularism and religion, one that Babbage's and Maxwell's scientific writings would extend and explore.

Indeed, according to Bernard Lightman, the nineteenth century was an "age of transition," and he cautions that the influence of religion on scientific discourse, far from undergoing a steady decline in the Victorian period, registered a heterogeneous, variable, and far from "monolithic" culture of belief, which lasted until the end of the century.[28] Numerous publications of the period— not only the *Saturday Magazine* but also the *Bridgewater Treatises,* the *Library of Useful Knowledge* volumes published by the Society for the Diffusion of Useful Knowledge, and Robert Chambers's bestselling *Vestiges of the Natural History of Creation*— exemplified the varied ways in which nineteenth-century Britons sought to reconcile a more traditional Christian theology to the findings of contemporary science.[29] As the statistical sciences provided both an available vocabulary and a precise numerical index for the place of chance and uncertainty in major events as in everyday life, and geological and natural histories extended both the temporal and causal range of explanatory narratives, theological debates over the place of divine intervention, human agency, and free will evolved into questions about providential oversight, chance, and probability for those negotiating this shifting, heterogeneous epistemological landscape. In this new realm of belief and understanding, contingency managed to be as important to the articulation of new scientific theories, such as Darwin's account of evolution, as to recalibrations of Christian faith. Given that providence, as many proposed, did not entail God's constant surveillance and interference, contingency provided an occasion for exploring spaces of possibility within a universe otherwise organized by both natural and divine laws, for investigating the potentialities between necessity and accident, and between a visible outcome and its alternatives.

If a religious discourse centered in divine providence constituted one perhaps unexpected arena for thinking contingently, then the past presented another. For contingency focused attention on time—its historical pastness, the process of its passage, and its malleability in and as narrative, the possibility of going back or stepping outside time. Romantics like William Wordsworth maintained what Sue Zemka terms a "durational aesthetic," an intimately sensed, reflective approach that placed remembered "spots of time" outside the reach of time itself, and the modernists, according to Jesse Matz, used narrative to cultivate an "ecology of time," a space for temporal restoration and management beyond the resources of the physical world.[30] The Victorians, too, invested time with meaning and an almost material significance—whether the slow time of broad chronological expanses and long causal trajectories, or what Jimena Canales calls the "microtime" that emerged through nineteenth-century scientific efforts to measure, scrutinize, and subdivide the moment into ever finer increments.[31] Beer argues that early nineteenth-century geology and natural history, in particular, looked to the affordances of narrative for the representation of gradual, extended events: "Because of [their] preoccupation with time," these disciplines recognized "inherent affinities with the problems and processes of narrative."[32] And in the intersections between early nineteenth-century scientific and literary writings Rebecca Stern identifies not only a greater interest in the passage of time, but an enhanced opportunity for exploring its plasticity and potential; no longer only linear or unidirectional, narrative temporality in both genres became, she explains, "multiple and mobile."[33] By the end of the century the technology of film would "make time," and hence the relations and manipulations of cause and effect, "visualizable" and available for analysis, according to Doane.[34]

But if the flicker was cinema's immediate reminder of time's arrow, the potentialities of one frame always being foreclosed by the appearance of the next, this book suggests that earlier technologies, such as prose narrative and the protean view, presented contingency as a means by which viewers might inhabit and arrest the forward momentum of time. Historical fiction mobilized contingency to reframe the past as the future,[35] while natural histories and geologies by William Buckland, Chambers, Lyell, and Darwin inserted readers into the past as though they were *in medias res*, and hence remade the past, even the unimaginably distant past, into a space where outcomes were as yet undetermined. They transformed the instant of suspended potential that modern film would render almost imperceptible and expanded it into a vast, present-tense landscape of possibility, as they also, by accelerating invisibly slow processes, made them visible. In expressing and arresting time, these works presented it as an object for collective contemplation: They allowed for the slow playing (and replaying, and reversing) of causal process, for the methodical distillation and magnification of all possibility sprung from a single moment. But their experiments also encompassed what we might call temporal detours, where conditional statements routed readers into an atemporal, dislocated space beyond the narrative's before-and-after structure. As if to point to the limitations of conventional narrative, they transformed the temporal into the spatial, the ephemeral into the material, and in doing so distorted—stretched, flattened, reversed—the otherwise fleeting instants of decision.

Organized around four sets of experiments with contingency, this book is not intended as a comprehensive survey of contingency's use in Victorian literature—indeed, the impossibility of such a task is part of its point. Rather, by examining a selection of works where disparate genres, media, and forms of knowledge intersect, it situates the intellectual threads linking Lewis Carroll's word games to Darwin's evolutionary theory, the language of popular children's works to life insurance policies and to the changing shape of Babbage's computational designs in the 1830s, within a shared, albeit unevenly textured, epistemological cloth. In this sense, it is also a history of the conditions and commonalities that characterized a mass reading culture in Britain from the 1820s to the early 1870s, when short-lived publications intended for immediate consumption, like classified advertisements and commemorative illustrations, were read alongside works that would eventually ascend to the gentleman's bookshelf and to literary and scientific canons. This approach is especially appropriate to early nineteenth-century Britain, when new technologies supported a booming print culture, with its greater efficiency and reduced cost of publication, expanded modes of image production, and widened circles of distribution.[36] These factors changed the kinds and quantities of works available to a wide range of consumers, and also allowed for some of the experimental publications I discuss here.

The book's first chapter examines Babbage's decision in the 1830s to cease work on his original calculating machine, the Difference Engine, and to design a new, more capable (yet never realized) Analytical Engine, and it reads this shift with relation to the broader conversations in which Babbage's other writings participated: about life insurance, natural history, and divine intervention. Collectively, I suggest, they signal Babbage's turn from a linear, predictable conception of futurity toward a contingent one, as well as a shift from the certainties of the arithmetic series to a kind of numerically expressed narrative. His early actuarial work and writings on life insurance delivered one means of representing, both in prose and through statistical tables, shifting and undetermined outcomes, but it was his later work on calculating engines that enabled him, with the assistance of Lovelace, to articulate a more fully formulated account of contingency and anticipation. Reading the output of each machine, Babbage attended to the complex story told by the numerical patterns produced by the Analytical Engine, in which not only the operator's intentions but also changing conditions and circumstances lay encoded, just as in his later years he would study the complex histories and imagined futures inscribed in tree rings and newspaper clippings.

In his rambling, schematic *Ninth Bridgewater Treatise*, Babbage likened the Analytical Engine's calculations to the work of creation: Both were set in motion through a higher-order, anticipatory program of directives and parameters, whose processes were nonetheless capable of proceeding without further intervention. The idea of a rational "watchmaker" who starts the world running and subsequently allows his well-designed mechanism to operate without further adjustment was a familiar one by the 1820s and 30s, and Babbage adapted that conceit to explore the larger questions that natural theology invited: about the legibility of design, about the role of chance and contingency within governed systems, and about the relationship between the predictability of the machine and its potential to express agency.

Geologists and natural historians like Lyell and Darwin shared Babbage's interest in contingent rather than teleological futures, but they were also determined to use them to challenge the natural theology Babbage's account seemed to support. In the second chapter, I investigate their redoubled emphasis on chance and secular causality and consider some of the reasons why Lyell's *Principles of Geology*, Eliot's *Adam Bede*, and Darwin's *On the Origin of Species* situated contingency not in the future (as Babbage had) but in the historical past. Reimagining history as replete with alternate possible outcomes served as a powerful way of resisting the foreclosed observations of their theologically inclined contemporaries, figures like Paley and Whewell. Lyell introduced contingency as a way of intervening in scriptural accounts of creation and of the deluge, while Eliot mobilized it to reinvent an otherwise predictable, melodramatic tale of seduction; through moments of contingency, they transformed familiar, pivotal scenes from the past into temporal and narrative openings. But if Lyell and Eliot were interested in the mechanism by which time ultimately enacted a foreclosure of suspended alternatives, Darwin proposed that nature might be a space not only of foreclosure—in the form of extinction—but also of multiplication and synchronicity. He encouraged readers to view the diversity of the natural world, in other words, as a proliferation of simultaneous alternatives, where the emergence of variants—of short and long hair, or of serrated and smooth leaves—might represent the divergent, unforeclosed paths of past moments of contingency.

Lyell, Darwin, and Eliot envisioned pasts and futures shaped by the weight of outcomes. A volcanic eruption, a species rendered extinct, a child born out of wedlock: All have significant consequences. But contingency, once released from temporal and causal constraints—when one alternative as opposed to another had no serious consequence, when time and processes were reversible—was a central element of the period's play. The third chapter analyzes the role of contingency in these playful, experimental genres and considers the ways in which contingency as both formal principle and operative mechanism moved across genres, between textual and spatial, narrative and cartographic, synchronic and diachronic modes of representation. Through readings of protean views and board games of the 1830s and 40s, Lewis Carroll's *Alice* books and word games, and children's publications that combined image and narrative in innovative ways, it demonstrates how each, often by borrowing from other genres like puzzles and maps, reinvented narrative, transforming its traditionally linear structure into one replete with divergent, parallel, and simultaneous paths. At the same time, these works instituted their own rules, circumscriptions, and logical structures.

From the visible alternatives of children's play, the final chapter turns to the realm of the invisible upon which Maxwell and Eliot focused their attention. In their writings, they recognized not only the unavailability of molecules and of emotions, respectively, to observation and empirical testing, but also a fundamental indeterminability characterizing their objects of study. What they advanced was a new epistemology, one based not in empirical ways of knowing but in probabilistic ones. In promoting this new methodology in the 1860s and 70s, Maxwell's writings turned away from the statistical averages that were the foundation of earlier thermodynamic research and focused instead on the range of possibilities represented by the statistical distribution. I read his famous thought experiment not in terms of the much-debated capacities of the "demon" but as a means of exploring the limits of chance, desire, and faith.

Eliot's final novel, *Daniel Deronda*, engages with a similar set of questions, as it repeatedly mobilizes the language of the empirical sciences as a metaphor not for knowledge but for its limitations. In the realm of human feelings and understanding, the novel proposes that observers accept uncertainty and cultivate a probabilistic stance, where the proliferation of narrative possibilities, a kind of statistical distribution of emotion and event, enables both sympathy—a willingness to imagine another's range of possible feelings—and also a renewed contemplation of the relationship between chance and individual belief. Significantly, through these experiments in epistemology, both Maxwell and Eliot envision the ways in which subjective and objective forms of knowledge might reconverge in probabilistic understanding.

As much as these engagements with contingency might seem to anticipate a more recent interest in uncertainty and a rejection of the determinism associated with the Victorians, these chapters demonstrate that contingency was, in fact, at the heart of decidedly nineteenth-century intellectual and cultural practices. It offered opportunities for thinking through the principles of chance and probability introduced by the statistical sciences, while it also invited reflection on the degrees of freedom available within the period's dominant histories, religious narratives, and natural laws. For scientists, novelists, publishers, and readers, these experiments with contingency tested and challenged, as they sometimes also reaffirmed, the conventions of form and genre, the rules of the game, the limits of the system.

CHAPTER 1

Anticipations of an Unpredictable Future

Nineteenth-Century Life Insurance and
Babbage's Calculating Engines

A SALES PITCH for life insurance addressed itself to the reader "whose income depends upon his own exertions, . . . to the private gentleman, having a family, and living on a moderate income; and to the person engaged in trade." For such individuals, the 1843 pamphlet reasoned, a policy was "absolutely essential; indeed, the almost innumerable modes in which it may be beneficially employed by every one, are now beginning to be so generally known and acknowledged, that it is not considered requisite to enlarge."[1] As if to prove this last point, when the same company advertised in 1854, it omitted the rationales and scenarios that appeared in its earlier version altogether. This revision over a period of little more than a decade registers a broader cultural shift in which life insurance, once a rarity, a specialized product that needed explanation at the beginning of the nineteenth century, became a relatively commonplace commodity half a century later.[2] In his overview of the industry's phenomenal growth, Lewis Pocock, the director of the Argus Life Assurance Company, counted a mere eight companies in existence in 1800, then sixteen by 1820, and more than forty at the time of writing in 1842 (though Timothy Alborn puts this last number at closer to ninety).[3] Elaborating on these statistics, Alborn reveals that the marketplace also expanded rapidly beyond the presumed clientele of earlier policies—the middle-class, Church of England gentleman—to include, by mid-century, women, Catholics, dissenters, and eventually members of the working classes as potential customers.

As it expanded its consumer base, the life insurance industry faced a corresponding demand for agents and actuaries. In the early decades of the nineteenth century, the statistical sciences upon which the preparation of complex tables of premiums and payouts depended were themselves only in a fledgling state, and skilled actuaries were relatively scarce.[4] So the directors of a newly formed entity like the Protector Life Assurance Company would have congratulated themselves on securing a reputable, Cambridge-educated mathematician to serve as house actuary in early 1824. As the company began to advertise in the daily newspapers, the actuary's work would have included consulting tables of mortality rates and preparing lists of insurance premiums. But the Protector, like a number of others, was itself a casualty of the intense competition among insurance companies in the 1820s; it folded only a few months later, before it ever formally opened for business.[5] Experienced actuaries were still in demand, but the Protector's mathematician chose not to pursue employment with other insurance companies and instead directed his energies elsewhere.

Although the actuary, Charles Babbage, then 32, turned his attention to the design of his most famous undertaking, the Difference Engine, he did not put his experience with the insurance industry behind him altogether. In 1826, as he was focusing on his new calculating engine, he wrote and published *A Comparative View of the Various Institutions for the Assurance of Lives*, intended as an explanatory work for a public not yet accustomed to the principles of insurance. This volume never made it past the first edition, and it could be considered at best only a modest success, receiving mixed responses from readers. While Babbage's father, a banker, enjoyed the book so much that he claimed to have read it three times through,[6] the reviews that appeared in reputable journals were more circumspect. The *Edinburgh Review*, for example, expressed disappointment at its dullness, calling it "a descent into the details of ordinary business," while the *Quarterly Review* was at least more receptive to its subject, hailing life insurance as of "more importance" and "more general utility" than any other British institution of the period.[7] As the demand for life insurance grew over the first half of the century, Babbage's *Assurance of Lives* was one among hundreds of publications to appear on the subject, which included pamphlets and promotional materials to more sustained examinations like his and Pocock's works. But Babbage's volume has been treated as a largely forgettable contribution to the genre and, according to historian Martin Campbell-Kelly, is "perhaps the least studied" within his oeuvre.[8]

Among historians of science and technology, Babbage's mundane actuarial efforts, which offered him the promise of a steady salary and position at a relatively early point in his career, have been treated as incidental to the daringly original work that would cement his reputation both during his lifetime and long after. And the discipline that has dominated research on Babbage, the history of computing, has focused on those writings that seem to anticipate twentieth-century technologies.[9] A number of scholars, including Gordon Miller, Richard Romano, and Simon Schaffer, have nonetheless looked more broadly at and offered historically situated readings of Babbage's writings; their studies have linked the period's political economy, and especially the principles of efficiency, systematization, and the division of labor he describes in his 1832 publication, *On the Economy of Machinery and Manufactures*, to his contemporaneous interest in automation and his designs for his calculating engines.[10] Campbell-Kelly is virtually alone in his attention to *Assurance of Lives*, in which he identifies premonitory signs of the author's genius for "encyclopedic knowledge" and his "systematic approach" to mathematical problems.[11] This chapter extends the work of these and other scholars through a reconsideration of Babbage's early actuarial work. It suggests that even as he left the insurance office and actuarial tables behind him professionally, his early experience with insurance remained a deeply embedded part of his intellectual life and informed the shape of his future endeavors, including his most ambitious work: his design for a successor to the Difference Engine.

Babbage's involvement in actuarial work, from 1824 to 1826, occurred at a period significant not only for the life insurance industry, which was gaining a prominent place within the consumer marketplace, but also for Babbage's own research, which would have been transitioning from a period of intense work on the Difference Engine in 1823 and 1824, and toward a proposal, which he would complete by the early 1830s, for his more complex Analytical Engine. But the alignments between his foothold in the world of insurance and his evolving computational designs are more than circumstantial. For just as life insurance promised, in the form of a policy available for purchase, the ability to accommodate uncertainty and contingency—which according to insurance writings were the defining conditions of modern existence—so too would the Analytical Engine account for shifting and unpredictable futures, a key feature that distinguished it from the earlier Difference Engine, whose output was, by design, linear and predictable. While Babbage never built this second engine, he explored its capacities in his 1837 *Ninth Bridgewater Treatise,* an unofficial addendum to the series of volumes that had been commissioned by the Earl of Bridgewater, works of popular science intended to reconcile recent findings to a narrative of Christian belief. Babbage's contribution, not only unsolicited but also unconventional in style and argument, made claims about the uncertain relationship between identifiable patterns in the past and an unrealized future in ways that disrupted aspects of the natural theology espoused by the original Bridgewater volumes.

By joining a narratological to a historicist reading of his other works—his *Assurance of Lives,* his *Treatise,* his memoir, and his scrapbook—I suggest that Babbage's understanding of what could be conveyed through the numerical series moved beyond the capabilities of the Difference Engine. He developed not only new technologies but also new ways of thinking about the expressive potential of numbers. The numerical sequence was no longer, in its ideal form, a reflection of reliability and predictability, but came instead to approximate narrative, in which contingency was at once a sign of authorial intention and a reflection of the complexity of the natural and social worlds. Through these disparate texts, he explored how the series, the collection, and the table might represent the discontinuities and unforeseen events that characterized modern life, and how two of the technologies he worked to actualize, life insurance and the Analytical Engine, mediated between present and future, and between the individual and a contingent, changeable world. His works situated both himself and his readers in a state of active anticipation, ever scanning the horizon for encoded patterns that might describe the past— whether these were just legible in a calculating engine's numerical output, in the growth rings of trees, or in the newspaper advertisements he gathered in his later years—and offer insight into the algorithms that might shape the future.

An Actuarial Prologue

Life insurance, in its barest form, was a commodity whose price varied in accordance with mortality rates. Eighteenth-century French mathematicians like Pierre-Simon Laplace had developed the theoretical foundations for the statistical sciences that underlay the principles of insurance, but in Britain statistics only emerged as a field with a coherent set of principles and purposes in the early decades of the nineteenth century, around the time when the nation's industry began to rely ever more heavily on those figures for its rapid growth. Even as late as 1830, as Mary Poovey notes, practitioners of the statistical sciences were still noncommittal regarding the use of numerical figures and tables, agreeing only that statistics should, as its etymology implied, provide data concerning the state.[12]

Babbage's 1826 *Assurance of Lives* was written for readers who would likely have had little experience interpreting statistical figures, much less the statistical tables that would become commonplace in popular journalism by the 1850s. Even a decade later, an article intended for a general audience, "Popular Illustrations of Life Assurance," would find it necessary to explain the basic principles of statistics with painstaking clarity: "human life is . . . of uncertain duration, and as our lives may be terminated within an hour, or protracted for many years, we have all of us a certain chance, or probability, (only to be expressed by figures,) of surviving to the end of every year," as it worked through a series of mental exercises, such as, "Suppose six counters, marked 1, 2, 3, 4, 5, 6, were placed in a box, and it was required to determine the chance of drawing out any one of them."[13] Published for a similarly uninitiated audience, Babbage's volume had multiple goals. With its attention to profit and costs, and its repeated critiques of business practices and ethics, Babbage's volume offered insight into the economic and professional considerations of the industry; but it also considered the principles of life insurance from the perspective of the individual consumer.[14] Like its journalistic counterpart, it explained the purpose of life insurance and also turned to both numerical and narrative representations to illustrate its operative principles.

Babbage opened his work with what he anticipated would strike many readers of the 1820s as a paradox: "Nothing is more proverbially uncertain than the duration of human life, when the maxim is applied to an individual; yet there are few things less subject to fluctuation than the average duration of a multitude of individuals."[15] By drawing attention to the distinctions between the certainties that made categories of events (births, accidents, and deaths) in large populations seem predictable in frequency, and the uncertainties that applied to the individual, Babbage pointed to the implicit duality of the statistic, one that was central to the success of companies purveying life insurance. Of any population of ten thousand persons, the occurrence of illnesses like tuberculosis would seem to follow predictable patterns and rates of occurrence, but such knowledge revealed little about whether you or your neighbor would fall ill. Life insurance drew its profits from the probabilistic space between the population's certainties and the individual's uncertainties, as well as, implicitly, from the relationship between past data and anticipations of the future. Moreover, as Babbage noted, against the "rate of mortality" these companies needed to weigh an additional probability: the "interest which will probably be made" from the premiums paid.[16] By reducing the effects of statistical outliers, actuarial data based on large numbers allowed them to formulate reliable estimates of the numbers that would fall ill or die, and to adjust their premiums accordingly. But for individual clients, there could be nothing other than uncertainty about their financial and physiological fates, against which the purchase of a policy was meant to provide a measure of protection.

With its attention to profit and costs, and its repeated critiques of business practices and ethics, Babbage's volume offers insight into the economic and professional considerations of the industry; but it also considers the principles of life insurance from the perspective of the individual consumer. To a readership unfamiliar with the conventions of insurance, Babbage explains the factors that might affect one's insurability—a history of disease, past vaccinations, type of employment—and enumerates the multiple reasons that might motivate individuals to insure, such as "marriage, the birth of children, or a variety of circumstances."[17] Indeed, he devotes several pages to describing scenarios in which an insurance policy might be worthwhile:

> A creditor who is secure of receiving his money, provided his debtor lives a few years . . . a person just entering into possession of an entailed estate, who wishes to raise a sum of money which he can gradually repay in the next five or seven years. . . . The heir to an estate which depends on his surviving an aged relative, [who] wishes to make a provision for some of his family or friends.[18]

These fragments of narratives invited novice readers to understand how the abstract principles of life insurance might apply to everyday life, as they also draw attention to the contingencies shaping the world they inhabited, where personal experience might be affected not only by factors of social class, geography, and occupation but also by sudden events, possible windfalls (inheritances or career advancements) and setbacks (illness or financial burdens). What he calls the "uncertain tenure of human existence," whether one's own or someone else's, is thus just one example among a range of other uncertainties—financial, familial, professional—that shape one's fate.[19]

The book's dual focus, with its first two chapters devoted to mortality and interest rate tables and the third focusing on the insurance policy itself, reflects the gap between statistical representations of populations and the significance of such data for individuals,[20] a gap that also effectively separates the past from the future. When discussing rates of mortality, for instance, Babbage turns to the "experience" of another company, the Equitable, "during the thirty years which terminated in 1800," and its observation that "the probabilities of life appear to have been equally favourable in every period."[21] Companies, he implies, draw on past patterns of mortality and on the assurance that such patterns will vary little across large populations from year to year. But as his treatment of the individual emphasizes, until the decisive moment—of accident, of death—in any given life, there can be no assurances, only a murky realm of speculation and unrealized futurity. Probability in this context implies possibility, a kind of prophesying about what lies ahead, and Babbage's narratives of creditors and would-be heirs left in suspense describe individuals ever poised on the threshold of an uncertain future, one shaped in large part by events beyond their control.

These visions of a contingent future—of the potential consequences of childbirth, mortality (one's own as well as that of others), investments, and accidents—persist as mainstays of insurance literature, gaining prominence in later works, which would make ever more explicit and strident claims upon the reader's attention. That Babbage includes them here as unsensational elements of his account, however, indicates the extent to which thinking contingently was central to the marketplace for life insurance: It was the vehicle by which insurance projected population data about casualties and mortalities in past years into a generalized sense of risk to which any and all were subject in the future.

Babbage's 1824 table of premiums for the Protector Life Assurance Company was typical of the genre, where one column displayed the client's age increasing in a linear sequence, but where adjacent columns for insurance premiums showed figures mounting in a far less steady fashion.[22] These latter columns reflected the complex probabilities affecting one's mortality with each passing year, or what Babbage described as the "value of contingencies depending on lives." These he represented in numerical rather than narrative form, and indeed, the complexity of the equations used to generate such tables, with their numerous variables and internal contingencies, register the impossibility of a linear or predictable future.[23] Still, readers needed no specialized knowledge of statistics in order to reach probabilistic conclusions; based solely on fairly straightforward financial calculations, they would realize that, for example, at age 66 there would be at least a one-in-twenty chance of not living out the year, or would consider that at age 46 they would need to die before the age of 70 in order to make the policy financially worthwhile. Like its narrative counterparts, the table encouraged readers to reflect on personal circumstances and possible outcomes, to occupy an unrealized future for a moment. Moreover, by allowing readers to determine the point at which a policy was not only reassuring but also financially sound, the actuarial table stripped those speculations to their barest form and directed readers into a specific calculus that might apply to their own lives.

Narratives for the Insurable Life

Eighteenth-century insurance schemes, historians tell us, were not altogether distinct from gambling.[24] In the early days of insurance, policies were commonly purchased for public figures or events. Thus one might purchase a policy for "the success of battles, the succession of Louis XV's mistresses, the outcome of sensational trials," for example, and as Lorraine Daston explains, while the insuring firm always had a broad sense of likelihoods, "statistics played no role in pricing"; only towards the end of the eighteenth century did insurers apply population statistics and encourage individuals to purchase coverage for their own lives.[25] Even then, the insurance company more closely resembled a mutual aid society, in which dues paid might fund surviving widows or children in the case of a member's death, or the tontine system, in which the sum of all payments would go to the single surviving member. Like private clubs, these groups approved memberships at their own discretion, often after a personal interview with the prospective purchaser.[26] Otherwise, insurance was often sold in short-term contracts to cover only specific periods of exceptional risk— the months or years of a purchaser's sea voyage, for example.[27]

But in the nineteenth century the insurance industry began to distance itself from this common association with unusual or speculative ventures; as one financial author put it, "nothing is less speculative in reality" than life insurance, which ought properly to be considered "an extended form of banking."[28] Central to this repositioning was the remaking of risk as a condition at once universal and quotidian. As population statistics reminded readers, risk was no longer to be thought of as a voluntary condition assumed by the daredevil or gambler, but regarded as an all-encompassing fact of modern life, touching not only the sailor and the industrial worker but also the quiet widow who seldom ventured from home as well as the infant still in its cradle—and not just at identifiably risky periods but at every moment of every day.[29] In a world where all individuals, regardless of class, age, or occupation, were subject to risk, purchasing an insurance policy, now available for general consumption, became a matter not of speculation but of prudence. As Daston argues, these early nineteenth-century insurance companies did more than simply sell policies. In convincing readers of the need for life insurance and training their minds "toward the long term, toward the future," they cultivated a market among the rising middle classes, whose financial futures, unlike those of the aristocracy, depended on salaried and waged earnings.[30] So, too, Babbage's *Assurance of Lives* all but excluded those at the economic extremes of society from consideration; his examples, with their references to a delayed expectation of money or to reliance on a regular, earned income, seemed to eliminate both the lower classes and the very wealthy as prospective clients for this new industry.[31] Insurance advertisements of the period likewise echoed the formulaic language of middle-class morality. A promotional pamphlet issued by the Alfred Life Assurance Company noted that insurance was a reliable indicator of "civilization," as well as of "prudence and forethought"; and in response to its own rhetorical question, "What is Life Assurance?" the Aegis Life Assurance Company Almanack answered that "It is the exercise of forethought, of prudence, of benevolence."[32]

By the 1820s, as one prospectus observed, life insurance had become "a general practice, an understood duty,"[33] and a later pamphlet from 1850 validated this assessment, declaring that "the principles of Life Assurance are so well known, and its advantages so justly appreciated, that little explanation is required. The duty of providing for the contingencies to which life is subject is universally admitted."[34] Still, promotional materials and financial publications continued to detail the principles of life insurance for a general readership, often by supplementing statistics with illustrative narrative examples. Private authors like Babbage participated in this practice, but so did companies, whose policies and prospectuses were often accompanied by lengthy justifications regarding the benefits of insurance.

These materials courted not the risk-seeker but his prudent, office-bound counterpart. The Edinburgh Life Assurance Company prospectus of 1849, for example, addressed itself explicitly to "Persons in the Church, the Law, the Army, the Navy, or in public offices, Medical and Professional men, and, in short, all whose incomes depend upon their lives."[35] These prospectuses and advertising materials reveal how the insurance industry helped to establish a rhetoric of contingency in the first decades of the nineteenth century, one that played a key role in defining and transforming the very meaning of risk for the public. They stressed that the risks against which policies provided security and stability were no longer the exceptional, often voluntary risks associated with foreign travel or labor, but the quotidian ones to which everyone, according to these companies, was exposed: indebtedness, disease, death.[36]

While Daston and François Ewald have detailed the philosophical and mathematical conditions that allowed for the success of the insurance industry, this chapter focuses on the rhetorical and narrative strategies by which company prospectuses shaped the reader into a consumer. For not only did these documents train audiences in statistical understanding, but through prose they also emphasized the universality as well as the inescapability of risk. By the 1840s, the middle-class public would have been somewhat familiar with statistical principles, in part through the public health and social reform efforts that both relied on and publicized them, but insurance companies also made generalizable, calculable risks feel personally relevant. For example, a Prudential Insurance policy prospectus invited the reader to ask himself,

Can he feel other than anxious at heart, with upwards of 30,000 persons perishing in this metropolis yearly . . . ? Let him take this fact home, and divide the entire population of those immediately about him, say one million and half, by this amount of mortality, and consider that one out of every fifty perishes annually, and how soon he and his may be included in this average.[37]

Through a canny rehearsal of the otherwise abstract disjunction between the law of large numbers and the uncertainties that exist at an individual level, the Prudential leads the reader through a step-by-step conversion of mortality statistics into the language of risk, a personal calculus best calibrated, it suggests, in the imaginative terms of narrative ("how soon?"). Through the rhetoric of risk, it enjoins the reader not only to understand but also to inhabit this statistical knowledge, even if only in a rudimentary way, to regard himself as "included" in the period's population statistics. At the same time, this narrative of inclusiveness was necessarily inflected by gender. For the ideal reader was often figured, as he is here, as male, someone "anxious at heart" not primarily for his own sake, but whose considerations are situated at "home," where the implied objects of his concern and the beneficiaries of the policy he will purchase—wife, children, unmarried sisters, widowed mother—tender an emotional appeal for security and subsistence.

Recognizing the value of life insurance was thus more than a function of one's social class; it entailed a set of attitudes, behaviors, and ethics. As Daston explains, in place of the gambler and lottery-player, for whom the future was matter for fantastical, and often incalculable, speculation, life insurance companies promoted a new type, a figure for whom insurance was a provision for the years to come and a calculable measure of foresight and good planning. Babbage, too, drew on this distinction, noting that "thoughtless people whose credulity is . . . duped by the splendid promises of the lottery" might be drawn to life insurance, but that it was intended rather for the thoughtful and "prudent," who turned to insurance "to provide against the uncertainty of life."[38] The review of Babbage's *Assurance of Lives* that appeared in the *Edinburgh Review* concurred, declaring that "*Security* is the grand and indispensable requisite . . . in this shifting scene of things."[39] Insurance thus demanded from the model individual an acknowledgment of life's contingencies, but at the same time it promised a measure of insulation from them. Effectively reaffirming the logic of regular labor that underpinned middle-class masculinity, life insurance placed a monetary value on the endeavors of the living and promised to extend that value in the form of a regular income and predictable lifestyle to the policy's beneficiaries.

This shift in attitude was not limited to the single act of purchasing insurance. As the author of the pamphlet, "Have You Insured Your Life? If Not— Why Not?" pointed out in an illustrative example, being thoughtful rather than thoughtless necessitated a complete transformation of the self:

> Here's a fellow clerk, say . . . who puts by his half-a-crown per week to secure £250 on his life. A mere drop or two of beer or a few cigars the less; a little more attention to the expenses of his household; a few minutes earlier in the morning; a walk instead of riding to the office; or one "little quiet party" in the year the less, is all he is required to do to spare the money. . . . How does this man feel when he looks round upon his family? . . . his happiness seems perfect.[40]

Recognizing the value of life insurance entails a series of behavioral changes in the clerk, the definitive lower-middle-class occupation of the time, but also one that was thought to be temporary, a position that allowed mobility.[41] Financial prudence is here a means of inhabiting one's social class, actual or desired, and also—in spite of the fact that many of these companies marketed their policies to both genders—one's masculinity. Financial planning by way of life insurance is not only the precursor to but the equivalent of ensuring familial happiness, a cumulative effect of everyday temperance, regular habits, domestic management, and seriousness of purpose. Moreover, it demands that the purchaser abandon the selfishness of his own life and of the present moment, his small sacrifices in the present allowing him to provide for others after his death. Significantly, the pamphlet contrasts the frugal, reliable clerk, not with the gambler, but with another outdated type:

> [T]he man who "trusts to Providence," . . . hopes—and, in his ignorance, perhaps he prays—that Providence will provide for those he leaves behind him. That is, he virtually expects that God shall work a miracle, though the age of miracles has passed and gone.[42]

Where God, like the gambling table, is represented as an unpredictable and unreliable external agency, the steady, incremental actions of the clerk and the steady, reliable income promised by his life insurance policy emerge as symbols of a reassuring predictability and a willingness to assert personal control over one's financial future.

In this turn from an old-fashioned religious faith to a more secular understanding of the future, the comfortingly familiar language of virtue offered the illusion of moral and financial continuity. These life insurance documents likewise reinforced lessons that would have been familiar from contemporaneous children's works, many of which read like updated versions of Bunyan's *Pilgrim's Progress*, the Christian hero's travails and temptations rescripted for a more secular nineteenth-century life. The modern condition of accident and risk, they emphasized, was manageable through the assertion of moral action, and what might be called accidents almost always occur as the result of bad decisions, which the reader might learn from and hence avoid. When, for example, in a series of ever more catastrophic episodes in Mary Elliott's 1819 *The Wax-Taper, or, Effects of Bad Habits*, a young girl damages a valuable piece of muslin by mistake or breaks a washbasin, or when the family's cat eats its pet bird, or when her infant sibling sets herself on fire, the narrator declares in a combination of rhetorical understatement and moral overstatement that these are "scrapes" produced by the girl's "silly habit of meddling with things neither needful nor proper for her."[43] Similarly, in an 1807 book entitled *The Second Chapter of Accidents*, a little boy, pridefully "desirous of shewing himself to all his friends" in his new clothes, disobeys the order not to leave the house's courtyard and ends up bumping into a "chimney-sweeper, and in striving to avoid the sooty lad, . . . fell into the kennel"; as if to reinforce its lesson about responsibility (as well as the need for maintaining social hierarchies), the narrator reminds readers that "This was in consequence of leaving the place assigned him to play in."[44]

While the emerging life insurance industry presented a somewhat more complex vision of the world, one in which unforeseen events like illness or death were understood as emptied of moral content—many of which would arrive at one's doorstep regardless of one's character—insurance narratives nonetheless appealed to a similarly straightforward set of moral equations:

Good people make good choices, and good choices lead to good outcomes. Moral decision making, that is, allowed for the transformation of the unpredictability of the world at large into the predictability of the private sphere. What is more, by "no longer resigning [individuals] to the decrees of providence and the blows of fate, but instead transforming [their] relationship with nature, the world and God," as Ewald puts it in his study of the socioeconomics of insurance,[45] insurance translated a still Christianized discourse of contemporaneous morality into a more abstract language, one that spoke in economic, even scientized, terms. Note, for example, the new meaning and form the word "providence" takes on in these documents. No longer the external force denoted with a capital *P*, the embodied Christian divinity who provides, it has been transformed into an internal attribute, embodied by the "provident" (especially as opposed to the "improvident") individuals themselves.[46] The Prudential Mutual Assurance, Investment, and Loan Association prospectus drew upon this latter, secular definition, declaring that insurance "command[s] the attention of the provident of all classes of the community."[47] An 1849 Edinburgh Life Assurance Company prospectus echoed this transition from religious to secular on its cover, which depicted a mother holding an infant in her arms. While reminiscent of a typical Madonna and child image, the pages within explain that they represent rather the earthly wife and child whose "happiness" depends on the reader's decision to "limit ... expenditure" in order to afford a policy.[48]

The clerk who saves his half-crowns, the husband who forgoes unnecessary purchases: Insurance prospectuses and advertising directed readers' attention to these embodiments of self-sacrifice, and especially to their place within what was at once a new moral and also a new temporal framework. They reminded readers, through both narrative and statistics, of the inevitable passage of years, of increasing age and an ever-encroaching mortality, and also encouraged them to manage their time through regular acts of saving and paying premiums. Gaining control over present behaviors, they implied, could lend control over the future as well. Ewald observes that, "[t]o calculate a risk is to master time, to discipline the future,"[49] and life insurance exemplified this maxim, providing its purchasers with a sense that the provident behavior they demonstrated through small acts of saving and self-restraint in the present might translate into a provision for the future. As the Catholic, Law, and General Life Assurance Company announced, "A Man Aged 25" pays "about NINEPENCE a week only!" for a policy, and that "[s]mall indeed must that man's income be who cannot spare by the exercise of an ordinary amount of frugality, such sums as these, to secure his family from the immediate pressure of poverty."[50]

Appealing to a secular logic of labor and political economy, the language in these pamphlets transformed a Christian narrative that would have been familiar to working men and women, in which incremental acts of faith and renunciation eventually lead to a greater reward beyond the grave. Here, those deeds acquire a calculable monetary value. What is more, in directing the mind away from the pursuit of immediate pleasures and toward an eventual reward, these pamphlets encouraged readers to plan for a future composed of both foreseeable and unforeseeable events. Perhaps appropriately, then, one of the insurance company's signature marketing tools was the calendar, a reminder of time's inexorability, the blankness of the future, and the power of insurance to provide some control over it. The Colonial Life Assurance Company, for instance, issued its 1852 prospectus in the form of an almanac, where a list of important dates in British history was printed throughout in verso, while a blank space for one's own "memoranda," presumably to be organized in similar date-by-date fashion, appeared just opposite. Through its juxtaposition of historical record and as-yet unscripted events, it served as a kind of metaphor for insurance itself, wherein knowledge of a known past always faced a reckoning with an unknown future.[51]

At the same time, insurance companies cast readers' minds into the future through rhetoric that depicted not so much a single road stretching visibly into the future, but multiple paths full of diverging possibilities. Indeed, the future defined by the insurance policy was one characterized by chance, probability, and uncertainty, and with a seemingly infinite number of decisive moments. And as prospectuses were revised over the first half of the nineteenth century, they revealed the ever-greater number of contingencies around which policies could be constructed and multiplied the numbers and types of tables featured within their pages. For instance, in 1846 the London Assurance Company listed four types of plans, one for the "Whole Term of any Single Life," a "lowest rate" plan, one "to be paid on the death of A, provided B be then living," and another "to be paid on the death of either A or B," while its 1854 edition included many more options adapted to different scenarios, such as policies for "Short Period Assurances . . . for the Terms of One, Three, Five, Seven, and Ten Years," accommodations for "Limited Number of Payments" and "Decreasing Premiums."[52]

These prospectuses and pamphlets also proliferated narrative contingencies and alternatives. The Legal and Commercial Life Assurance Society, for instance, declared that the policies being offered "embrace every description of contingency that the varied circumstances of human life involve," and the prospectus for the Metropolitan Counties and General Life Assurance company asserted that they "have endeavoured to meet every case, and to embrace every contingency connected with the duration of human life."[53] Another prospectus prescribed insurance

> for the clerk, whose income fails with his office—for the creditor, whose sole security is the life of his debtor—for the husband, whose only income is his wife's jointure—for the dependent upon an annuity during the life of another—for the tenant bound to repairs, or to pay fines for renewals—for those parents, or guardians, who have paid apprentice fees, and such apprentice dies, and it then becomes an object to regain the money so expended.[54]

A fourth advertised that insurance could provide a young man with "a handsome sum to settle on his wife, should he ever marry; should he require a loan, an old Policy becomes an ample security; should he wish to sell it after the lapse of years, it is a bank note."[55] Yet another listed the circumstances surrounding individuals who died unexpectedly: "A widow lady, aged 53, assured her life for £600, and died 19 days after paying her first premium. . . . A tradesman, aged 39, assured his life for £500, and within 23 days fell a victim to Typhus Fever"; as it eventually concluded, "persons in the enjoyment of good health may be cut off contrary to all human expectation," and that while those individuals "appeared to be in the possession of a sound constitution, yet, in less than a year after the issuing of their policies they were *all dead*."[56]

While these companies emphasized the moral necessity of purchasing insurance, the world they depicted was far from the one outlined in early nineteenth-century children's literature, where "scrapes" and "accidents" are morally overdetermined and by extension, avoidable. By contrast, they describe a future filled with unpredictable outcomes: unexpected costs, unanticipated responsibilities, and sudden deaths. If, as historians Roger Cooter and Bill Luckin have claimed, the modern concept of "accident" emerged in Britain in the 1830s as a category of event without any necessary moral or causal content,[57] then the entrance of life insurance into the everyday lives of early Victorians surely contributed to the growing consciousness of this category of "accident." These prospectuses repeatedly depicted a world in which events occur without a discernible reason; they shifted the moral significance that might once have been attached to misfortunes or windfalls from the moment of occurrence to the moment of anticipation, where the individual's decision to ensure a steady income for his family, regardless of what might happen, became a measure of moral worth. In this sense, morality, like one's probable life expectancy, became something almost calculable, legible through one's financial foresight and the regularity of one's insurance premiums and payouts.

Furthermore, while some prospectuses relied on accounts of ostensibly real-life cases—the 53-year-old widow, the tradesman who died of typhus—many others relied more explicitly on the conventions of fiction. Babbage's *Assurance of Lives*, for example, invited readers to exercise their imaginations in conjuring persons or populations: "If we were to take . . . ten thousand infants just born," he wrote, "suppose . . . only six thousand of these remain alive, perhaps at the age of twenty."[58] Understanding statistics, he suggested, necessitated the reader's acceptance of certain premises upon which a set of speculations might operate, as well as a willing suspension of disbelief in order to visualize that hypothetical population. But later narratives mobilized these hypothetical individuals in more explicit ways, drawing less on a sensibility enabled by statistical awareness than one cultivated by a familiarity with the conventions of fiction. With their everyman protagonists—the clerk, the concerned husband, the young man who has not yet inherited his fortune—they sketched, in a few lines, versions of the more elaborate Bildungsroman to which readers would have been accustomed. These hopeful characters, too, looked to a future replete with possibility, and their very anonymity encouraged identification across a broad spectrum of readers: This *could* be you, or at least someone *like* you, they seemed to suggest.

These publications encouraged readers to engage with these fragments of fiction-making, inviting them to imagine any number of scenarios and outcomes for these would-be protagonists, to follow their hypothetical illnesses, deaths, and inheritances through multiple narrative outcomes, and by extension, to envision still others beyond the printed page. Indeed, even works that referred readers to ostensibly real-world examples seem designed to prompt the reader to generate in response his or her own, personalized spectrum of hypothetical narratives concerning the possible failures, injuries, and burdens that might occur in the weeks, months, or years to come—to proliferate a whole range of contingent outcomes beyond the examples offered. The final page of the Railway Passengers' Assurance Company prospectus, for example, lists daily activities, and next to them, the unlikely accidents that befell their participants.

The effect was to introduce the unanticipated into the imagination, and to suggest, by way of the seemingly improbable, an array of possible outcomes for any given moment. One might reasonably expect, for instance, that in sailing one might risk overturning or drowning, but the Railway Passengers' Assurance prospectus noted that dangers inhered even in simple, everyday acts. Thus, the act of "Walking" resulted in one banker in Langport "Crossing road" and being "knocked down by cart"; a London solicitor who went "hunting" might have expected to be injured by a stray shot, but in fact, received a "Blow from branch of tree"; even "At Home," an unlucky draper was not safe from accident, as his "Foot caught in carpet."[59] By contrast, the readers of the Metropolitan Counties and General Life Assurance Society prospectus received not a list, but this direct challenge:

> Reader! You may be young; you may be strong; your intentions may be good. . . . Candidly, and in a spirit of kindness, let me ask you, reader, have you ever calculated the average duration of human life? . . . . Consider also the accidents, the daily accidents, which occur, and from which none of us are exempt, and then gravely demand of yourself—"In case I become an early victim to the grave, how have I provided for my family? how can I be certain that I may live even another year to add to the little savings I have already made? or that health may be conferred on me, to enable me to continue my present profitable exertions?"[60]

Abandoning the third-person hypothetical clerk or creditor, with whom readers might identify, this prospectus addresses them with the interpellative "you." It enjoins them, suspended as they are in the present moment, to contemplate a range of uncertain futures, a horizon of shifting circumstances and fortunes. If statistical percentages and probabilities seemed hopelessly abstract to lay readers, then narrative, though perhaps lacking in mathematical precision, nonetheless invited readers to inhabit this indeterminacy in a more accessible way, by multiplying in the imagination the alternatives that might emerge at any given moment in time.

From the Law of Differences to Irreducible Futures

As the life insurance policy worked its way into the heart of everyday, middle-class life over the course of the century, the British public also became more fluent readers of that other major component of the prospectus: the statistical table. Babbage understood the importance of the table, not just to the insurance industry but also to the period's other economic, scientific, and geographical endeavors. Indeed, his interest in table-making, and his awareness of the challenges associated with the process, preceded and also extended beyond his work for the Protector. Numerical tables of any sort, he knew, were the end product of many stages of human labor: arithmetical calculations done by hand (often by women workers known as "computers"), transcription of those calculated figures into a table, and transfer from the handwritten table to the typeset and finally printed page. The process was labor-intensive and error-prone; journalist Dionysius Lardner decried the quantity of errata found in printed tables and the various points at which—even with the most capable minds and hands at work—they might enter the process.[61]

Babbage designed the Difference Engine in the early 1820s as a solution to this problem. Mechanizing the operation from start to finish, it incorporated numerous functions into a single machine: computing, tabulating, printing. Still, as Herbert Sussman observes, the true "significance of Babbage's calculating engine lies in that it is not physical but mental activity that is done by the machine."[62] In an early "trial" that pitted a capable "friend" against a prototype of the machine, the engine, tasked with both calculating and recording the results into a table, easily matched the human, whose sole job was to transcribe;

as Babbage proudly noted, "thirty numbers of the same table were calculated in two minutes and thirty seconds: as these contained eighty-two figures, the engine produced thirty-three every minute."[63] The machine thus represented an ideal of efficiency and accuracy to which the human could only aspire.

The operations of the engine were premised on what Babbage termed the "method of differences," the principle by which the solution to an nth-order equation might sequentially be reduced to a linear function, and hence, ultimately, to a constant. Thus, for the polynomial[64]

$$f(x) = x^2 + x + 41$$

where x represents a series of integers (n, $n + 1$, $n + 2$, and so on), the difference between any given $f(n)$ and $f(n+1)$ might be expressed through the linear function

$$f(x) = 2x + 2$$

In other words, the results of a sequence of numbers run through an exponential function might be tabulated using a series of much simpler calculations. Babbage's friend and supporter, stockbroker Francis Baily, marveled that the machine's design would allow it to calculate up to "four orders of differences" through a "principle well known to be, at once, simple and correct in its nature,"[65] and a triumphant Babbage, referring to this same "principle," announced that "the method of differences has now, for the first time, been embodied into machinery."[66]

As both Baily and Babbage discerned, the new invention translated the results of higher-order equations into a sequence of predictable, constant differences, remaking a more complex calculus into simple arithmetic. Baily elaborated:

> A machine to add a number of arbitrary figures together is no economy of time or trouble; since each individual figure must be placed in the machine. But it is otherwise when those figures follow some law. The insertion of a few at first determines the magnitude of the next; and these of the succeeding. It is this constant repetition of similar operations, which renders the computation of tables a fit subject for the application of machinery.[67]

Babbage likewise described the certainty of this mathematical future, where figures not yet calculated could be predicted based on fixed laws: "[T]he equation of differences being given, I can, by setting an engine, produce, at the end of a given time, any distant term which may be required. . . . I can produce the numerical result which it is the object of that law to give."[68] For both, a knowable future rested on the existence of a single, transcendent law, such that the 51st term, or the 2,051st term, could always be calculated and known in an instant; it suggested that the future could be predicted in terms of a constant relationship to the past or to the present. The Difference Engine, then, represented not only the relentless accuracy of mechanism, but also the reassuring certitude of an inexorable law operating in spite of the fluctuations of time, circumstance, and human labor.[69]

This promise of accurate and easily reproducible tables met with an enthusiastic response. Noting that the engine would benefit a range of professions—the "surveyor, the architect, the builder, the carpenter, the miner, the gauger, the naval architect, the engineer, civil and military"—Lardner stressed "the truly national importance" of this "perfect and easy means of producing those tables."[70] The British government concurred, and beginning in 1823, it authorized a series of payments to Babbage for the engine's construction. Over the next ten years, by Babbage's estimate, the government would invest around £17,000 in the Difference Engine, a sum that Babbage, who had by 1827 inherited his father's considerable estate, liberally supplemented in turn with his own fortune.[71] By 1833, however, after a series of disagreements with his engineer Joseph Clement, and with dwindling funds, Babbage stopped work on the Difference Engine.[72] The partially completed, functioning fragment remained at Babbage's private residence, where, if it generated no tables of "national importance," it drew at least the admiration of visitors.

But behind his decision to abandon work on the Difference Engine lay another reason: his growing interest in a new project. The strength of the Difference Engine, he had come to realize, was also its weakness. In generating tables based on a single polynomial, the machine was, as Lord Byron's daughter, young mathematician Ada Lovelace, put it, an "expression of one particular theorem of analysis," but as she also recognized, "its operations cannot be extended so as to embrace the solution of an infinity of other questions."[73] As the author of

A Comparative View of the Various Institutions for the Assurance of Lives, Babbage would likewise have recognized that the Difference Engine was ill equipped to produce and print tables such as those required by the insurance industry, which necessarily accommodated a shifting, multivariate rather than linear future. As the construction of the Difference Engine became mired in difficulties, both practical and financial, Babbage conceived of a new machine, called the Analytical Engine, which was to surpass his first invention in numerous ways. He brought these ideas forward for the first time in 1834. In a cautious letter to the prime minister, he acknowledged the government's previous support and summarized his progress to date on the Difference Engine, before turning to what he admitted was "a subject of great difficulty," which he knew might imperil further funding for the first, stalled project: his proposed design for a "totally new engine possessing much more extensive powers, and capable of calculations of a nature far more complicated."[74] In spite of these ambitious claims, the new engine received little attention from the government, and, as Babbage had feared, funding for the earlier one ceased altogether.[75]

The Analytical Engine consumed Babbage's attention between 1833 and 1846, and although he devised numerous plans and designs for it during these years, it received no financial support and was never built.[76] Yet despite its lackluster reception by the government, his designs found several champions, including Lovelace and a number of mathematicians—Giovanni Plana, Luigi Menabrea, and Ottaviano Mossotti—in Italy.[77] In 1843 Lovelace published her English translation of Menabrea's 1842 "Notions sur la machine analytique de M. Charles Babbage," along with her own extensive explanatory notes (which on their own were more than three times as long as Menabrea's original document), as "Sketch of the Analytical Engine."[78] As these works revealed, the new calculating machine had a number of advantages over its predecessor. First, it was capable of a wider array of mathematical functions, including multiplication and division. Second, it could handle multiple operations at once and store the results of one computation while a second (or third, or fourth) was underway.[79] Third, through the feeding of cards into the machine, an innovation inspired by Jacquard's automated loom,[80] the calculating functions to be executed could be determined in advance by its operator—to be followed in a particular order and to meet a specified set of circumstances. This early version of a computer program meant not only that the machine was capable of what is now known as looping, where the output from one calculation might be reintroduced as input into the same or another calculation, but also that it could change course without the operator's intervention, "on the occurrence," Lovelace explained, "of any specified contingency."[81]

For Babbage and his interlocutors, the new engine's capabilities, no longer limited to mere table-making, might be understood as analogous to other complex processes such as the developmental changes of the organism, the earth's transformations over a period of millennia, or even the creator's divine plan as it unfolded over time. Lovelace, for example, referring back to the French textile technology that inspired Babbage's mechanism in describing the Analytical Engine's ability to combine multiple functions, writes that "We may say most aptly that the Analytical Engine *weaves algebraical patterns* just as the Jacquard loom weaves flowers and leaves."[82] But after likening the engine's numerical output to floral designs on textile, she extends her analogy to include the generation of nature itself; for the engine's mathematical functions, as she puts it, speak the same "language through which alone we can adequately express the great facts of the natural world, and those unceasing changes of mutual relationship which, visibly or invisibly, consciously or unconsciously to our immediate physical perceptions, are interminably going on."[83] The progression of Lovelace's analogies also implicitly distinguishes the Analytical Engine from its predecessor. While the method of differences produced a sequence whose linearity represented the reliability and relentlessness of mechanism, the capabilities of the new machine could best be understood through natural, temporal, or linguistic metaphors, and through additional dimensions across which difference and variation might reveal themselves.[84] But where Lovelace and Menabrea make these comparisons only fleetingly, focusing instead on the engine's mathematical potential, Babbage elaborates upon them with a similar set of analogies in his 1837 *Ninth Bridgewater Treatise: A Fragment*, a meandering contemplation of the relationship between Christianity and mathematics.

Babbage composed the treatise as his own independently published contribution to the *Bridgewater Treatises on the Power, Wisdom and Goodness of God as Manifested in the Creation*, a series of eight volumes published from 1833 to 1836 at the behest of the Earl of Bridgewater's posthumous commission. Written by some of the period's leading scientific and theological experts, the treatises were, according to Jonathan Topham, intended as "a largely nontechnical and religiously conservative compendium of contemporary science."[85] They extended and complicated existing arguments about natural theology, especially those set forth in William Paley's by-then canonical *Natural Theology*, originally published in 1802; specifically, by examining recent findings in a range of areas including geology, physiology, natural history, and astronomy, they aimed to show how natural laws existed in alignment with a larger, divine plan.[86] Recognized as an important contribution to popular scientific knowledge, the series was widely read as well as widely used in educational institutions.[87] In the years during and following their publication, a small flurry of works, in addition to Babbage's *Ninth*, would claim the status of unofficial contributions to the series, such as J. S. Bushnan's 1834 *Introduction to the Study of Nature, Illustrative of the Attributes of the Almighty, as Displayed in the Creation* and Charles Mountford Burnett's 1838 *The Power, Wisdom, and Goodness of God, as Displayed in the Animal Creation*.[88]

Babbage's volume makes its arguments in a fashion at once encompassing and incoherent, veering from reflections concerning divine providence and the occurrence of miracles, to musings on such subjects as the human desire for fame, French probability theory, and the rate at which heated granite expands. Recent assessments of the *Ninth Bridgewater Treatise* have been largely dismissive, characterizing it as "fragmentary," "idiosyncratic," and a "Tristram Shandy of a book."[89] Nonetheless, his biographer Doron Swade deems it his "most philosophically rewarding work," and Alan Liu reads both its original and revised versions as searching accounts of the possibility of free will within a determined system.[90] But where the incalculability of the human becomes legible for Liu by reading around the edges of Babbage's published text, I argue that the central concern of *Treatise*—as of the nineteenth-century natural sciences more generally, from the *Bridgewater Treatises* to Darwin and beyond—is the status not of will but of chance within a providential worldview. For all its idiosyncrasy and unconventionality, it is, I suggest, something of a sequel to his *Assurance of Lives*, an extension and experimental expansion of his earlier actuarial reflections on the principles of contingency and the incalculability of the future.

Most immediately, the *Ninth* was a response to William Whewell, who had argued, in his official contribution to the Bridgewater series, that natural history (or what would come to be known as the biological sciences) could provide insights into the creation that mathematics could not.[91] Babbage disagreed, arguing that the laws of mathematics were uniquely equipped, being pure rather than dependent on the senses as the other sciences were, to reveal Christianity's "first class of truths."[92] But Babbage's contribution also used mathematics in ways that unsettled some of the foundational premises of the official Bridgewater volumes. While it demonstrated affinities with the natural theology of Paley and Whewell, his inconsistent claims about and metaphors for the nature of divine agency at times advanced a different set of theories to describe its scope and its relationship to chance.[93]

At points his language affirms a theology that seems to come in undiluted form from Leibniz: a belief that God possesses both the foresight and vision to have anticipated the need for complexity and to have accommodated all contingencies at the moment of creation. Yet in explicating these principles, Babbage's language often veers in another direction. Paley had famously compared God to a watchmaker, but Whewell chose a governmental analogy, calling him a "legislator" of natural laws.[94] In the *Ninth,* Babbage returns to the technological: For him, the earth functions like a calculating machine, with God as its designer and operator. But while Paley sets the analogy aside once it has served its purpose, Babbage's calculating machines continue to loom large throughout, threatening to transcend any merely metaphorical status in his text. Was the Analytical Machine to be understood as a figure for the enormity of the creation, a material example that serves a theological claim,[95] or—as readers of the *Ninth* might legitimately have asked—was the creation the example by which they might better understand the workings of the machine?

Babbage begins by considering how a single plan might account for the range of types and multiple transformations observable in nature: the emergence of the butterfly from the branch-bound caterpillar, for instance, or the variety of forms in the vegetable world, and the sheer range of speciation.[96] The distinction he draws between misguided accounts of God "as perpetually interfering, to alter for a time the laws He had previously ordained" and a vision of God as possessed of "foresight . . . the highest attribute of omnipotence," is a response to those who, like William Buckland—author of *Geology and Miner-alogy Considered with Reference to Natural Theology*, one of the volumes in the official *Bridgewater* series—espoused a theory of "Creative Interference," by which God asserted "direct agency" in the creation of each of the "new forms of organic life."[97]

For Babbage, the need for interference was a mark of inferior design. At the opening of chapter 8, for example, whose purpose is to illuminate the "attributes of the Deity," he explains the role of divine providence in governing the natural world: "[I]t is more consistent with the attributes of the Deity to look upon miracles not as deviations from the laws assigned by the Almighty . . . but as the exact fulfillment of much more extensive laws than those we suppose to exist."[98] By the second paragraph, he translates this theological question into a mathematical, then a technological one, as he turns to a comparison of two different calculating machines, the first requiring the operator's intervention to produce an observed change, the next operating under a set of prearranged laws. Both generate an apparently predictable sequence of numbers, a series of squared integers, broken only by a single cubed number. The operator of the latter machine, however,

> has the power to order *any* number of such apparent deviations from its laws to occur at any future periods, however remote, and that each of these may be of a different kind . . . there can be no doubt that the observer would ascribe to the inventor far higher knowledge than if . . . he were to intervene, and temporarily to alter the calculations of the machine.[99]

In other words, the machine capable only of "one particular theorem" (to borrow Lovelace's terminology)—like the Difference Engine—was necessarily inferior, while the machine capable of responding to "the occurrence of any specified contingency" (to adopt Lovelace's description of the Analytical Engine), whose operator might charge it with expressing any number of theorems, approached the divine. Campbell-Kelly writes that, "Babbage saw God as the programmer of a divine algorithm,"[100] but so too, Babbage figured the programmer of the Analytical Engine as endowed with a god-like capacity. Yet the parallels between the prudent consumer of life insurance, for whom a policy would both acknowledge and manage the contingencies of everyday life, and this superior entity are evident here as well, especially in Babbage's application of the language of life insurance writings—"foresight"—to theological questions in his volume's opening.[101]

In drawing these comparisons, Babbage implies that where the Difference Engine's unchanging series revealed only mechanism, the sequence of numbers generated by the Analytical Engine should be understood, as indeed Lovelace had likewise suggested, as a kind of narrative, with a legible temporal and causal structure. Its confrontations with contingency, like the "miracles" observable in the natural world, are encoded as discontinuities in an otherwise continuous pattern; these are the legible traces of the moments in which agency and chance, design and accident, converged. From his university days when, as a founder and member of the Analytical Society he compared the forms of notation used in the period's calculus texts, he had been interested in how abstract mathematical principles might best be communicated in linguistic form and on the printed page. So too, his *Assurance of Lives* juxtaposed tables showing the "value of contingencies" and prose illustrations of life's uncertainties, as if to imply that numbers and narrative might be extensions of each other. The *Ninth* actively pursues this parallel between numerical and narrative forms of representation. Thus while Babbage regarded mathematics, according to historian William Ashworth, as an ideal "mental technology" that could take the place of a less precise and potentially unwieldy biblical verse,[102] the *Ninth Bridgewater Treatise*, through its complex network of analogies—where the engine and natural theology, and an output of numbers and nature itself, might serve as examples of each other—also elaborates on Lovelace's contention that numbers might serve as a form of "language," that a sequence of calculations might convey meaning in both articulate and legible ways. For like the scriptures, the engine's numbers could render a historical process visible, albeit in coded form, by communicating through its sequential patterns the relationship between past and present, as well as expectations for the future.

Babbage was nonetheless inconsistent about the exact nature of God's "program" for earthly complexity, an inconsistency that the fragmentary quality of his treatise only exacerbated. Perhaps for this reason, the *Ninth Bridgewater Treatise*, in spite of the established reputation of its author, was, as Walter

Cannon explains, embraced neither by proponents of natural theology nor by advocates of a new, more secular geohistory.[103] For while Babbage refuted William Buckland's conception of a God who guided the world amidst changing conditions through repeated acts of intervention, would Babbage's vision align with that of Leibniz's God, who had already examined all contingencies and who had already chosen among them a single script for the future? At times, the *Ninth* seems to point in this direction. Babbage, for example, classifies divine knowledge as the capacity

> to have *foreseen*, at the creation of matter and of mind . . . all these changes, and to have provided, by one comprehensive law, for all that should ever occur, either to the races themselves, to the individuals of which they are composed, or to the globe which they inhabit . . .[104]

And this is the version of natural theology, Liu suggests, to which the *Ninth* adheres, one in which "history, slaved to natural determination, can be read forward and backward all along the illimitable tracks of the great program."[105] Babbage would certainly have had contemporaneous British arguments in favor of natural theology in mind. In Note C to his *Treatise*, citing Laplace's account of divinity in his 1814 "Philosophical Essay on Probabilities"—"for it [God's intelligence], nothing would be uncertain and the future, as the past, would be present to its eyes"—he alludes to the existence of a transcendent, providential vision in whose eyes the contingencies of the future were, like "the past," already foreclosed.[106]

Yet elsewhere Babbage implies that these possible futures remain unrealized and undetermined, even to an all-knowing entity. As he explains in the preface to the first edition, God might be "intimately cognizant of the remotest consequences of the present as well as of all other laws," but this means merely that the divine plan "should require no future intervention to meet events unanticipated by its Author."[107] In this rendering, even God inhabits a world of "events unanticipated," of contingencies untested, and yet—and here that God differs markedly from Buckland's—one in which such contingencies demand "no future intervention." In this alternate account of the creation, divine agency is distinct from both omniscience and determinism. Again, Babbage elaborates on this claim by turning to the technological. The availability of chance and free will, he explains, might be understood through the operations of his new calculating engine, whereby a new function could

> be made to take place at a time not foreseen by the person employing the engine. For example: when calculating a table of squares, it may be made to change into a table of cubes, the first time the square number ends in the figures 269696; an event which only occurs at the 99,736th calculation; and whether that fact is known to the person who adjusts the machine or not, is immaterial to the result.[108]

In a world where God's plan encompasses eventualities without determining them, the unanticipated occurrence of the number 9,947,269,696 (the square of 99,736) represents the moment of contingency. What was at stake in that possibility, as both Babbage and Lovelace recognized, had implications for an understanding of both computational and natural design. As Whewell and, at points, Babbage himself, took pains to demonstrate, what looks like chance is merely an effect of our mortal perspective, of the necessarily limited and fragmented knowledge available to us. But the *Ninth* also posits that chance might not be a function (only) of epistemology, but might have ontological standing, and what is more, it suggests that admitting this fact does not constitute a negation of design, but rather its reimagining. A superior design, whether divine or technological, that is, would be able to accommodate the operations of a truly unforeclosed future.

The Analytical Engine, Babbage ventures, might offer one mechanism by which to accomplish this, but as he would have known, life insurance offered another. In Ewald's words, "Insurance can be defined as a technology of risk,"[109] and like insurance, the Analytical Engine was a technology defined by its ability to admit indeterminacy, the unpredictable and unknown. Indeed, as Babbage well knew, whether one was the actuary preparing tables of premiums or the customer purchasing a policy, anticipating the future was not the same as knowing or determining it. Rather, by thinking contingently, one exercised the kind of foresight that ensured that "no future intervention" would be required, even when "events unanticipated" happened to occur. A good algorithm, like a good insurance policy, could at least offer an assurance that all possibilities and eventualities would be encompassed by it.

Thus even when theological questions had been set aside, the nature of the Analytical Engine's ability to respond to contingency was a matter of great interest to Babbage and his circle; more particularly, they asked, did intellectual agency reside in the engine's operator, or in the engine itself—and if the latter, what was its extent? In his 1837 essay, "On the Mathematical Powers of the Calculating Engine," Babbage's only publication devoted solely to the Analytical Engine, he cautioned that the "analogy between these [mechanized] acts and the operations of mind" were merely "convenient and expressive," rather than indicative of the engine's intellectual powers;[110] Menabrea, too, was circumspect on this point: "[T]he machine is not a thinking being, but simply an automaton which acts according to the laws imposed upon it," he wrote in his 1842 essay.[111] But Lovelace endorsed the analogy, again drawing on the language of "contingency" that pervaded contemporaneous writings on life insurance: "The engine is capable, under certain circumstances, of feeling about to discover which of two or more possible contingencies has occurred, and of then shaping its future course accordingly."[112] For her, the capacity of the personified engine, like that of its operator, to navigate a realm of undetermined outcomes and contingencies constituted a form of agency and freedom. Nor was Babbage himself wholly resistant to this reading, for when an Italian physicist, Professor Mosotti, later questioned "how the machine could perform the act of judgement sometimes required during an analytical enquiry, when two or more different courses presented themselves," Babbage seemed to affirm the possibility of agency in his reply: "It is not even necessary that two courses only should be possible. Any number of courses may be possible at the same time; and the choice of each may depend upon any number of conditions."[113]

Crucially for Babbage and his respondents, "thinking" (as opposed to mere mechanism) *was* thinking contingently, activated in the moment of what they termed "choice," in the engagement with shifting circumstances and the evaluation of alternatives that might arise, the consideration of any number of undetermined "future courses" of action. Just as what distinguished the "prudent" individual from his "thoughtless" counterpart, so he had argued in *Assurance of Lives*, was the former's acknowledgment of the "uncertainty of life,"[114] the "thinking" engine was designed to operate with a similar set of uncertainties. Unlike the Difference Engine, then, which presupposed a predictable and known future, both life insurance and the design of the Analytical Engine envisioned a world in which the future did not necessarily adhere to patterns established in the past; this new realm required instead an active and repeated weighing of conditions, circumstances, and contingencies at every moment. Years earlier, in its review of *Assurance of Lives*, the *Edinburgh Review* had described life insurance as a means of responding to the "shifting scene of things,"[115] and Babbage's Analytical Engine responded to this "shifting scene" as well—a landscape of chance, uncertainty, and possibility.

For Babbage, then, where the linear output of the Difference Engine reflected the reliability of the machine, the numbers generated by the Analytical Engine, with their series of repetitions and divergences—a long sequence of squares followed by a cube, for example—were far more articulate, telling a kind of story about shifting circumstances and conditions, alternatives considered, and paths taken. Indeed, if we look to Marie-Laure Ryan's "fuzzy-set definition" of narrative—which applies to a work with, at minimum, "spatial," "temporal," and "mental" dimensions, whose posited realm "undergo[es] significant transformations . . . caused by non-habitual physical events," and whose "participants" are "intelligent agents" capable of "purposeful actions"[116]—then the way Babbage and his supporters read the following hypothetical sequence of numbers is as a form of narrative:

1

2

3

4

5

· · ·

· · ·

· · · · ·

· · · · ·

99,999,999

100,000,000

(regularly as far as) 100,000,001

100,010,002 (the law changes)

100,030,003

100,060,004

100,100,005[117]

The sequence suggests a responsive agency, with moments of "feeling" and "choice" (to borrow Lovelace's and Babbage's words, respectively) behind the shifting pattern of figures. Where prose accounts of accidents and sudden deaths enabled, for his contemporaries in the insurance industry, an elaboration of what statistical tables communicated in numbers, Babbage was interested in the converse: the means by which the temporal and causal complexity of a process might be expressed as a numerical sequence. Through their erratic progress over time, the numbers in an insurance rate table could convey, perhaps more precisely than any story rendered in prose, the contingencies governing individual lives.

In turning his attention from actuarial principles to the contingencies shaping other, much longer histories in the *Ninth Bridgewater Treatise*, Babbage also extended the kinds of stories that numbers could tell—including those revealed in the geological record and through the perpetuation of ocean waves and even sound waves over millennia.[118] All of these, he suggested, constitute the left traces of longer narratives, whether in the form of granite layers or "ripple-marks" in sediment and air, and thus "bear equally enduring testimony" to the past.[119] For Babbage, history, through periods of both uniformity and discontinuity, could become legible through the inscription of sequences— encoded, as it were—in the natural world, in the same way that a history of agency and contingency might be read in the Analytical Engine's numerical output. Thus within trees he located a narrative of the earth's history and, significantly, a narrative whose encryption in the form of tree rings might subsequently be translated into another language.[120] Trees, he explained, bore the "indelible records of past events" at their core, "every shower that falls, every change of temperature that occurs, and every wind that blows...; slight, indeed, and imperceptible, perhaps, to us, but not the less permanently recorded in the depths of those woody fabrics."[121] Such sequential changes in climate and condition were not only legible in the tree's rings, he asserted, but they, in turn, might also be converted into a sequence of letters, "*o L L s o o o o s L L o o*," denoting "ordinary," "large," and "stinted" rings.[122] Significantly, where the numerical narratives that served as his examples focused on a single moment of contingency, the sudden occurrence of 9,947,269,696 or of 100,010,002 in an otherwise seemingly predictable sequence, Babbage's tree rings told a story that more closely resembled that found in life insurance, of ever-changing conditions and multiple variables, where every moment bore the possibility of a future distinctly different from the past.

The actuarial table, the output of the Analytical Engine, even a sequence of letters or numbers could be understood, according to Babbage, as forms of narrative shorthand. Trained readers might come to decipher periods of stability, shifting circumstances and conditions, and decisive events—an encoded history of contingency, just legible in the world around them, in patterns of mortality, the products of mathematical functions, and the growth rings of trees.

Late Scraps

By the 1840s, Babbage had resigned from his position at Cambridge and ceased work on the Analytical Engine. Now in his 50s, he turned his attention to a range of seemingly disparate endeavors, such as essays on submarines, lighthouses, taxation, and deciphering; a "Table of the relative frequency of occurrence of the causes of breaking of plate glass windows"; a renewed plan to complete the Difference Engine; and a sustained personal campaign against the street noise that, he argued, disrupted his work.[123] Campbell-Kelly characterizes these productions as the work of a "spent" and disappointed genius,[124] and scholarly attention to these later examples from Babbage's oeuvre drops away in corresponding measure.

It was during these years that he participated in one of the more popular pastimes of the period, one that appealed as much, if not more, to women than to men: the keeping of a scrapbook. Commercially available scrapbooks of the first half of the nineteenth century generally offered blank pages upon which their owners could mount clippings, images, lines of verse, or memorabilia from an evening's entertainment; they could also add personal embellishments in the form of freehand drawings, inscriptions in prose or verse, and even scraps of lace, hair, embroidery, or flora. In addition, scrapbook pages often showed signs of collaborative, communal effort, where solicited contributions from friends and relatives marked the "wider networks of sociability" for which the volume served as a "tangible memorial."[125]

But even this material record of Babbage's leisure hours reveals the idiosyncrasies of its owner. In a genre often employed and read as a form of feminine self-expression, Babbage's album elaborates on some of the abiding concerns of his professional life, and like his earlier *Ninth Bridgewater Treatise*, it was an aggregation of fragments. Yet the album contains next to nothing from its owner's private pen, being instead composed entirely of pieces cut from newspapers and journals.[126] And where, for example, the scrapbook of his male contemporary, American economist and social scientist Henry Carey, was similarly lacking in handwritten detail (though it did bear signs of personal ownership through its gathering of articles and reviews concerning its owner's publications),[127] the contents of Babbage's album look, by contrast, impersonal. Like other examples of the period, it reveals an appreciation for poetry and riddles ("Why is love like a potatoe [*sic*]?" clipped from a newspaper); he also seems to have been fond of printed images, which included the sentimental (a woman cradling a lamb), the exotic (stylized renditions of Chinese art), as well as classical and military portraits.[128] Still, some of the book's contents more clearly reflect Babbage's intellectual interests. An image of the Temple of Serapis in Italy was likely a visual reference to his 1847 essay on the geology of the site; announcements of new devices and mechanisms—such as the electric telegraph and Baranowski's "Ready Reckoning Machine"—and notices for exhibitions both major ("the Great Exhibition") and minor ("A Grand Spider Show") mirror his continuing interest in the period's scientific ventures.[129]

But Babbage reserved the majority of his scrapbook's pages for advertisements he had cut from newspapers, and specifically, from the sections of the *Times* that, as one contemporaneous observer proclaimed, were more "frequently thrown aside unread" than otherwise.[130] In some cases, these were commercial notices, but more often they were announcements placed by private citizens, sometimes advertising items lost and found: "LOST, on Thursday evening, the 13th inst., at Polish Hall, Guildhall, a LADY's POCKET HAND-KERCHIEF, trimmed with wide Brussels lace, very rich. Whoever has found the same and will bring it to 14, Berners street, Oxford street, will be RE-WARDED," and "LOST, on Monday evening, a TABBY CAT with a brass collar. Whoever will bring the same to 32, Wimpole street, will receive TEN SHILLINGS REWARD."[131] Others advertised for lost persons: "E. B., who left his home, at Islington, on Monday last, is affectionately requested to COMMU-NICATE with his friends, who are suffering great anxiety on his account";[132]

"H. P. C. is earnestly requested to SEE the PARTY who is broken-hearted by his unaccountable conduct. The secret is safe. Write, or they cannot live—M. H.";[133] or "G. T. L.—Pray WRITE to me. I have full authority to promote your object without requiring your return, and wait the opportunity to do so.—J. A."[134] Still others telegraphed responses or advice to unknown parties: "Z. Y. YES. You are deceived, be cautious," for instance, and "TO 'ALETHE.'—I don't. Appoint a place, and S. will write."[135]

Each scrapbook page appears to have been organized around a loose thematic focus—persons, objects, animals—but whether a consistent pattern governed their assembly and placement within each page is unclear. The lost "tabby cat" item, for example, appears with other advertisements concerning dogs and cats; he had excised that announcement along with the one that was printed immediately after it, regarding a lost "FAWN-COLOURED ITALIAN GRAYHOUND," from the 27 January 1843 *Times*, but the subsequent item, advertising "DOGS of FASHION" for sale, comes from the 5 April 1843, issue, and the next, "FOUND ASTRAY, a large MASTIFF," was cut from the 16 January 1844, paper.[136] Another page (Figure 1.1) adopts a loosely alphabetical arrangement, where messages from "A. C." precede an article about the disappearance of "Adela Villiers," and subsequently, a telegraphic announcement from someone calling themselves a "A FRIEND to JUSTICE."[137] The organizing theme of another scrapbook page, however, is more elusive: a lost manuscript, a "SPANISH FAN" "TAKEN" from Devonshire House, a request for the address of "J. MENZIES."[138]

What drew him to these announcements, rather than to the equally intriguing scenarios that other, unchosen entries in those same issues of the *Times* conjured, such as the "GOLD BRACELET, set with malachite stones" lost at Ascot, for example, or the earnest search for "DAVID CROSS, who about the years 1838, 1839, or 1840, was living as footman in the family of the late Alderman Venables"?[139] These pages encourage us to ask, as Roger Cardinal did when contemplating twentieth-century Dadaist works assembled out of scrap paper, what these "dead letters spell . . . out," and whether the patterns we see are the operations of chance or of "expressive intent."[140] Babbage's assiduous collecting of thousands of these advertisements for his scrapbook—into which he occasionally placed entire columns intact and at other times pieced numerous

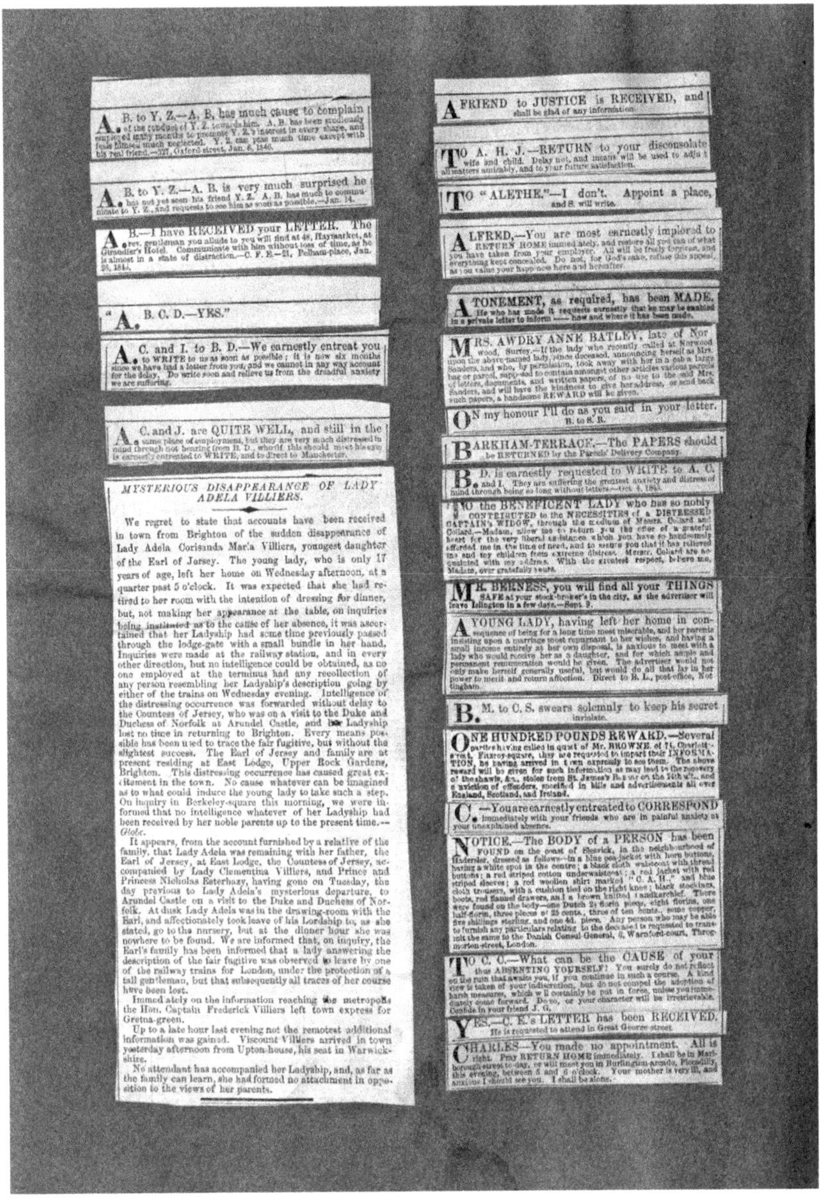

A B. to Y. Z.—A: B, has much cause to complain of the conduct of Y. Z. towards him. A.B. has been studiously treated in many months to presume Y. Z. can put much time except with his real friend.—227, Oxford-street, Jan. 6, 1846.

A B. to Y. Z.—A. B. is very much surprised he has not yet seen his friend Y. Z. A. B. has much to communicate to Y. Z., and requests to see him as soon as possible.—Jan. 14.

A H.—I have RECEIVED your LETTER. The ever, gentleman you allude to you will find at 48, Haymarket, at Gunselier's Hotel. Communicate with him without loss of time, as he is almost in a state of distraction.—C. F. R.—21, Pelham-place, Jan. 20, 1841.

"A B. C. D.—YES."

A C. and I. to B. D.—We earnestly entreat you to WRITE to us as soon as possible; it is now six months since we have had a letter from you, and we cannot in any way account for the delay. Do write soon and relieve us from the dreadful anxiety we are suffering.

A C. and J. are QUITE WELL, and still in the same place of employment, but they are very much distressed in mind through not hearing from D. D.; should this should meet his eye is earnestly entreated to WRITE, and to direct to Manchester.

MYSTERIOUS DISAPPEARANCE OF LADY ADELA VILLIERS.

We regret to state that accounts have been received in town from Brighton of the sudden disappearance of Lady Adela Corisanda Maria Villiers, youngest daughter of the Earl of Jersey. The young lady, who is only 17 years of age, left her home on Wednesday afternoon, at a quarter past 5 o'clock. It was expected that she had retired to her room with the intention of dressing for dinner, but, not making her appearance at the table, on inquiries being instituted as to the cause of her absence, it was ascertained that her Ladyship had some time previously passed through the lodge-gate with a small bundle in her hand. Inquiries were made at the railway station, and in every other direction, but no intelligence could be obtained, as no one employed at the terminus had any recollection of any person resembling her Ladyship's description going by either of the trains on Wednesday evening. Intelligence of the distressing occurrence was forwarded without delay to the Countess of Jersey, who was on a visit to the Duke and Duchess of Norfolk at Arundel Castle, and her Ladyship lost no time in returning to Brighton. Every means possible has been used to trace the fair fugitive, but without the slightest success. The Earl of Jersey and family are at present residing at East Lodge, Upper Rock Gardens, Brighton. This distressing occurrence has caused great excitement in the town. No cause whatever can be imagined as to what could induce the young lady to take such a step. On inquiry in Berkeley-square this morning, we were informed that no intelligence whatever of her Ladyship had been received by her noble parents up to the present time.—Globe.

It appears, from the account furnished by a relative of the family, that Lady Adela was remaining with her father, the Earl of Jersey, at East Lodge, the Countess of Jersey, accompanied by Lady Clementina Villiers, and Prince and Princess Nicholas Esterhazy, having gone on Tuesday, the day previous to Lady Adela's mysterious departure, to Arundel Castle on a visit to the Duke and Duchess of Norfolk. At dusk Lady Adela was in the drawing-room with the Earl, and affectionately took leave of his Lordship to, as she stated, go to the nursery, but at the dinner hour she was nowhere to be found. We are informed that, on inquiry, the Earl's hopes have been informed that a lady answering the description of the fair fugitive was observed to leave by one of the railway trains for London, under the protection of a tall gentleman, but that subsequently all traces of her course have been lost.

Immediately on the information reaching the metropolis the Hon. Captain Frederick Villiers left town express for Gretna-green.

Up to a late hour last evening not the remotest additional information was gained. Viscount Villiers arrived in town yesterday afternoon from Upton-house, his seat in Warwickshire.

No attendant has accompanied her Ladyship, and, as far as the family can learn, she had formed no attachment in opposition to the views of her parents.

A FRIEND to JUSTICE is RECEIVED, and shall be glad of any information.

T O A. H. J.—RETURN to your disconsolate wife and child. Delay not, and means will be used to adjust all matters amicably, and to your future satisfaction.

T O "ALETHE."—I don't. Appoint a place, and it will write.

A LFRED.—You are most earnestly implored to RETURN HOME immediately, and restore all you can of what you have taken from your employer. All will be freely forgiven, and everything kept concealed. Do not, for God's sake, refuse this appeal, as you value your happiness here and hereafter.

A TONEMENT, as required, has been MADE. He who has made it requests earnestly that he may be enabled in a private letter to inform — how and where it has been made.

M RS. AWDRY ANNE BATLEY, late of Norwood, Surrey.—If the lady who recently called at Norwood upon the above-named lady, since deceased, announcing herself as Mrs. Saunders, and who, by permission, took away with her in a cab a large bag or parcel, supposed to contain amongst other articles various papers of letters, daguerreotypes, and written papers, of no use to the said Mrs. Saunders, and will have the kindness to give her address, or send back such papers, a handsome REWARD will be given.

O N my honour I'll do as you said in your letter. B. to R.B.

B ARKHAM-TERRACE.—The PAPERS should be RETURNED by the Parcels' Delivery Company.

B D. is earnestly requested to WRITE to A. C. and I. They are entering the greatest anxiety and distress of mind through being so long without letters.—Oct. 9, 1845.

T O the BENEFICENT LADY who has so nobly CONTRIBUTED to the NECESSITIES of a DISTRESSED CAPTAIN'S WIDOW, through the medium of Messrs. Collard and Collard.—Madam, allow me to return you the case of a grateful heart for the very liberal assistance which you have so handsomely afforded me in the time of need, and to assure you that it has relieved me and my children from extreme distress. Messrs. Collard are acquainted with my address. With the sincerest respect, believe me, Madam, ever gratefully yours.

M R. BERNESS, you will find all your THINGS SAFE at your stock-broker's in the city, as the advertiser will leave Islington in a few days.—Sept. 3.

A YOUNG LADY, having left her home in consequence of being for a long time most miserable, and her parents insisting upon a marriage most repugnant to her wishes, and having a small income entirely at her own disposal, is anxious to meet with a lady who would receive her as a daughter, and for which ample and permanent remuneration would be given. The advertiser would but only make herself generally useful, but would do all that lay in her power to merit and return affection. Direct to B. L., post-office, Nottingham.

B. M. to C. S. swears solemnly to keep his secret inviolate.

O NE HUNDRED POUNDS REWARD.—Several parties having called in quest of Mr. BROWNE, of 74, Charlotte-street, Fitzroy-square, they are requested to impart their INFORMATION, on having arrived in town personally to no them. The above reward will be given for such information as may lead to the recovery of the estate, &c., stolen from St. James's Bazaar, on the 21st inst., and a variety of offenders, most of it in his said advertisement in all over England, Scotland, and Ireland.

C.—I you are earnestly entreated to CORRESPOND immediately with your friends who are in painful anxiety at your unexplained absence.

N OTICE.—The BODY of a PERSON has been FOUND on the coast of Sussex, in the neighbourhood of Hastings, dressed as follows—in a blue pea-jacket with horn buttons, having a white spot in the centre; a black cloth waistcoat with steel buttons; a red striped cotton under-waistcoat; a red jacket with red striped sleeves; a red woollen shirt marked "C. A. H.," and blue cloth trousers, with a cushion tied on the right knee; black stockings, boots, red flannel drawers, an I a brown knitted handkerchief. There was found on the body—one Dutch 2s. 6d. piece, eight florins, one half-florin, three pieces of 25 cents, three of ten cents, some copper, five shillings sterling, and one 4d. piece. Any person who may be able to furnish any particulars relating to the deceased is requested to transmit the same to the Danish Consul-General, 6, Warnford-court, Throgmorton-street, London.

T O C. C.—What can be the CAUSE of your thus ABSENTING YOURSELF? You surely do not reflect on the ruin that awaits you, if you continue in such a course. A kind have is taken of your indiscretion, but do not compel the adoption of harsh measures, which will certainly be put in force, unless you immediately come forward. Do so, or your character will be irretrievable. Confide in your friend J. O.

Y ES.—C. E.'s LETTER has been RECEIVED. He is requested to attend to General George-street.

C HARLES.—You made no appointment. All is right. Pray RETURN HOME immediately. I shall be in Marlborough-street to-day, or will meet you in Burlington-Arcade, Piccadilly, this evening, between 5 and 6 o'clock. Your mother is very ill, and anxious I should see you. I shall be alone.

FIGURE 1.1 Page from Charles Babbage's scrapbook (c. 1847–51), n. p. Kress Collection, Baker Library, Harvard Business School.

individual advertisements into a kind of collage—seems to do more than re-constitute a version of the front page of the *Times*. But if so, what "expressive intent" underlies their meticulous arrangement?

One obvious reading is biographical. By offering insight into the personal intimacies of others, they suggest a readerly voyeurism, an impulse to witness in other lives fragmentary reflections of his own sense of sorrow over lost intimacies, perhaps with those family members who died in 1827: his wife, his father, and two of his sons. Taken from another perspective, these advertisements might serve as material examples of the invisible "library" of spoken words that, as Babbage hypothesized in the *Ninth Bridgewater Treatise*, hung in the particles of the air; embedded in unseen sound waves, "in their mutable but unerring charac-ters . . . [they] stand for ever recorded, vows unredeemed, promises unfulfilled, perpetuating in the united movements of each particle, the testimony of man's changeful will."[141] As testimonials to incompletion and misunderstanding, these advertisements also offer a refracted perspective into the "vows unredeemed" and "promises unfulfilled" in Babbage's scientific life, the unfinished projects and unrecognized efforts, the professional disappointments, the importuning letters, often unanswered, to prospective sponsors and supporters.

These interpretations cast Babbage as something of a late Romantic, who recognized the emotional power that lay in the moment arrested, the intention or desire forever unfulfilled, where beauty "cannot fade, though thou hast not thy bliss." But these scraps also shed light on Babbage the actuary and designer of the Analytical Engine, for whom the narrative fragment was the sign of an interrupted series, in which the past was, at least for a moment, severed from a legible future. Where Keats might have celebrated incompletion for its constancy and permanence, Babbage was interested in the mathematical and epistemological challenge that lay in calculating the relationship between one element in a series and the next. Whether through the study of the fragmented histories of the geological record, signs of divine intention in the natural world, or a numerical series *in medias res*, readers inhabited a moment of suspension between a past that could be interpreted and decoded and a future available only to anticipation and speculation.

The Analytical Engine, both in its design and in what it demanded of its users, exemplified this state of anticipation, of looking forward to the potentialities and contingencies of the future. As Babbage wrote in 1837, one of its features was an innovative mechanism that allowed the machine to, in his words, "anticipate" the possible carriage of a digit from one column (as it approached the number nine) to the adjacent column, an operation that put the engine into a state of readiness without determining its next move.[142] "Anticipation" described the condition of the engine's observer as well, who might witness a long series of squares and yet might discover that the "next number which shall appear on those wheels, and which you expect to find a square number, shall not be so."[143] So too, Babbage explained, the reader who observes a "series of natural numbers, 1, 2, 3, 4, 5, etc." up to 100,000,001, will have become "firmly convinced that the engine . . . will continue whilst its motion is maintained, to produce the same series," and instead finds that "the next number . . . instead of being one hundred million and two, is one hundred million *ten thousand* and two."[144] Babbage's series, in this sense, takes on the qualities of narrative, where one figure and the next operate within a temporal and causal framework, where each number in a series suspends the observer in a moment of uncertainty and speculation, until fulfillment arrives in the form of the next number.

Computer scientist Seth Bullock writes that for Babbage, the engine's purpose was never "to produce some end product; rather, the ongoing calculation [was] itself the object of interest,"[145] and the clippings in Babbage's scrapbook suggest the other ways this process of "ongoing calculation" might express itself. Consider, for example, the repetition of items, producing the effect of a visual and temporal stutter, in the lower left corner of one of its pages, where he includes each of four copies of the advertisement, "To E. L.—Why did I not see you last Monday, the 9th? Pray, let me see you, if possible, before you go to N. W., or write, as I am most anxious—W.," an item that appeared in the *Times* on consecutive days for a full week.[146] This he followed with four copies of the sequel, as printed again on consecutive days the following week, "To E. L.—I have RECEIVED your LETTER, with its enclosure. When do you return? Pray write again, and more fully, as I am very anxious.—W" (Figure 1.2).[147]

The careful tracking of the item's iteration as it was reprinted day after day, and of its next installment, reflects Babbage's own experience of anticipation—scanning the paper every day to learn how "W." was faring with his or her

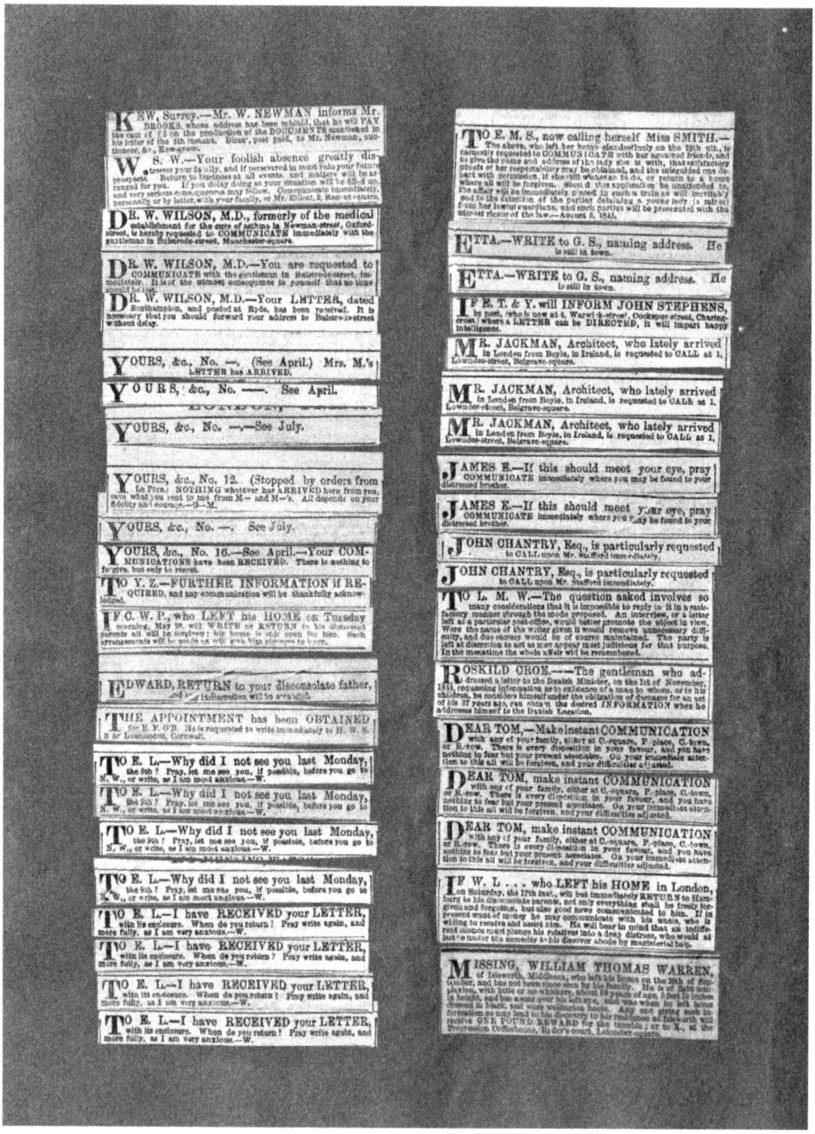

KEW, Surrey.—Mr. W. NEWMAN informs Mr. BROOKS, whose address has been withheld, that he will PAY the sum of £5 on the production of the DOCUMENTS mentioned in his letter of the 5th instant. Direct, post paid, to Mr. Newman, auctioneer, &c., Kew-green.

W. S. W.—Your foolish absence greatly distresses your family, and if persevered in must ruin your future prospects. Return to business at all events, and matters will be arranged for you. If you delay doing so your situation will be filled up, and very serious consequences may follow. Communicate immediately, personally or by letter, with your family, or Mr. Elliott, 2, Regent-square.

DR. W. WILSON, M.D., formerly of the medical establishment for the cure of asthma in Newman-street, Oxford-street, is hereby requested to COMMUNICATE immediately with the gentleman in Bulstrode-street, Manchester-square.

DR. W. WILSON, M.D.—You are requested to COMMUNICATE with the gentleman in Bulstrode-street, immediately. It is of the utmost consequence to yourself that no time should be lost.

DR. W. WILSON, M.D.—Your LETTER, dated Southampton, and posted at Ryde, has been received. It is necessary that you should forward your address to Bulstrode-street without delay.

YOURS, &c., No. —. (See April.) Mrs. M.'s LETTER has ARRIVED.

YOURS, &c., No. ——. See April.

YOURS, &c., No. —.—See July.

YOURS, &c., No. 12. (Stopped by orders from Le Père.) NOTHING whatever has ARRIVED here from you, save what you sent to me from M— and M—'s. All depends on your fidelity and courage.—G—M.

YOURS, &c., No. —. See July.

YOURS, &c., No. 16.—See April.—Your COMMUNICATIONS have been RECEIVED. There is nothing to forgive, but only to regret.

TO Y. Z.—FURTHER INFORMATION if REQUIRED, and any communication will be thankfully acknowledged.

IF C. W. P., who LEFT his HOME on Tuesday morning, May 20, will WRITE or RETURN to his distressed parents all will be forgiven; his home is still open for him. Such arrangements will be made as will give him pleasure to learn.

EDWARD, RETURN to your disconsolate father, and your indiscretion will be arranged.

THE APPOINTMENT has been OBTAINED for E. F. O'B. He is requested to write immediately to H. W. S. near Launceston, Cornwall.

TO E. L.—Why did I not see you last Monday, the 9th? Pray, let me see you, if possible, before you go to N. W., or write, as I am most anxious.—W.

TO E. L.—Why did I not see you last Monday, the 9th? Pray, let me see you, if possible, before you go to N. W., or write, as I am most anxious.—W.

TO E. L.—Why did I not see you last Monday, the 9th? Pray, let me see you, if possible, before you go to N. W., or write, as I am most anxious.—W.

TO E. L.—Why did I not see you last Monday, the 9th? Pray, let me see you, if possible, before you go to N. W., or write, as I am most anxious.—W.

TO E. L.—I have RECEIVED your LETTER, with its enclosure. When do you return? Pray write again, and more fully, as I am very anxious.—W.

TO E. L.—I have RECEIVED your LETTER, with its enclosure. When do you return? Pray write again, and more fully, as I am very anxious.—W.

TO E. L.—I have RECEIVED your LETTER, with its enclosure. When do you return? Pray write again, and more fully, as I am very anxious.—W.

TO E. L.—I have RECEIVED your LETTER, with its enclosure. When do you return? Pray write again, and more fully, as I am very anxious.—W.

TO E. M. S., now calling herself Miss SMITH.—The above, who left her home clandestinely on the 29th ult., is earnestly requested to COMMUNICATE with her agonized friends, and to give the name and address of the lady she is with, that satisfactory proofs of her respectability may be obtained, and the misguided one depart with permission, if she still wishes so to do, or return to a home where all will be forgiven. Should this application be unattended to, the affair will be immediately placed in such a train as will inevitably lead to the detection of the parties detaining a young lady (a minor) from her lawful guardians, and such parties will be prosecuted with the utmost rigour of the law.—August 6, 1846.

ETTA.—WRITE to G. S., naming address. He is still in town.

ETTA.—WRITE to G. S., naming address. He is still in town.

IF E. T. & Y. will INFORM JOHN STEPHENS, by post, (who is now at 4, Warwick-street, Cockspur-street, Charing-cross,) where a LETTER can be DIRECTED, it will impart happy intelligence.

MR. JACKMAN, Architect, who lately arrived in London from Boyle, in Ireland, is requested to CALL at 1, Lowndes-street, Belgrave-square.

MR. JACKMAN, Architect, who lately arrived in London from Boyle, in Ireland, is requested to CALL at 1, Lowndes-street, Belgrave-square.

MR. JACKMAN, Architect, who lately arrived in London from Boyle, in Ireland, is requested to CALL at 1, Lowndes-street, Belgrave-square.

JAMES E.—If this should meet your eye, pray COMMUNICATE immediately where you may be found to your distressed brother.

JAMES E.—If this should meet your eye, pray COMMUNICATE immediately where you may be found to your distressed brother.

JOHN CHANTRY, Esq., is particularly requested to CALL upon Mr. Stafford immediately.

JOHN CHANTRY, Esq., is particularly requested to CALL upon Mr. Stafford immediately.

TO L. M. W.—The question asked involves so many considerations that it is impossible to reply to it in a satisfactory manner through the mode proposed. An interview, or a letter left at a particular post-office, would better promote the object in view. Were the name of the writer given it would remove unnecessary difficulty, and due secrecy would be of course maintained. The party is left at discretion to act as may appear most judicious for that purpose. In the meantime the whole affair will be remembered.

ROSKILD CROE.——The gentleman who addressed a letter to the Danish Minister, on the 1st of November, 1844, requesting information as to existence of a man to whom, or to his children, he considers himself under the obligation of damages for an act of his 37 years ago, can obtain the desired INFORMATION when he addresses himself to the Danish Legation.

DEAR TOM,—Make instant COMMUNICATION with any of your family, either at C.-square, P.-place, C.-town, or B.-row. There is every disposition in your favour, and you have nothing to fear but your present associates. On your immediate attention to this all will be forgiven, and your difficulties adjusted.

DEAR TOM, make instant COMMUNICATION with any of your family, either at C.-square, P.-place, C.-town, or B.-row. There is every disposition in your favour, and you have nothing to fear but your present associates. On your immediate attention to this all will be forgiven, and your difficulties adjusted.

DEAR TOM, make instant COMMUNICATION with any of your family, either at C.-square, P.-place, C.-town, or B.-row. There is every disposition in your favour, and you have nothing to fear but your present associates. On your immediate attention to this all will be forgiven, and your difficulties adjusted.

IF W. L . . . who LEFT his HOME in London, on Saturday, the 17th inst., will but immediately RETURN to Hamburg to his disconsolate parents, not only everything shall be freely forgiven and forgotten, but also good news communicated to him. If in present want of money he may communicate with his uncle, who is willing to receive and assist him. He will bear in mind that an indifferent silence must plunge his relatives into a deep distress, who would at last be under the necessity to discover his abode by magisterial help.

MISSING, WILLIAM THOMAS WARREN, of Isleworth, Middlesex, who left his home on the 20th of September, and has not been since seen by his family. He is of light complexion, with little or no whiskers, about 65 years of age, 5 feet 10 inches in height, and has a scar over his left eye, and was when he left home dressed in black, and wore wellington boots. Any one giving such information as may lead to his discovery to his residence at Isleworth will receive ONE POUND REWARD for the trouble; or to X., at the Progression Coffeehouse, Ryder's-court, Leicester-square.

FIGURE 1.2 Page from Charles Babbage's scrapbook (c. 1847–51), n. p. Kress Collection, Baker Library, Harvard Business School.

inquiries after "E. L.," to see whether anxieties had been quelled or uncertainties resolved; similarly, these accumulated fragments also speak eloquently to the larger narrative of W.'s and E. L.'s lives, a relationship shaped by its own anticipations, of appointments missed, uncertain journeys, and periods of waiting. Collectively these clippings reenact the irresolution and contingency of disparate moments in time and reveal an interest in what a narrative opening, as opposed to a conclusive end, might allow. For not only does the seemingly meticulous sequencing of these fragments invite readers to look for larger patterns—lost cat, lost dog, found dog—and to guess at what the next item in the series might have been, but the individual fragment—with its coded, open-ended plea, seeking and imploring—also induces a similar sense of anticipation to that experienced by the Analytical Engine's observers, situated as they were between the certainties of a known present and an unknown future. Like the "vows" and "promises" that hang upon the air, these advertisements were lasting records of specific instants, in which the act of looking toward the possibility of fulfillment—of cherished belongings restored, friends reunited, safety assured—had not yet found the certainty of resolution.

Whether in the form of tree rings, a sequence of numbers generated by the Analytical Engine, or words suspended in the air or in print, the world bears its encoded record of a moment, as it also gestures toward the uncertainty of what is to come. The *Ninth Bridgewater Treatise* might have claimed to exalt "the power and knowledge of the great creator,"[148] but significantly, it seems to have located evidence of that "power and knowledge" less in the evidence of what the creator had planned and achieved than in what remained unrevealed and unrealized. For Babbage, it was in that space of possibility and contingency, where God's laws, the "testimony of man's changeful will," and the openness of chance coexisted, that the evidence of an ever-more complex algorithm might become legible to mortal eyes.

CHAPTER 2

Past-Tense Futures

History and Temporality Rewritten in Lyell, Eliot, and Darwin

CHARLES LYELL'S THREE-VOLUME *Principles of Geology* opens with a seemingly straightforward definition of its subject: "Geology is the science which investigates the successive changes that have taken place in the organic and inorganic kingdoms of nature."[1] Elaborating on the exact nature of this "science" a few sentences later, Lyell qualifies his statement, now implying that geology might best be understood not by analogy with other sciences but with another discipline altogether, that of "history."[2] In fact, he contends, geology is a hybrid of scientific and historical modes of study and knowledge. The geologist, by analyzing visible layers of earth and stone, applies methods of scientific study to a natural historical record, the cumulative signs of change and progress legibly embedded in the rocks and other formations before the observer's eyes.

Lyell was not alone in identifying the affinities between scientific and historical modes of investigation.[3] As Jonathan Smith points out, John Herschel, making a similar claim in his *Preliminary Discourse on the Study of Natural Philosophy* just a few months after the publication of Lyell's first volume in 1830, described political history as the beneficiary of methodological advances in natural history.[4] The way the latter prioritized gradual and uniform causes, Herschel ventured, might serve as a useful model for political history, too, which more than a "mere record of tyrannies and slaughters," could provide a nuanced "archive of experiments, . . . gradually accumulating towards the solution of the grand problem."[5] Lyell, as Smith and others have observed, shared this gradualist conception of history, one that he extended in *Principles* into a broader argument about causality—what Whewell would come to call "uniformitarianism"—in which he asserted that the earth's history had been shaped by slow processes operating in a constant and recurring way throughout time, rather than by the *deus ex machina* catastrophes and miracles more consistent with a biblical account of causal phenomena.

Lyell's opening paragraphs emphasize that uniform causes permit the observer to "institut[e] a comparison between the present and former states of society,"[6] but by the third paragraph of *Principles*, Lyell shifts his focus from continuities across time to moments of decisive discontinuity:

> We often discover with surprise, on looking back into the chronicles of nations, how the fortune of some battle has influenced the fate of millions of our contemporaries, when it has long been forgotten by the mass of the population. With this remote event we may find inseparably connected the geographical boundaries of a great state, the language now spoken by the inhabitants, their peculiar manners, laws, and religious opinions. But far more astonishing and unexpected are the connexions brought to light, when we carry back our researches into the history of nature. The form of a coast, the configuration of the interior of a country, the existence and extent of lakes, valleys, and mountains, can often be traced to the former prevalence of earthquakes and volcanoes, in regions which have been long undisturbed.[7]

In its tracing of warfare "long . . . forgotten" and "the former prevalence of earthquakes" in "regions . . . long undisturbed," this passage attests to the power of deep causal forces, but it also alludes to a different conception of history, be it political or geological, beneath the surface of visible coastlines or human memory, one unmoored from a sedimented, stable conception of all that has "taken place."[8] This vision, with its attention to the contingencies inherent in causal phenomena, whether in "the fortune of some battle" or in the eruption of a volcano, verges on the counterfactual. Conjuring spectral visions of the other "language[s]" that might have been "spoken" or the "religious opinions" that might have taken hold, these implied contingencies reframe history in terms of chance and complex causality rather than determination. History, in Lyell's rendering, is an amplification and extension of "fortune," where the consequences of one long-lost event might have encompassing and lasting effects for the "fate of millions."

Lyell's opening allusion to military history—the effects of battles on languages, customs, and boundaries—was particularly apt for the post-Napoleonic moment in which he was writing. As Catherine Gallagher explains, the act of thinking through counterfactuals in order to improve performance on the battlefield, of considering how a range of strategies and maneuvers might have produced different outcomes, was a well-accepted practice among military historians by the early nineteenth century.[9] If the period's histories allowed and invited such counterfactual speculations about what might or might not have happened in war, *Principles* implies, then so too might geologists apply a similar approach to events such as earthquakes, floods, or volcanic eruptions that shaped the earth's surface over time. But as Lyell develops his argument over the succeeding 1,400 pages, it becomes clear that his chosen analogy, while striking, also works imperfectly. For while the counterfactual history he evokes, like the military strategizing of the period, centered on identifiably decisive turning points, on the idea that a single battle's outcome might have redirected "the fate of millions," Lyell's geohistory is one that transforms contingency, even over the millennial spans he discusses, into something quotidian, a regular, natural condition.

An awareness of historical contingency, Martin Rudwick contends, was central to nineteenth-century geology. Echoing Lyell's analogy, he writes that "the earth's own history," like the "human historiography" of late modernity, came to be seen as "ineluctably *contingent,*" in which contingency was not an exceptional but rather an unexceptional state: "It became clear that at every turn, geohistory could conceivably have taken a different course."[10] But where Rudwick assigns an awareness of contingency to the early nineteenth-century discipline as a whole, including those works that adhered to biblical accounts of the earth's history, this chapter investigates Lyell's original contributions to a historical methodology shaped around secular contingencies. For in suggesting that geological history might operate like military history—a matter of wholly secular causes and effects—Lyell rewrites a narrative that for other natural historians of his and earlier decades had necessarily been based on another master narrative, that of the Bible, in which processes and consequences were understood to be shaped by divine fiat rather than by chance.

So-called catastrophists and uniformitarians, both reaching for a unifying theory to explain the continuities observable in geological and natural history, developed opposing accounts of the causal processes that could result in the changes for which rock and fossil records provided mounting evidence. For catastrophists, the historical record was a decidedly discontinuous one, punctuated by moments of intervention, of ordained apocalyptic events and miracles, in an otherwise stable, perfectly ordered world.[11] But for figures like Lyell (despite what the word "uniformitarian" might imply),[12] the very constant of the natural world was change. So, too, for Charles Darwin, his intellectual heir, the challenge would lie in demonstrating how natural processes, whose very slowness gave the illusion of an unchanging world, could yet generate the variety now observable in all its earthly grandeur, from the peaks of the Andes to the depths of the Pacific Ocean, the delicate wings of the butterfly to the massive bones of long-extinct beasts.

Adelene Buckland argues that for Lyell, "Writing was not simply a means of imagining or publicizing geology, but rather was a kind of scientific practice," and James Secord advances a similar claim, positing that Lyell's uniformitarianism, with its insistence on secular, knowable causalities, offered not so much a description of the geological past, but a stance strategically necessary to an emerging discipline. As he puts it, it was "a method, not a doctrine about the shape of earth history."[13] For Lyell, contingency operated in a similar fashion, as a methodological tool rather than a descriptive practice. With its suppositional, speculative potential, it could never be mistaken for a form of evidence or an assertion about things as they actually were. Instead, as a useful premise about the operations of chance, contingency served as a strategy that Lyell and others mobilized at both stylistic and narrative levels. Indeed, the association Lyell conjures in his third paragraph between history and contingency is one he pursues throughout *Principles*, in whose pages contingency becomes an essential, regular element not just of the earth's past but also, crucially, of historical narrative more generally. By drawing attention to moments of possibility, the language of contingency renders the earth's slow causes and processes legible for readers, and by emphasizing the unforeclosed quality of outcomes, it not only enables the removal of divine intervention and teleologies from causal processes but also illustrates how a set of uniform, natural laws might be reconciled to the workings of chance. Through narratives of contingency, that is, Lyell transforms *Principles* into a kind of virtual laboratory for thinking about historical processes: one in which he (and his readers) take the place of chance, varying conditions at will, from moment to moment, in order to examine their effects, isolate both causes and consequences, and suspend the ordinary fixities, scale, and directionality of historical time.

This chapter retraces a loose genealogy across several generations of historians diversely and broadly defined, including Paley, Whewell, and Lyell, as well as George Eliot and Darwin, who looked to contingency as a test case, a measure of the degree to which histories might be rescripted in accordance with a religious or secular worldview. The patterns of imaginative and historical endeavor these writers adapted from one another have been ably examined by other scholars. Gillian Beer, George Levine, Martin Rudwick, Sally Shuttleworth, Jonathan Smith, among others, have detailed the magnitude of Lyell's influence on Darwin's thinking about deep time and the uniformity of causes, as well as the impact of Darwin's *Origin of Species* on the rhetoric and emplotment in Victorian novels by Dickens and Eliot. While acknowledging these historically recognized relationships, this chapter investigates a looser network of affinities and shared strategies that allowed older narrative formulae to be revised and reinvented to open interstitial spaces of possibility within seemingly foreclosed historical narratives.[14] While Levine credits Darwin's resistance to "teleological explanation" for "in effect changing the way his culture could think,"[15] this chapter considers the linked contributions that Lyell, Darwin, and Eliot all made to an epistemology shaped around new conceptions of temporality and causality in historical narrative. In strategically undoing the determinations of history, their narrative experiments suspended temporality and the drive toward closure as they transformed the past into a realm for thinking about alternate futures.

This chapter takes its cues from critical work across a range of disciplines and genres: Mary Ann Doane's examination of contingency in early cinematic media, Hilary Dannenberg's narratological taxonomy of contingent forms,

Gallagher's study of late eighteenth- and early nineteenth-century military counterfactuals, Levine's and Beer's analysis of Darwin's narrative practices, and important work by historians of science on geological histories of the period. Through the use of contingency, Lyell, Eliot, and Darwin rescripted once familiar genres and reshaped the conventions of historical representation. This is not to imply that such experiments were exclusive to these three figures, or to suggest that we might trace a simple genealogy from one figure to the next; rather, this chapter draws attention to them as significant examples of the experiments in contingent histories that emerged in the early decades of the nineteenth century. For just as Lyell repurposed the signature elements of biblical rhetoric and the familiar components of the deluge narrative to experimental ends, so too in *Adam Bede* did Eliot rewrite the determined, clichéd plot of melodrama—delusion, seduction, and downfall—for a nonprovidential world. History, whether in biblical, geological, or novelistic form, might best be understood, they imagined, not from the grand perspective of an omniscient, teleologically driven retrospection, but from the many moments of chance awaiting excavation from within the framework of a historical retelling.

Lyell's Experimental Landscapes

Biblical accounts of the earth's history never went away, according to Rudwick, who rightly observes that geohistories of the early nineteenth century were necessarily a hybrid genre, a blending of different narrative traditions, both Christian and secular.[16] And what was true for the period's geohistorians reflected the scientific culture more broadly. Aileen Fyfe and Bernard Lightman have argued that the sharp divide often understood to exist between religion and science is an artifact of our more recent ideological investments, and that in the first several decades of the nineteenth century in particular, the two resided, often amicably, along a continuum of belief. As discussed in the previous chapter, that continuum, a space of reconciliation and renegotiation in the 1820s, 30s, and 40s, encompassed a number of works, including the *Bridgewater Treatises* and Babbage's own explorations of the place of agency and chance within design. The complex, textured relationship between religious belief and scientific research likewise informs this chapter's approach to the period's natural and geological histories, and its reading of how figures like Paley, Whewell, William Buckland, and Lyell reimagined both the rhetorical and thematic elements of biblical narrative—specifically the creation, deluge, and apocalypse—to accommodate the period's new geological findings and methods.

By the time he published *Natural Theology* in 1802, Paley was already known for his inquiries into religious and moral matters: his 1785 *Principles of Moral and Political Philosophy* and his 1794 *A View of the Evidences of Christianity*. All three works had a place in the curriculum at Cambridge, where Paley was a respected lecturer and clergyman, but *Natural Theology* easily surpassed those earlier publications in influence and readership. As Jonathan Topham notes, while the volume was in many ways behind the scientific times, it was nonetheless recognized as a significant contribution to popular conversations about natural history; by the 1850s there were more than 90,000 copies in circulation.[17] In place of the absolute ruler more suited to the *ancien régime*, Paley compared the divine creator to an up-to-date industrialist; his authority over natural processes was technological and managerial, a setting of the machinery ("a stocking-loom, a corn-mill, a carding-machine") in motion, even as its operator might seem absent.[18] But unlike Babbage—who would make a similar comparison decades later, but for whom contingency, in the form of those "events unanticipated by its Author," had an important place within any design[19]—Paley held that the process of creation could admit no alternative outcomes. For him, contingencies were always foreclosed by a divine, encompassing vision, such that,

> chance is excluded from the present disposition of the natural world. Universal experience is against it. What does chance ever do for us? In the human body, for instance, chance, i.e. the operation of causes without design, may produce a wen, a wart, a mole, a pimple, but never an eye. Amongst inanimate substances, a clod, a pebble, a liquid drop, might be; but never was a watch, a telescope, an organized body of any kind, answering a valuable purpose by a complicated mechanism, the effect of chance.[20]

He mobilizes experimental hypotheses only to demonstrate that thinking contingently leads to developmental dead ends. Through a methodically articulated set of oppositions, between the useless and the useful, the amorphous and the organized, the ugly and the admirable, he suggests that we can discern the work of intelligence and intention in natural structures.

For Paley the outcomes he observes in the natural world, such as organs and organisms and formations of land and water, are not the productions of open-ended chance but of divine judgment and decision. Any contingency he or we might imagine is absorbed into the superior "intellectual agency" which "*chus*[es] out of a boundless variety of suppositions which were equally possible, that which is [most] beneficial";[21] to entertain alternate suppositions, the possibility of a different corporeal structure or climate pattern, for example, is an exercise in futility. He illustrates this point on repeated occasions, venturing naive speculations only to reveal their failure. He writes, for instance,

> If both bones had been joined to the cubit or upper arm at the elbow, or both to the hand at the wrist, the thing [turning the hand] could not have been done, . . . [I]f the centripetal force had changed . . . if, at double the distance, the attractive force had been diminished to an eighth part, or to less than that, the consequence would have been, that the planets, if they once began to approach the sun would have fallen into his body.[22]

A close examination of nature, he concludes, whether the arrangement of the bones in the body or the principles of physics, reveals "intelligence and design," and effectively "excludes every other hypothesis" from consideration.[23] To imagine the viability of alternate forms in nature is not only to question God's knowledge and wisdom, then, but also to reveal by comparison the weakness of the human capacity for creative and intellectual agency. Where God's encompassing vision has perceived, seemingly in an instant, what is best "out of a boundless variety of suppositions," our speculations are consistently stunted, destructive formations, yielding death and catastrophe.

Whereas Whewell and others writing in the decades following updated Paley's account of natural theology, to emphasize the importance of natural laws rather than the judgments of a divine creator, many nonetheless echoed Paley in warning readers against the kind of hypothesizing that implicitly questions the rational, providential order of the natural world.[24] While Whewell, for example, views the speculative hypothesis as a fundamental element of scientific study, in which conjectures based on inductive reasoning might lead to reliable conclusions within the space of a controlled scientific inquiry,[25] he demonstrates that counterfactual speculations about the natural world can only be counterproductive. According to his 1833 *Astronomy and General Physics Considered with Reference to Natural Theology*, arguably the most successful and widely read of all the *Bridgewater Treatises*,[26] there can be no viable alternatives to what he represents as an ideal universe. To speculate about other possibilities, Whewell suggests, echoing Paley, is to doubt the perfection of natural systems, such as the order of the seasons and the arrangement of the planets, and is necessarily to conjure an imperfect, even chaotic and destructive world. He writes, for example, that, "[i]f the summer and the autumn were much shorter, the fruit could not ripen; if these seasons were much longer, the tree would put forth a fresh suit of blossoms to be cut down by the winter,"[27] and throughout, other hypothetical conditions produce similarly unhappy outcomes. In a discussion of physical laws, for instance, Whewell indulges in speculation only to follow almost immediately with what amounts to a dismissal of any such propositions: "[I]f the intensity of gravity were to be much increased, or much diminished, if every object were to become twice as heavy or only half as heavy as it now is," the disastrous result would be found in "motions too quick or too slow, wrong positions, jerks and stops, instead of steady, well conducted movements."[28] To imagine these aspects of nature as somehow contingent rather than necessary is an offense not only, or even primarily, to the agency of their creator, as Paley would have it, but more so to the very idea of a rationally ordered universe. In contemplating the natural world, Whewell declares with satisfaction, "how unlike chance everything looks."[29]

Even as Paley's and Whewell's texts referred to contingency in affirming the working of rational and legible causalities, noting that fruit requires warm weather to ripen and the hand's movement requires a radius and an ulna, their arguments ultimately insisted upon its foreclosure by divine judgment, whose omniscient agency reserved for itself the management of any number of possible alternatives and the wisdom to select among them. The foreclosure of alternatives—the degrees of narrative freedom limited by a providential teleology—was, as George Levine writes, a central characteristic of the sciences of the early nineteenth century.[30] Even where explicit claims about a divine "author" might be absent, readers understood that, as Lightman puts it, references to "the laws of nature or the natural order" implied the presence of an overseeing entity.[31]

In fictional works, the ideological counterpart to natural theology's emphasis on order and design was what Thomas Vargish calls the period's "providential aesthetic," an investment in the meaningfulness of narrative structure and closure, and in which a comprehensive sense of order and purpose necessarily discouraged the imagining of alternative courses.[32] But while Vargish and others, such as Leland Monk and Stephen Kern, suggest that providentialism served as the prevailing perspective for most Victorian writers, others have argued that contingent and counterfactual thinking—different ways of recognizing that another outcome might have been possible—was a feature of prose narrative from as early as the eighteenth century. Levine, as mentioned earlier, associates the "growing nineteenth-century dissatisfactions with closure" with Darwin's *On the Origin of Species*, and Doane locates the emergence of interest in contingency in a similar place, in Darwin's mid-century theories of natural selection in particular, as well as in the contemporaneous mathematics of Charles Sanders Peirce and in thermodynamic research.[33] In these, Doane suggests, we see signs of a "modernity" that "valorize[s] the contingent, the ephemeral, chance."[34]

Considering contingency by way of the counterfactual narrative, Dannenberg credits Neal Roese and James Olson when she writes that "the urge to counterfactualize is an intrinsic mode of human thought" and reflects a fundamentally "human urge for *narrative liberation* from the real world."[35] But elsewhere, placing counterfactuals within a loosely organized chronology, she recognizes that counterfactuals served as "a key realist strategy" in the eighteenth century, and in the nineteenth they "beg[a]n to evolve and proliferate," in a transformation she links to the cultural shift from religious to secular epistemologies.[36] As she explains, "if history is no longer following a divinely preordained course, then *divergence* from the actual historical course of events becomes more conceivable."[37] Others have offered a still more specific literary and epistemological genealogy. Gallagher, in her analysis of military counterfactuals, argues that in "the late eighteenth century . . . strong secular reasons adduced for counterfactualizing history,"[38] while Debra Gettelman and Andrew Miller show how versions of counterfictional thinking contributed to the shaping of readerly emotional investments and to characters' acts of self-realization in mid-Victorian novels, respectively.[39]

Lyell's conception of history was part of his larger effort to, as he contended elsewhere, "free . . . science from Moses," and this secularizing impulse is evident not only in his claims about geology but also in his framing of it as historical narrative.[40] Specifically, by comparing the long history of the earth to the recognizably secular outcomes on the battlefield—matters of strategy, numbers, circumstances of terrain and environment, and available technologies—the opening paragraphs of *Principles* asserted that secular causalities operated in geohistory as well. Land and sea take shape through rationally available causes, the eruptions, tidal patterns, shifts in climate, and other natural, observable phenomena that operated in the past as they do in the present. Yet in rejecting the possibility of exceptional phenomena and divine intervention, Lyell does not reject contingency; rather, he reclaims authorial power over and through its potential. For where, Rudwick explains, the "pervasive theme" of Christian theology was that "the course of events might have been otherwise," that sense of contingency within the Bible was always already foreclosed and contained by the supremacy of God's own "freedom of action."[41] *Principles* removes the operation of alternatives that inheres in that "otherwise" from the purview of divine authority, and in so doing, situates "freedom of action" within a field delimited only by the finitude of rational, legible causalities. At the same time, Lyell absorbs the providential attentiveness to detail that characterized natural theology, in which the shift from summer to fall, the shape of the ulna, and the distance between planets were all equally worthy of divine contemplation, and he adapts it to a geohistory in which every moment, even one seemingly insignificant, bears the possibility of an "otherwise." That potentiality, effectively a counterpart to the period's frequentist statistics, which reframed the once exceptional event—homicide, illness, death—as regular occurrences within a longer, more comprehensive view, likewise remakes catastrophism's catastrophes into events that could be seen as, in Lyell's words, "part of the regular and ordinary course of Nature."[42]

These multiple goals may have been unusually ambitious ones, but Lyell demonstrated the skill of a master strategist in laying his arguments before the public. Like other geological works written for a wide, nonspecialist audience during this period, *Principles of Geology* addressed itself to a respectable, middle-class readership, one often possessed of theologically conservative tendencies, and to this end, Lyell not only chose an established, highly respectable publisher, John Murray, for his monumental work but also ensured that favorable reviews appeared in a range of mainstream publications.[43] Moreover, the *Principles'* savvy navigation of an intellectual landscape dominated by biblical accounts of the earth's creation on the one hand and scientific ones on the other—a landscape that Rudwick, Aileen Fyfe, and Lightman have encouraged us to think of as continuous rather than sharply demarcated or opposed—was one important contributor to its lasting impact. And where Rudwick implies that the language of "creation" was a kind of default, a ready *lingua franca* for both scientists and lay writers of the period,[44] Secord discerns in Lyell's appeals to the rhetoric of Christian theology a canny attempt to appeal to a conservative readership.[45] So, too, his discussion of events like volcanic eruptions enhanced the appeal of his work to a range of audiences, those for whom apocalypse had theological meaning but also those whose appetite for archaeological treatises and displays in various media had been whetted by relatively recent eruptions on the Continent and elsewhere. While spectacles representing morally and theologically significant scenes of apocalypse, such as "the Fall of Babylon," continued to be popular during this period,[46] paintings as well as immersive depictions of events outside theological interpretation, such as the reenactment of Vesuvius's eruption at Surrey Zoological Park, which drew thousands of spectators,[47] reflected a broad willingness to view such catastrophes as secular events, as part of a "history" understood as both "contingent and unpredictable."[48]

Yet in addition to appealing to a popular audience, Lyell's work also needed to chart a path across unstable professional ground. As Smith reminds us, since its founding in 1807, the Geological Society of London had sought to distance itself from speculative, "armchair theorizing" and to remake itself as an empirical science based in "fieldwork and observation."[49] Yet *Principles* employed elements of both—its uniformitarian claims necessarily drawing on observation of present processes and the visible results of past ones, while its extension of those claims into the realm of speculative or counterfactual futures drew on the author's own imaginative, creative role. To judge by sales and readership,

Lyell's venture was a successful one. Multiple editions appeared over the ensuing decades in both Britain and the United States, and his readers constituted
a varied and illustrious constellation of Victorian intellectuals: Thomas Car-
lyle, Harriet Martineau, John Ruskin, Charles Darwin, George Eliot, Herbert
Spencer, John Stuart Mill.[50]

Ralph O'Connor points out that Lyell's achievement was inseparable from
the very quality of his narrative authority, and specifically, his considerable
"rhetorical gifts," something he shared with his onetime instructor, William
Buckland, a successful scientific author in his own right.[51] But where Buckland,
who had penned one of the *Bridgewater Treatises*, was explicit in his appeals
to a higher textual authority (such that the earth's layers were themselves the
"unfolding records of the operations of the Almighty Author of the Universe,
written by the finger of God himself"),[52] Lyell asserted a different kind of
authorial power, placing himself in the role of creator, repeatedly enacting,
animating, and illuminating—and inviting the reader to do the same. In this
sense, while Lyell may have departed from an adherence to the Bible as an
explanatory document, it was nonetheless central to *Principles* as a template
for the construction of a historical narrative. For like Paley and Whewell, Lyell
was rescripting a familiar, identifiable history, related in the Book of Genesis,
through the language of scientific discourse. Indeed, two of the primary events
driving the biblical narrative, the creation and the apocalypse, also provided
the plots through which he explored the limits of natural history.

Just as William Buckland reconstructed deep history through his writing
and thereby lent it the kind of compelling immediacy more often found in the
period's panoramic displays and theatrical events,[53] Lyell's prose offered an
immersive experience. His repeated invocation of "we" throughout *Principles*
holds readers close, involving them in the unfolding acts of creation being
described. Critics have read such lines as an assertion of poetic agency, a kind
of self-authorizing challenge to divine authority, rendered in language that
O'Connor describes as approaching a Byronic virtuosity.[54] Even as these visions of deep history confronted a geological sublime, a temporal and spatial
dimension within which both readers and historian might seem insignificant
indeed, Lyell's prose asserts "the agency of the creator, in this rhetorical instance, [the geologist] himself."[55] But where critics like J. M. I. Klaver and

Virginia Zimmerman frame such assertions as specific and relatively isolated occurrences,[56] I argue that rewriting acts of creation in a secular mode is a central characteristic of Lyell's prose, as well as the key to understanding the broader function of his temporal and narrative experiments.

To be sure, the language of Christianity recurs throughout Lyell's work, with references to the "Author of Nature," to a "Creative Intelligence" and "Infinite and Eternal Being."[57] But Lyell seizes upon the contingent quality of the earth's surface, the sense of possibility that inheres in its forces, shape, and condition, in order to assert his own ability to shape and reshape those elements. Consider, for example, the shifting use of the word "let" in a passage from chapter 8:

> Let us suppose that the laws which regulate the subterranean forces are con-
> stant and uniform. . . . Let us then imagine the quantity of land between the
> equator and the tropic in one hemisphere to be to that in the other as thirteen
> to one. . . . Then let the first geographical change consist in the shifting of
> this preponderance of land from one side of the line to the other, from the
> southern hemisphere, for example, to the northern. . . . if, at another epoch,
> we suppose a continuance of the same agency to transfer an equal volume of
> land from the torrid zone to the temperate and arctic regions of the northern
> hemisphere, there might be so great a refrigeration of the mean temperature
> *in all latitudes*, that scarcely any of the pre-existing races of animals would
> survive, and, unless it pleased the Author of Nature that the planet should be
> uninhabited, new species would be substituted in the room of the extinct.[58]

What begins as the explicit language of hypothesis in the first two sentences ("Let us suppose . . . Let us then imagine") becomes, by the third sentence, something different, where supposition starts to test not only the limits of the imagination but also the limits of creation in accordance with natural laws. Significantly, with that phrase, "let the . . . change consist," Lyell also reformulates what he elsewhere calls the "fiat of the Almighty,"[59] familiar through its repetition in the Book of Genesis. Notably, this passage still admits a place for that other "Author of Nature," but it is a permissive rather than creative role. Whereas for Paley there could be only one "Author" and alternative outcomes could end only in catastrophe, Lyell reframes the function of his own "authorship" as imaginative rather than determinative, one operating through

contingency to allow for the proliferation rather than the foreclosure of hypothetical effects, and under which any consequences are to be understood not
in terms of morality or theology but rather in terms of biology and geology.

Adelene Buckland writes that "Lyell's world is thronging and alive with
change, change in all directions, at all times, by all possible means," and for
her, contingency functions as a productively disruptive force in *Principles*; it
opens up the sealed causalities of biblical or traditional historical narrative and
breaks the links that other writers had used to join those elements into what
Secord calls a "continuous 'story of the earth.'"[60] For that reason, Buckland
emphasizes the fragmentary quality of *Principles*, what she also characterizes
elsewhere as "anti-narrative" in its fundamental resistance to plot.[61] Yet while
Lyell's work broke with the grand, "continuous" narratives of natural theology,
his writing nonetheless mobilizes the force of narrative as a key component of
his argument. Not only does he allude to earlier narratives even as he rewrites
them, but he also relies on the inferential, temporal, and causal dimensions that
the very principles of narrative supply even as he remakes those principles in
radically experimental ways.

For those who looked to the Bible as an authoritative history, the signal
event that eclipsed other biblical narratives in significance was the deluge.
This was the sole event for which empirical evidence could be sought in the
geological record, where the nineteenth-century earth sciences might, it was
thought, verify the truth of the Bible as a historical document.[62] Indeed, Lyell
reminds us, investigators through much of the Christian era had insisted that
"the deluge was the only great catastrophe by which considerable change had
been wrought on the earth's surface" after creation, though as early as the seventeenth century Robert Hooke had had the temerity to deem "the favourite
hypothesis of the day ('that marine fossil bodies were to be referred to Noah's
flood') wholly untenable."[63] Even so, respected works of the nineteenth century
still turned to the Noachian record as a historical reference point and the basis
for geological investigation. While William Buckland did not adhere to a literal
account of Genesis,[64] his 1824 *Reliquiae Diluvianae* nonetheless centered on a
detailed analysis of the bones and sediment found in a local cave as proofs,
he concluded, that a "diluvial current" like the one described in Genesis was
"the only adequate cause that can be proposed" to explain the distribution of

clay, pebbles, and fossils in southern England.[65] This "incontrovertible body of facts," not mere theological assertions but the products of scientific investigation, supported the "admission of an universal deluge."[66]

Not surprisingly, then, the deluge serves as a key event in Lyell's argument as well, but he repeatedly mobilizes the flood narrative, especially in Volume I, to different ends. By first alluding to the many records of major floods—in ancient Egyptian and Greek testimonials, in the Koran, and in recent accounts throughout North America and Europe—he dissociates it from its status as a singular event in Judeo-Christian history.[67] Indeed, using the fragmentary quality of the geological record to question the narrative continuities that were an essential part of biblical accounts, he draws attention to the indeterminacies in the historical record, moments that then serve in *Principles* as opportunities for speculative reflection. As Adelene Buckland rightly observes, the earth's "limited and provisional data set" posed "a specifically modern epistemological problem," and Lyell's text draws attention to these limitations rather than attempting to resolve them.[68] His new geology, in the absence of empirical data, invested imaginative labor with professional credibility,[69] but it also broadened the scope of what might be considered experimental science. In *Principles* those experiments take place on the page, his theory of uniform causes serving as the apparatus upon which to mount different combinations of conditions and circumstances, inviting both author and reader to weigh alternatives and hypothesize about outcomes. For Lyell, the "freedom of action" (to borrow Rudwick's formulation again) that once belonged to God now inheres in the contingencies Lyell himself activates on the page. But as freely as his prose runs from suppositions to multiplied conditionals, Lyell's contingencies do not allow for 360-degrees of freedom; they themselves are now circumscribed by a new set of factors: natural laws, uniform causes, and the allowances of the geological record itself.

In response to William Buckland's contention that the "secondary strata" in England provide evidence that once "there was sea where now the principal chain of Europe extends,"[70] Lyell declares, toward the end of *Principles*, that the geological record provides no evidence of the "strictest interpretation of the scriptural narrative."[71] From this assessment he ventures beyond the past into the realm of the unrealized, writing that "we may certainly anticipate great

floods in future" for whose "sudden escape of the confined waters," he emphasizes, "[n]o hypothetical agency is required" to explain.[72] Another speculative
statement, "[s]hould Lake Erie remain in its present state until the period when
the ravine recedes to its shores, the sudden escape of that great body of water
would cause a tremendous deluge,"[73] illustrates this point, as it likewise removes
the "Deluge" from its place in Buckland's theologically driven account, and
remakes it into a "deluge" whose occurrence is both contingently and rationally
determined. These accounts of the flood as a recurring, regular event enable
Lyell to affirm the repetitive rather than directional shape of natural history,
and to emphasize the role of secular and uniform, rather than divine, causalities.

Perhaps more striking, however, is the way in which *Principles* reframes not
just the flood as an event but its status as a master narrative. Jonathan Smith
has commented on the temporal flexibility of Lyell's prose, the ease with which
he moves between past and present as a way of underscoring the uniformity of
geological processes over time.[74] But his narrative experiments do more than
point to the continuities between history and the present: They also perform a
radical redirection of the deluge narrative, not only removing it from its biblical
contexts but from ordinary temporal and geographical registers altogether; they
rescript what was once familiar to readers and render it nearly unrecognizable.
The recent geological and archaeological discoveries of which readers would
have been aware undoubtedly aided Lyell in these reorientations, for with
their unfamiliar animal and plant forms, they rendered the past as alien as the
unrealized future and perhaps just as ripe for narrative reinvention. Thus in one
such passage, Lyell frees the flood not only from biblical history but from any
identifiable history, recasting it in an atemporal realm of speculation:

> Let us suppose those hills of the Italian peninsula and of Sicily, which are of
> comparatively modern origin . . . to subside again into the sea, from which
> they have been raised, and that an extent of land of equal area and height . . .
> should rise up in the Arctic ocean, between Siberia and the north pole. . . .
> But let the configuration of the surface be still further varied, and let some
> large district within or near the tropics, such as Mexico for example, with its
> mountains rising to the height of twelve thousand feet and upwards, be con-
> verted into sea, while lands of equal elevation and extent are transferred to

the arctic circle . . . let the Himalaya mountains, with the whole of Hindostan, sink down, and their place be occupied by the Indian Ocean.[75]

Note how, as before, the language begins in a speculative, inclusive mode ("Let us suppose") before shifting to a more authoritative stance, such that the ensuing litany of commands, "let the configuration of the surface . . . let [it] be converted into sea . . . let the Himalaya mountains . . . be occupied by the Indian Ocean," again acquires the quality of the signature fiats of Genesis ("Let there be light").[76] This assertion of creative agency is only the beginning, as the passage also rewrites geography, rearranging the earth's surface into an unrecognizable landscape. A geography described in modern (rather than biblical) terms—the lands of Mexico and the Himalayas—becomes a new oceanic bed, and the flood, too, is transposed from the past tense, the tense of foreclosure (Genesis 5: "And the waters of the flood were upon the earth"), into a temporality suspended within the present, the conditional, and the subjunctive. Undoing the teleological ends of biblical narrative, it rescripts the diluvian narrative in an imaginary and temporally unsituated future.

Another version of the biblical flood narrative in the second volume follows Lyell's (now) signature pattern, where the language of supposition transforms into a recognizable form of edict:

[L]et us suppose every living thing to be destroyed in the western hemisphere, both on the land and in the ocean, and permission to be given to man to people this great desert, by transporting into it animals and plants from the eastern hemisphere . . . herbivorous animals in their turn must be permitted to make considerable progress before the entrance of the first pair of wolves or lions. Insects must be allowed to swarm before the swallow could be permitted to skim through the air and feast on thousands at one repast.[77]

Here he omits any explicit reference to a watery destruction, but his account of human agency in repopulating a decimated earth alludes to an equivalent event, now told from a postdiluvian perspective. This second passage makes vague reference to another agency, possibly divine, but it sutures the sense of enforcement conveyed through the repeated formulation "must be" to a permissive ("permitted" and "allowed") rather than authoritative language, making its outcomes possible rather than determined. Lyell's version at once unsettles the certainties of a determined biblical past and also defamiliarizes that once familiar narrative by transposing it into the atemporal language of hypothesis and possibility.

If such language, as Secord suggests, makes *Principles* seem "profoundly ahistorical,"[78] it was also, I propose, counterhistorical, not so much a rejection of history, but—in the spirit of military histories and speculative fiction—a deepened engagement with history through the envisioning of alternate trajectories and temporalities. By rescripting narratives that had previously existed in an indelible past, Lyell shapes geological equivalents of those military speculations to which he referred in his opening lines, those contemplations of "how the fortune of some battle has influenced the fate of millions of our contemporaries . . . the geographical boundaries of a great state, the language now spoken by the inhabitants."[79] Freed from the determinations of a known outcome, such speculations invest history with contingency. Indeed, they engage in the kind of activity that William Makepeace Thackeray's narrator in *Vanity Fair* famously ascribed to readers "who like to lay down the History-book, and to speculate upon what MIGHT have happened in the world, but for the fatal occurrence of what actually did take place"; such speculations, Thackeray continues, constitute "a most puzzling, amusing, ingenious, and profitable kind of meditation."[80] In *Principles*, Lyell likewise reinvents the historical past as a space of contingency, but he does so even more insistently than Thackeray. For where the novelist pauses strategically, just before the Battle of Waterloo, Lyell encourages readers to look upon every aspect of geological history and to see there a landscape of both past and future possibility. Indeed, for him the past looks a great deal like the future, and this not only because his theory of uniform causes emphasizes temporal continuity, but also because at every turn he invites us to inhabit the past as though from the perspective of an undetermined present, a moment from which we might contemplate any number of alternate futures.

Time Suspended in *Adam Bede*

Such moments, almost by definition, exist in an alternate temporal realm. They cannot exist in the past tense, nor do they, technically, exist in the future. Military counterfactuals, Gallagher tells us, tended to employ "past-tense hypothetical conditional conjectures" as they pointed to the pivotal moment and to the alternate route that history might have taken: "'If Napoleon had not tarried in Moscow but had swiftly marched on St. Petersburg, then he might have conquered the world,'" her example reads.[81] But Lyell, in inviting us to imagine nature's alternate routes, suspends the temporal, spatial, and even causal coordinates that made the counterfactual instrumental to military thinking.

The counterfactual histories and fictions Gallagher discusses focus their investigations around pivotal battles or leaders; thus Napoleon, Hitler, and the Battle of Waterloo are recurring figures in these speculative dramas.[82] By contrast, *Principles* identifies historical pivots nowhere and everywhere, every geography and every moment bearing the potential for a transformative event. All are part of the "ordinary course of nature" he describes. In his hands the past-tense conditional is less the targeted exercise it was for his military counterparts than a generative force that takes readers out of time altogether. In this passage, for example,

A more correct idea will be formed of the dimensions of the two streams, if we consider how striking a feature they would now form in the geology of England, had they been poured out on the bottom of the sea after the deposition, and before the elevation of our secondary and tertiary rocks. The same causes which have excavated valleys through parts of our marine strata, once continuous, might have acted with equal force on the igneous rocks, leaving, at the same time, a sufficient portion undestroyed, to enable us to discover their former extent. Let us then imagine the termination of the Skaptâ branch of lava to rest on the escarpment of the inferior and middle oolite, where it commands the vale of Gloucester. The great plateau might be one hundred feet thick, and from ten to fifteen miles broad, exceeding any which can be found in Central France. We may also suppose great tabular masses to occur at intervals, capping the summit of the Cotswold Hills between Gloucester and Oxford, by Northleach, Burford, and other towns. The wide valley of the Oxford clay would then occasion an interruption for many miles; but the same rocks might recur on the summit of Cumnor and Shotover Hills, and all the other oolitic eminences of that district.[83]

The passage opens with a "past-tense hypothetical conditional" ("had" these streams of lava "been poured out on the bottom of the sea") followed by a repeated use of "then," typically signaling a temporal and causal sequence. But rather than tracing a single, identifiable causal trajectory, what follows is a proliferating series of contingencies, conditionals, suppositions, and possibilities, an ever-widening range of second- and third-order "mights," and through them, a temporal reinvention of the past. "Might have" morphs into "might be," the past into an indeterminate alternate futurity. If this is history, it's one that refuses teleologies and determined ends. Instead, the passage implies, understanding it comes by looking not into the past but into an undetermined future. Marked with modern names (Gloucester and Oxford), the geography might be recognizable, but the passage otherwise situates us outside time.

The temporal plasticity that characterizes Lyell's prose thus goes beyond the "special kind of conditional mode" typically found in military histories;[84] and it also enacts a more specific set of operations than what Thomas Huxley characterized, broadly, as "retrospective prophecy,"[85] wherein a scientist investigating the past assumes a visionary rather than empirical, objective stance. For Lyell, as for Eliot, to whose work this chapter now turns, the alternate future is situated neither in the past nor in the future, but in moments of suspended temporality that are replete with possibility and potential.

Set in an agricultural English past, *Adam Bede* has no obvious, identifiable historical referent to stir the memory; in spite of the specific date Eliot's 1859 novel assigns to its opening, 18 June 1799, no Jacobite uprising or French Revolution anchors it to a particular time or location. Rather, its primary means of conveying a sense of temporal historicity lies in the narrator's intermittent references to the pastness of these events ("Sixty years ago—it is a long time," as he intones at one point, echoing the formulaic intervention of Sir Walter Scott's narrator in *Waverley*),[86] as well as in his focus on Adam, in whose working lifetime the shift from a rural system of patronage to professional, entrepreneurial labor reflects a broader historical transition among the rising working and middle classes of his time and places the novel at a recognizable, if loosely defined moment in British history.[87] But while Eliot's novel lacks the explicit focus on political history that Georg Lukács identified as one of the defining features of historical fiction, it nonetheless has much in common, as Eve

Kosofsky Sedgwick and Hao Li have reminded us, with other works that, like *Waverley* or *Barnaby Rudge*, are more frequently cited examples of the genre.[88]

Indeed a number of recent critics have treated the genre less in terms of political content than in terms of narrative performance, a balancing of foregone historical conclusions with a novelistic sense of possibility. As Katie Trumpener puts it, "the historical novel presents a violent struggle between different possible future worlds derivable from the same past, a process complete only when a particular present subsumes the past, with all its historiographical and narrative possibilities";[89] similarly, for Ian Duncan, historical fiction as pioneered by Scott "provide[s] the only place where we may catch the echoes and shadows of those possibilities, not so much shut down as subject to perpetual deferral" through their very telling.[90] Crucially, like *Waverley*, *Adam Bede* conjures a past "sixty years since," a temporal span at the outer threshold of personal memory for nineteenth-century readers, according to Carolyn Steedman, where remembering gives way to forgetting, first-person testimony to mediated accounts.[91] The occasional moments of retrospective narration via characters now supposedly in old age serve to underscore the plot's historicity, even as it reminds readers of the ways in which that past was once present. Whether Scottish rebels confronting defeat, French aristocrats ascending to the scaffold, or an unmarried woman facing pregnancy alone, these historical novels situate a contingent futurity and the contemplation of alternate outcomes in the past.

In *Adam Bede*, the narrator speaks about events that occurred at the turn of the previous century, but (to follow Duncan's and Trumpener's assertions) it is these retrospective moments, when the narrator refers to a foreclosed present even as he narrates an as-yet unforeclosed past, that most obviously align Eliot's novel with the genre of historical fiction. The passages with which he interrupts the plot to offer proleptic retrospection ("the neighbours from Hayslope . . . who told Hetty Sorrel's story by their firesides in their old age, never forgot to say how it moved them")[92] remind us that we are always moving toward what is—from his perspective, at least—a known conclusion, all while he withholds the fullness of that knowledge from us. What is more, the very conventionality of the novel's plot amplifies this relationship between past and present. For while much of the plot—a poorer lover betrayed for the sake of a wealthier one, a rural beauty seduced and abandoned—has a timeless quality, it also represents a largely foreclosed space, where the familiar story Eliot unfurls for us, a popular history of class relations and sexual desire, seems always to move, through the characters of Arthur Donnithorne and Hetty Sorrel, toward a foregone conclusion.[93] As Duncan posits, Scott's historical fiction "entertain[s] the very possibilities it is ostensibly, programmatically, shutting down,"[94] and *Adam Bede*, too, negotiates that space on at least two levels, between a telling suspended in the narratorial moment and a story whose course and outcome are already embedded in cultural memory.[95]

The novel in fact plays cannily with the tensions between its own predictability and the "possibilities" that animate it. Chapter 17 offers an explicit reflection on the project of realism (that "rare, precious quality of truthfulness" found "in many Dutch paintings").[96] And while it frames its vision within the foreclosed framework of a remembered history, "a faithful account of men and things as they have mirrored themselves in my mind," it also opens that historical vision to the contingencies expressed in the varieties of the human form.[97] Thus "the high-shouldered, broad-faced bride" and the "elderly and middle-aged friends" with their "very irregular noses and lips" reflect at once both typology and difference; as the narrator tells us, these "squat figures, ill-shapen nostrils, and dingy complexions are not startling exceptions," but rather—and here he sounds something like Lyell—a part of the "ordinary course of nature."[98]

But this more famous account of realism in chapter 17 is itself mirrored in an implicit reflection on the subject in chapters 12 and 13, where the language of contingency works toward a similar twofold purpose, unsettling the teleology and closure associated with historical fiction by conjuring, through the present tense and the invocations of chance, the effect of a realist mode. Here, as Arthur and Hetty begin their fateful convergence, Eliot's narrator muses on the novelistic possibilities that lie between foreseeable and unforeseeable outcomes. He first sketches, through the perspective of Arthur's character, a conventional vision of what lies ahead: "[A]ll his pictures of the future, when he should come into the estate, were made up of a prosperous, contented tenantry, adoring their landlord, who would be the model of an English gentleman—mansion in first-rate order, all elegance and high taste—jolly housekeeping—finest stud in Loamshire—purse open to all public objects," all of which support his declaration that, "You perceive that Arthur Donnithorne was 'a good fellow.'"[99]

In a break with tradition and an idealized squirearchy, however, that future will not be realized. Notably, at the moment when the chapter reroutes us through an alternate, though still conventional narrative of desire and sexual ruination, it makes a point about the introduction of contingency into Arthur's narrative. Just as Lyell had reformulated the sedimented conclusions of the biblical deluge for a secular readership, Eliot's narrator invites us to reimagine the conventions of narrative written for a probabilistic, rather than providential, age. Indeed, he follows Arthur's own certain vision of the future, a certainty he seems to affirm, with musings on the very unpredictability of futures more generally:

> The chances are that he will go through life without scandalizing any one; a sea-worthy vessel that no one would refuse to insure. Ships, certainly, are liable to casualties, which sometimes make terribly evident some flaw in their construction, that would never have been discoverable in smooth water; and many a "good fellow," through a disastrous combination of circumstances, has undergone a like betrayal.[100]

The narrator's act of imagining a divergent future removes us from a traditional teleology based in social class to a set of contingencies. And where the act of planning ahead, that sign of moral character for middle-class Britons, might help to obviate personally ruinous outcomes like bankruptcy or extramarital pregnancy, the language of insurance and accident serves as a reminder that contingency and chance can operate without regard for moral or providential considerations. In addition, just as Lyell rewrote a narrative his readers might have regarded as set in a determined past, Eliot's narrator introduces contingency into a conventional story whose ending we think we already know. For even as the narrative gives us not the story of the "good fellow" but sends us down another conventional path, that of the thoughtless cad who impregnates an innocent country maid, it succeeds in framing this past future as an open-ended one.

The "historiographical and narrative possibilities" that reside in that past future (to borrow Trumpener's words again) emerge most fully in these two chapters, whose titles, "In the Wood" and "Evening in the Wood," refer to the wooded grove of the Donnithorne estate, where Hetty and Arthur happen upon each other. Described as a "delicious labyrinthine wood" of "narrow, hollow-shaped earthy paths,"[101] with its multiplicity of symbolic routes and its sudden turnings, the wood signifies not only the realm of moral ambiguity these two characters confront, but also the multiplication of narrative alternatives, those secular contingencies dividing the "good fellow" from the seducer, the innocent maid from the fallen woman. If traditional literary associations between narrative and spatial journeys allow us to read this terrain as charged with symbolic potential, it also anticipates what Dannenberg has suggestively described as the more recent narratological practice of "mapping . . . narrative time and plot structure" in coordination, where images of branching, splitting, and forking mark moments of narrative divergence or convergence.[102] When Arthur decides "which of the paths would lead him home" at the end of chapter 13,[103] readers intuit that he contemplates a landscape at once narrative, geographical, and psychological.

Where Lyell's *Principles* used contingency to transform the imperceptibly slow causalities of geological history into legible, compressed narratives, Eliot's *Adam Bede* moves in the opposing direction, mobilizing the language of contingency to slow the fleeting instant, to remake it into an expansive, enveloping present.[104] In these scenes, the play of possibility serves as a means of representing the emotional texture of interiority, a character's subjective experience of the moment through a dense thicket of interpretations and surmises conveyed through indirect discourse. Arthur's silent resolution, for example, takes this form, tracing the temporal and causal outcomes of an as-yet unrealized action: "If he lunched with Gawaine and lingered chatting, he should not reach the Chase again till nearly five, when Hetty would be safe out of his sight in the housekeeper's room; and when she set out to go home, it would be his lazy time after dinner, so he should keep out of her way altogether."[105] In this formulation, which recalls the past-tense hypotheticals of historical fiction, we see Arthur imagining an alternative future, one that tellingly relies less on his own moral commitments than on an imperfectly conceived idea that chance might exert its own form of agency. At another moment, he considers that he and Hetty

> would get too fond of each other, if he went on taking notice of her—and what would come of it? . . . he might give himself up to thinking how immensely agreeable it would be if circumstances were different—how pleasant

it would have been to meet her this evening as she came back, and put his arm round her again and look into her sweet face. He wondered if the dear little thing were thinking of him too.[106]

This contemplation of alternatives and possibilities—which we know to be counterfactual, where "circumstances" are not "different," where Hetty will not "be safe out of his sight"—operates as an elaboration of interiority, and a similar passage, related now with the immediacy of the present tense (an example of what Sue Zemka terms Eliot's "presentification"[107]), introduces us to the play of contingencies within Hetty's mind as well:

> She is at another gate now—that leading into Fir-tree Grove. She enters the wood, where it is already twilight, and at every step she takes the fear at her heart becomes colder. If he should not come! O how dreary it was—the thought of going out at the other end of the wood, into the unsheltered road, without having seen him. She reaches the first turning towards the Hermitage, walking slowly—he is not there. . . . She walks on, happy whenever she is coming to a bend in the road, for perhaps he is behind it. No.[108]

Significantly, while historical fiction is typically, according to Trumpener, organized around "clear historical thresholds," a key battle or act of political resistance,[109] Eliot's novel transforms the everyday, conventional plot into one replete with thresholds. For Eliot's characters, the lived instant is densely populated by possibility and contingency. The narrator, too, participates in this proliferation of counterfactual speculations: "If Hetty had known he was there, she would not have cried: and it would have been better; for then Arthur would perhaps have behaved as wisely as he had intended."[110] The keywords of this mode—"if," "should," "would"—situate us and the characters within an atemporal present, a moment that cannot easily be aligned with the novel's primary temporal schema. Yet at the same time, these passages perform a version of the narratological "mapping" Dannenberg describes, as they repeatedly invoke and entwine spatial and temporal circumstances (Hetty leaves early, Arthur reaches the grove late) in order to represent the play of chance and the possibilities arising from any given moment of contingency.

In *Principles of Geology*, discontinuities of verb tense enable Lyell to make a point about the uniformity (rather than uniqueness) of causes; even as he ushers us into a speculative future, causalities behave as they do in the present and as they have in the past, in a knowable and rational fashion. In *Adam Bede*, Eliot offers a similar, universalizing commentary about the role of the conditional and contingent in human nature, as manifested in Arthur's retrospective self-justifications ("If Irwine had said nothing, I shouldn't have thought half so much of Hetty")[111] and in Hetty's recurrent wishful thinking. Critics have suggested that such hypothesizing is at many levels fundamental to Victorian fiction, to its own realizing processes and realist ends. As Beer puts it, "[p]lot in nineteenth-century fiction . . . projects the future and then gives real form to its own predictions. . . . it shares the nature of hypothesis, which by its causal narrative seeks ultimately to convert its own status from that of idea to truth,"[112] and Gallagher claims that such projections actively involve the reader as well, such that we are invited to

> form and discard hypotheses about them [characters], but we do not take the information we get as a continuous and systematic set of counterfactual hypothetical conjectures. . . . Realist fictions, to be sure, tend to dwell on the unactualized possibilities in a character's history, for exploring hypothetical conditionals creates both suspense and the simulacrum of personhood.[113]

In this sense, Eliot's narrator draws attention to the contingencies that contribute to an effect of realism and to a realist notion of selfhood located within it. The sense of open-endedness he generates lends itself to the immersive experience of novel reading.

But where the effect of realism depends, as Gallagher suggests, on our ability to set aside the determinations of traditional narrative, to imagine that the future is not already known, the use of such conditionals in a historical fiction like *Adam Bede* also functions as a kind of commentary on and practice in the very process by which fiction more generally achieves this temporal plasticity—this novel in particular being, Zemka asserts, "self-reflexive about" its own "temporal pacing."[114] Just as Lyell's prose formulations, slipping from the historical to the suppositional mode ("let us suppose") and then to the atemporal realm of the contingent ("might" and "would"), push readers into a rabbit hole of alternate histories and futurities, Eliot's novel consciously exercises our ability to inhabit a space outside the past tense of its own historicity, a space neither past nor future. In this sense its shifts into indirect discourse anticipate the action of film, where "the present as contingency has been seized and stored" as the past, Doane asserts; "[y]et this archival artifact becomes strangely immaterial; existing nowhere but in its screening for a spectator in the present, it becomes the experience of presence."[115] The technology of film, that is, possesses a past-tense materiality at odds with its present-tense experiential contingency, where each frame seems to rest on the threshold of some already determined yet also unknown futurity. What the visual immersiveness of film comes close to erasing, though—as it encourages viewers to ignore its own mediations—the medium of Lyell's and Eliot's prose draws attention to: the clunky apparatus of tense serves as a reminder of the temporal back and forth that the evocation of contingency demands.

The Romantic antecedents to these examples of temporal play are familiar to us. William Wordsworth, for example, in whose poetry memory and anticipation often worked in tandem, enacted its mirror image; in "Lines Written a Few Miles Above Tintern Abbey," for example, the speaker famously performs a kind of future retrospection: "in after years/ . . . with what healing thoughts/ Of tender joy wilt thou remember me."[116] Here the future holds the possibility of looking back to the present, and by extension the experience of the present acquires permanence through a deepened awareness that it bears the "spots of time" with which the individual might be "nourished and invisibly repaired" at some point in the months or years to come.[117] Passages in Eliot's novel, too, mirror this feeling of anticipatory potential; such moments, Zemka observes, are associated with a rural sensibility whose displacement by industrial, urban temporality is imminent.[118] When, for example, Mr. Poyser tells Hetty that "It'll serve you to talk on, . . . when you're an old woman—how you danced wi' th' young Squire, the day he come o'age,"[119] he enacts a similar move across time, a proleptic expression of retrospective longing whose certainty about the future, and about the subjectivities and conditions actors will inhabit ten, twenty years from now, adheres to predictable patterns. But complicating the reader's relation to such prophecies, Eliot makes this moment function with what we might more accurately call the refraction of double retrospection. For rather than encouraging us to look back as Poyser does, her historical fiction encourages us to look back to a moment when such looking back is possible—and in doing so, it serves as a reminder of our own extradiegetic perspective, from which past and future exist in contingent, rather than determined, relation. Indeed, she suffuses Poyser's reflection, which would otherwise read as a kind of proleptic nostalgia, with irony. It is not just the author and narrator who know the future, as Beer suggests above, but also readers who implicitly already inhabit it. We know that the old age Poyser naively envisions for Hetty will likely not be realized in the way he imagines, and that knowledge serves as a reminder of the ways in which contingency shapes history more generally. Likewise when the (intermittently intradiegetic) narrator mentions a conversation with "Adam Bede, to whom I talked of these matters in his old age,"[120] he performs a similar straddling of diegetic and temporal layers. By referring to a foreclosed endpoint that readers have not yet attained, his statement invites readers to consider the multiple contingencies through which the narrative present might be joined to the narrative future he conjures.

In other words, if the Romantic example frames this temporal relationship through the voice of prophecy, a sense of assurance regarding both present and future subjectivities, its Victorian counterpart implicitly posits that relation as one of contingency, where the shape of the future remains uncertain and as yet undetermined. Under what circumstances might Hetty look back as "an old woman" to the celebration of Arthur's majority? What combinations of choices and chances might yet lead to that feeling of retrospective contentment? Eliot's version of history exercises several degrees of temporal and narrative flexibility: It invites us to look not only from an intradiegetic future back in time to a (similarly intradiegetic) present, but also from the intradiegetic past into a future that aligns with the (largely extradiegetic) present. As it moves us from one moment to another, the novel also moves us as it were inside and outside its historical registers. To read the novel is to be invited into history's undetermined futures, to step outside its narrative momentum and to imagine its moments of unrealized potentiality and alternative outcomes.

While Eliot's novel adheres to the traditional prescriptions of Victorian narrative, dispensing lessons to be learned and expected moral (and legal) judgments upon its characters, it might be tempting to see in the language of contingency the potential for liberation from the narrative conventions and cultural impositions of the mid-Victorian period. Indeed, the critical consensus around contingency supports such a reading: Doane writes that "[c]ontingency appears to offer a vast reservoir of freedom and free play . . . its lure is that of resistance itself—resistance to system, to structure," and Dannenberg reads such moments in Eliot's work in a similar fashion, as proto-feminist experiments in narrative resistance, where "divergent plot patterns . . . analyze the reality of marriage by representing the deep conflicts of aims, wishes, and values that create unsuccessful and unhappy marriages."[121] Kern, too, locates the representation of chance and contingency within a larger history of scientific and epistemological progress, one characterized by a less absolute and "increasingly probabilistic" stance.[122]

Adam Bede, however, offers a more complicated account of contingency's relationship to structure and system. Its historical perspective differs in this fundamental way from the historicity of *Principles of Geology*, in which Lyell, in rewriting the earth's narrative trajectories, diverged from a determined biblical history to resist the temporal and causal frames of earlier accounts. The plot of Eliot's novel sticks to a largely familiar script, one that is, in the end, not only generically but also historically and morally determined, in which marriage and professional success are still, reliably, virtue's rewards. Within this context contingency operates not as a form of "resistance to system," for such thinking is often both futile—any projected sense of futurity, as the novel reminds us, is always part of what is already past—as well as undirected. Rather, contingency functions as a component of the system, one necessary to, rather than subversive of, the period's subject formation and social functions.

Gettelman has shown how the act of imagining served as a site for disciplinary "exercise[s]" in Eliot's fiction more generally.[123] For even as these works often conjured "a *multiplicity* of images" for readers (what she calls the "counterfictional" that will go unrealized), they discouraged readers from "taking the novel's act of imagining into their own hands."[124] Focusing on a specific subset of such imaginings, Andrew Miller has considered how the contemplation of optative identities that often occurs in Victorian novels, the envisioning of alternate lives or identities, enables a necessary process of self-consolidation. But in *Adam Bede*, the very act of thinking contingently, even if exercised to no specific end, has value. While the life insurance documents discussed in Chapter 1 supplied an array of ready-made futures in order to cultivate a specific (and monetizable) awareness of contingency, Eliot's novel exercises the capacity for transforming every moment into a potentially pivotal one, for imagining even the small shifts in outcome as a result of departing late or early or choosing this path rather than that one. Indeed, the imprecision of Hetty's visions is something the novel attributes to her small experience with fiction: "Hetty had never read a novel . . . how then could she find a shape for her expectations?"[125] Fiction, then, and the counterfictional—those second-order moments in which the novel reminds us of the value of fiction—enable the process by which the everyday contemplation of minor contingencies becomes the basis for a subjectivity defined by causal consciousness, an awareness of one's temporal and spatial embeddedness within the complex causal frameworks of the world.

Thus exemplifying more than a sign of foresight or prudent planning, thinking contingently implies an understanding that every instant might constitute a crossroads, a moment for looking around the bend, casting oneself into multiple imagined futures. What is more, just as these epistemological templates constitute interiority among Eliot's characters, so too do they suggest that the reader might cultivate their own subjectivity through a similar plasticity and fluid temporality of narrative, of a future imagined as the present, of the past reimagined as the future, of multiple futures at once. In this sense, thinking contingently has a normative, though not necessarily moral, purpose, where in the mere fact of existing at any given moment lies an imperative to conjure any number of narratable futures. Through the process of generating hypotheses and alternatives, and the proliferation of narratives, the self takes shape in a present that is always temporally labile. While these moments of temporal unmooring can momentarily free both characters and readers from some of the exigencies of plot, they also delineate what might be regarded as a new means of inhabiting the self, through a subjectivity necessarily oriented toward an undetermined future and given shape through a complex narrative framework.

Darwin's Alternatives

Early in his landmark work *On the Origin of Species*—like *Adam Bede,* also published in 1859— Darwin cautioned that readers contemplating nature's evident diversity might be "tempted to attribute their proportional numbers and kinds to what we call chance. But how false a view is this!"[126] In his refusal

to credit "chance" with agency, Darwin echoes the language of natural theology, which had employed a similar rhetorical pattern of false assumption
followed by an emphatic dismissal of any reference to chance.[127] But where
Paley, for example, had done this to emphasize the role of divine intention
in the productions of the natural world, Darwin looked to Lyell and Thomas
Malthus, whose works were among his primary influences in writing *Origin*,
to shape a secular theory to explain diversity and speciation. Like them, he
insisted on the operation of rational, uniform causal factors—the principles
of inheritance, competition between species, limited resources—even if their
exact mechanisms or dynamics were not always knowable in any particular case. While nature did not wield chance in a capricious fashion, chance
nonetheless played a significant role in his natural history. As George Levine
contends, "[c]hance for Darwin was a force, despite his own resistance to
it."[128] Indeed, in emphasizing that causal uniformity was neither teleology
nor determination, *Origin* repeatedly turns to the rhetoric of contingency
and chance to enforce the idea that the direction, pace, or exact means by
which change might occur was a highly chancy, contingent affair. As Darwin
acknowledged a few chapters later, "natural selection can do nothing until favourable variations chance to occur," and later, elaborating on this point, he
explained, "the existence of each species depends" on "many complex contingencies" (a formulation he judges worthy of repetition later in that same
chapter), such as "the variability being of a beneficial nature, . . . the power of
intercrossing, . . . the rate of breeding."[129] The variations that occur throughout nature, the diversity they represent, the possibilities of speciation they
enable: For Darwin these reflect the role of chance and contingency in natural processes, all operating in accordance with natural law.[130]

Other critics have also gestured to the significance of these "complex contingencies" in Darwin's work. Barry Allen observes that Darwin, in rewriting older
accounts of biblical contingency, produced what was "a really contingent history" in secular terms.[131] Beer likewise emphasizes that "Deviance, divergence,
accidentals, were the foundation for sustained change" in his argument, and
in Doane's words, *Origin* draws attention to the fact that "evolutionary change
hinges upon an aberration, a contingent difference."[132] In the remaining pages
of this chapter, however, I focus not just on the way contingency functions

as a key component in Darwin's arguments about speciation, but also on the way *Origin*, like *Principles of Geology* and *Adam Bede*, mobilizes a new mode of thinking, for, to turn again to George Levine's formulation, "Darwin was in effect changing the way his culture could think."[133] Here I elaborate on Dannenberg's observation that the "evolutionary maps" that appear in chapter 4 of *Origin*, with their branching, diverging paths, resemble "the divergent patterns of counterfactual narrative" found in fiction,[134] in order to consider how Darwin placed contingency at the center of an experimental narrative and epistemological practice. Shifting between prose and visual forms of argument, he played with the transpositions from one mode to another in representing contingency's potential, from graphic into grammatical expression, from temporal depth into spatial dimension.

Origin, much like its forebear, *Principles of Geology*, is an unconventional history, merging historical and experimental modes throughout, and looking as much to the future as to the past.[135] Indeed, if the record of a geological or natural past can only offer an incomplete account of what has occurred, the future Darwin outlines is imperfect and uncertain as well, and for him, that uncertainty manages to be productive, a realm ripe for both actual and stylistic experiments. But if Lyell's chosen rhetoric was that of the Old Testament fiat, then Darwin's language was not only that of a similar "godhead, 'author of all things,'" as Beer asserts,[136] but also that of the domestic scientist, testing hypotheses and designing and managing experiments in his own garden or home.[137] In this guise, he plays a modest local authority, much like the English workers whose experiments in breeding and grafting he foregrounds in the early sections of *Origin*. Thus the first chapter introduces readers to the principles of natural selection by alluding to familiar figures, those of the gardeners and breeders who habitually look among their seedlings and offspring and, "when a slightly better variety has chanced to appear, select . . . it, and so onwards."[138] Darwin presents himself as a like figure, a humble practitioner of "little" experiments, armed only with the implements of a typical English kitchen and a willingness to wait and observe:

> I have tried several little experiments . . . : I took in February three table-
> spoonfuls of mud from three different points . . . I kept it covered up in my

study for six months, pulling up and counting each plant as it grew; the plants were of many kinds, and were altogether 537 in number; and yet the viscid mud was all contained in a breakfast cup![139]

In developing this analogy between natural history and ongoing experiment, *Origin* extends its experimental stance back into a form of narrative practice, inviting readers into that speculative moment of possible outcomes. Just as we might wonder how many varieties of plants might be contained within our own little tablespoon of mud or how fully the traits of one sheep might be transmitted to its offspring, Darwin's prose asks us to contemplate the longer futures of nature's own eventualities, where heritable morphology becomes something malleable, no longer *form accompli* but a realm of speculative potential: "The bones of a limb might be shortened and widened to any extent, and become gradually enveloped in thick membrane, so as to serve as a fin; or a webbed foot might have all its bones, or certain bones, lengthened to any extent, and the membrane connecting them increased to any extent, so as to serve as a wing."[140] Here, nature rather than the professional breeder is the agent of selection, but the passage implies that his own (and by extension, the reader's) imagination can act with a similar creative, experimental agency, testing the limits of morphological change and continuity, where one form might become another.

Indeed, like Lyell's *Principles*, Darwin's *Origin* proliferates such hypothetical possibilities throughout, transforming the conventions of natural history, with its implicit focus on the past, into an exploration of alternative outcomes and futures conveyed through a layering of conditionals and subjunctives. "If an animal can in any way protect its own eggs or young, a small number may be produced, and yet the average stock be fully kept up; but if many eggs or young are destroyed, many must be produced, or the species will become extinct," he writes at one point, and at another, "if humble-bees were to become rare in any country, it might be a great advantage to the red clover to have a shorter or more deeply divided tube to its corolla, so that the hive-bee could visit its flowers."[141] For Darwin, such speculations emphasize not only the uniformity of natural laws (subsistence, reproduction, competition) to which populations, as well as readers' imaginations, must always adhere, but also the web of causalities by which species, geographies, and generations are so contingently joined together. Hence, "[i]f we wished to increase [a species'] average numbers in its new home, we should have to modify it in a different way to what we should have done in its native country; for we should have to give it some advantage over a different set of competitors or enemies," he observes. These moments become, in effect, exercises in thinking through causes and effects, a lesson Darwin underscores when he concludes that, "It is good thus to try in our imagination to give any form some advantage over another."[142]

But where contingency's alternatives animate the margins and interstices of fictional narrative—the mights and might have beens that surface often fleetingly, and only in the characters' or readers' imaginative spaces—they are by contrast at the forefront of Darwin's history. Although most of the narrator's speculations in *Adam Bede* necessarily lead nowhere in terms of narrative outcomes, the breeder's experiments with one group of pigeons or dogs can, by contrast, generate multiple viable lines. In other words, moments of contingency for Darwin lead not to an exclusionary choice but to multiplication, and thus provide one means by which his natural history unsettles the usual teleologies of narrative. As George Levine reminds us, in Darwin's vision, nature entertains and indeed requires variety, multiplicity. For Beer, too, observing that *Origin* "warms the random, with its meagreness and inconsequence, into profusion,"[143] evidence of Darwin's taste for multiplicity resides in his use of lists; there are, as she notes, "Ribston-pippin or Codlin-apple," "leaf-eating and bark-feeding insects," and "pouters, fantails, runts, barbs, dragons, carriers, and tumblers," instances of a stylistic signature that revel in nature's abundance.[144] While a number of these are joined by "or," many employ "and," a reminder that multiplicity is also simultaneity, an extension of nature's alternatives in parallel trajectories through time. These alternatives—the humble-bee and the hive-bee, the sphinx-moth and the beetle—are in effect nature's thought experiments, whose undirected modulations of form might be understood as the equivalents of the breeder's directed "what ifs," where the possibility of a white petal and a pink one, a longer leg and a shorter one, have given rise to the Myanthus orchid and the Catasetum, the "greyhound, bloodhound, terrier, spaniel, and bull-dog."[145] Where in fiction such alternatives can exist only in the realm of the atemporal and the unrealized, in Darwin's account they have been and can continue to be realized in abundance in the natural world.

As examples of multiplicity in Darwin's writing, these alternatives and lists reflect the ways in which two historical modes, the synchronic and the diachronic, usually treated as distinct, nonetheless converge in nature, and he elaborates on the hybrid quality of the natural record elsewhere, too. For instance, in likening nature to a historical narrative, albeit one only partly legible to us, Darwin writes that, "following out Lyell's metaphor, I look at the natural geological record, as a history of the world imperfectly kept . . . only here and there a short chapter has been preserved; and of each page, only here and there a few lines."[146] Nature is here an object in the present moment, a text to be read, but one where the traces of elisions and erasures and forgetfulness allude to a deeper, more complete narrative history that extends back in time. An analogy a few chapters later makes a more forceful effort to join these two visions of the past, where he finds in "every complex structure and instinct . . . the summing up of many contrivances, each useful to the possessor, nearly in the same way as when we look at any great mechanical invention as the summing up of the labour, the experience, the reason, and even the blunders of numerous workmen,"[147] a passage suggesting nature's purposive, accretive qualities, the organism a "summing up" of all that has come before, a compilation of historical memory. These examples emphasize the dual nature of *Origin*'s vision, in which a living being—like a book, a mechanical invention—is at once a material object in a particular moment in time and also a diachronic, cumulative record of the past.

In its spatialization of temporality, Darwin's famous diagram of speciation in chapter 4 of *Origin* (Figure 2.1) recalls the "geological maps" of his predecessors, Lyell and William Buckland, as well as of William Smith and Alexander von Humboldt, which transformed "a historical understanding of the earth and of life" into a simulacrum of the geological record, often a cross-section of exposed rock and earth, in which the past was made legible in a single, synchronic array.[148] But his image aligns as well with the diachronic, narrative elements of his own prose, cataloguing not only the multiple forms that populate the earth but also a historical vision whose essence is contingency, where decisive moments mark the division between past and future, between one form or species and another. Like Eliot's metaphor of the grove, a symbolic space of choice in which the taking of one path precludes the taking of another, Darwin's

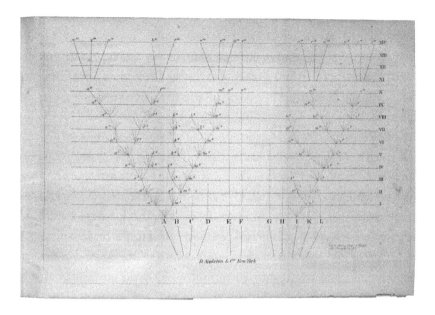

FIGURE 2.1 Diagram from Charles Darwin, *On the Origin of Species*,
foldout facing page 108 (New York: D. Appleton and Co., 1860). Courtesy
of the Thomas Fisher Rare Book Library, University of Toronto.

treelike image points to the ways in which one alternative might have excluded
another through competition or predation; the early extinctions depicted in
lines d^4 and s^2, for example, as they emerge from the lineage of species A at the
left side of the diagram, represent such lost lines. But significantly, the image
also illustrates the historical simultaneity of alternate paths, the species (a and
m) whose development might be traced through multiple nodes of divergence
and intermediate forms (a^7, a^8, a^9, and m^7, m^8, m^9) and that coexist in the same
temporal dimension.

In the style of this "branched diagram," Heather Brink-Roby identifies the
value of a representational mode "relatively free from the limitations . . . of
language,"[149] and here, to be sure, the diagram encompasses the multiplicity and
simultaneity of evolutionary paths with an economy that cannot be matched
by conventional narrative. At the same time, Darwin's experimental prose both
anticipates and approximates the branched form of the diagram, not only by
adopting the stance of the mathematical proof in preceding paragraphs, as

Brink-Roby observes—"Let A to L represent the species of a genus"[150]—but also and more insistently throughout *Origin* by proliferating hypotheticals and speculations, by effectively suggesting that every moment might constitute a point of contingency, where the play of environmental and morphological variables might generate another outcome. The rhetoric here, like the diagram at first glance, collapses and flattens the slow temporalities of natural historical processes: Its mathematical approach—where whole species are reduced to letters and genealogies are reduced to a line—lends it an abstract, atemporal quality. But on the next page Darwin reconstitutes these divergences and outcomes within an extended diachronic history. He reintroduces the temporal frame otherwise absent from his diagram in increasing, stepwise intervals—"the horizontal lines in the diagram, may represent each a thousand generations," or even "ten thousand generations"—in order to establish a scale that exceeds the usual temporalities of the historical imagination.[151]

Whether through image or through words, *Origin* invites readers to view the natural world, too, through the lens of a history dense with divergences, alternatives, and extinctions. Like the extraordinary "sixth-order hypotheticals" that appear in Carl von Clausewitz's version of the Napoleonic Wars, with its multilayered counterfactuals,[152] natural history, Darwin suggests, is the cumulative result of so many moments of contingency extending back in time. His diagram makes this point in the form of a spatialized history, where the very diversity legible in nature's present moment is also a register of the "many complex contingencies," as he puts it elsewhere, that characterize nature's long history. The language of abundance that *Origin* turns to throughout and also returns to in its conclusion, the "endless forms" that "have been, and are being, evolved," the "entangled bank" crowded with "elaborately constructed forms, so different from each other,"[153] conjures not only a synchronic vision of plenitude but also a diachronic narrative of contingency, possibility, and multiplication. To share Darwin's view of nature is to recognize that the multitude of forms before us can only be the result of many divergent and parallel paths traced through a common history, where those alternative trajectories have taken on—quite literally—lives of their own.

CHAPTER 3

Pivotal Moments, Diverging Paths

*Visual Narratives in Board Games, Protean
Views, and Carroll's* Alice *Books*

"If it had grown up," she said to herself, "it would have
made a dreadfully ugly child: but it makes rather a
handsome pig, I think."

Lewis Carroll, *Alice's Adventures in Wonderland,* p. 56.

ALICE'S DEADPAN ASSESSMENT of the pale bundle in her arms takes a
form repeated throughout *Alice's Adventures in Wonderland* and *Through the
Looking-Glass*, perhaps most absurdly in Tweedledee's sequence of causal
propositions ("if it wasn't so, it might be; and if it were so, it would be; but as
it isn't, it ain't"), where his terse summation, "That's logic," might do for them
both.[1] Through these and other examples, Lewis Carroll satirizes the language
of adult rationality by pressing it to its irrational limits, as he reveals that causal
argument and inference lead again and again to inane or fantastical conclusions.
Alice's statement, with its past-tense conditional that projects two alternatives,
takes the form of the historically situated counterfactual and counterfictional
narratives discussed in the previous chapter. Yet for Lyell and Eliot, the weighing of possible narrative outcomes held potentially catastrophic consequences
like earthquakes, floods, or extramarital pregnancies in the balance, while in
Carroll's topsy-turvy narratives there is no lasting "counter-." Because one

trajectory need not foreclose the other, the products of Alice's imaginative process—ugly baby and handsome pig—need not be, and indeed are not, mutually exclusive. Her words might frame the baby as the counterfictional outcome, but play makes futile any attempt at determining which might be actual and which merely hypothetical. As readers, we sense that if she and we were simply to wander the spaces of Wonderland for long enough, we'd come across that baby once again. Consequences matter in Lyell's and Eliot's adult worlds of natural and moral history, but Wonderland establishes a different logic, in which the choice of one alternative outcome over the other—playfully, maddeningly—can have none for either plot or character.

Proposing that we think about the process of play as a form of narrative, Marie-Laure Ryan, Kenneth Foote, and Maoz Azaryahu characterize nineteenth-century games as "sequences of formal moves prescribed by rigid rules," in contrast to contemporary digital games, which "simulate . . . the randomness of life, rather than the teleology of narrative."[2] I too suggest that we read the temporal and causal dimensions of mid-Victorian board games, children's stories, and visual entertainments in narrative terms. But I take issue with the characterization of nineteenth-century play as "rigid" and "formal," arguing instead that the seemingly weightless contingencies at the center of William Spooner's board games and protean views and Lewis Carroll's fictions invite dysteleological engagements with chance. Rather than accepting the either-or logic of their adult counterparts, these gamelike works envision a space of simultaneity, of both-and variants sprung from a single point of divergence. In adapting non-narrative modes of representation found in the period's mathematics, cartography, and visual culture in their reinvention of narrative, these works question the temporal, causal, and spatial exigencies of conventional forms, as they also articulate their own narrative rules and causal limits.

The realm of play this chapter delineates is thus somewhat different from that found in other critical accounts. While some have read in these works anticipations of modern cinema or postmodern literature, others adopting a more historically situated approach have emphasized their imperial dimensions, where play's primary purpose was to train children for lives of colonial adventure and rule. Taking a broader view of Victorian play, Matthew Kaiser considers how the principles at its center, its "ludic multiplicity" and "endless waves of variability," encompassed and informed multiple aspects of nineteenth-century culture, including its economics, sciences, and literature.[3] This chapter navigates between claims that Victorian play expressed an open-ended "multiplicity" and assertions that such games enforced adherence to purposeful political and ideological ends. By attending to the formal and material conditions of play, it considers the role of contingency's turning points and pivotal moments amid the period's shifting evaluations of historical and experiential knowledge.

Examples from three popular genres are the focus here: illustrated board games from the first half of the nineteenth century, Carroll's *Alice* books, and the transforming "protean view" of the 1830s and 40s—a static image that, when held to the light, displayed an alternate scene. All three draw attention not primarily to outcomes but to contingency as a process, to the points of transition, transformation, or divergence between one state and another. Suspending the forward momentum of traditional novelistic or historical narrative and its insistence on closure, these works invite readers and viewers to imagine a condition in which alternatives need not exclude each other, but rather, where two (or more) might be equally viable and available. In this chapter I consider the way in which visual genres, in particular, allowed for the unsettling of the temporal and causal directionalities of traditional narrative.

The nineteenth-century board game, whose eighteenth-century precursors generally focused on moral lessons, permitted engagement with a more causally and spatially complex realm, and this chapter traces the way other, contemporaneous forms of visual representation, such as popular cartography, allowed publishers to reimagine surfaces for play. The game's new spatial logic—of multiple possibilities within a finite, enclosed field—shared and perhaps even made available a set of visual and narrative conventions for writers like Carroll. His *Alice* books, while explicitly alluding to the game of chess and implicitly to the mathematical questions that dominated his scholarly life, merged a ludic sensibility with a structured exploration of contingency. Mobilizing a logic of alternatives at the level of word, sentence, and character, Carroll's works reimagined the developmental narratives of contemporaries like Darwin and Max Müller, positing genealogies without extinction, where generations of proliferating alternatives might circulate in a synchronic present. That vision of simultaneity informs the alternatives on offer in Spooner's protean views as well, where before-and-after images of a single scene, while emphasizing the inevitability of historical transformation, of a volcanic eruption or a building on fire, also allowed for the reversal of historical narrative and the virtual co-existence of two otherwise irreconcilable outcomes in a single object.

In Lyell's geological and Eliot's fictional accounts, the very fact that one outcome precluded another lent weight to moments of contingency. But Carroll's and Spooner's works, not unlike Darwin's *On the Origin of Species*, emphasized the proliferative potential of contingency, its capacity to multiply alternatives. Still, Darwin's vision of a profuse, generative nature operated within, and indeed, depended upon the directionality of time, the inexorability of whose forward movement propelled the processes he described: selection, extinction, adaptation, evolution. By contrast, the gamelike publications discussed in this chapter situate contingency apart from the moral considerations of Eliot's Hayslope and the temporal concerns of natural selection, and instead, in a space where the moment of divergence no longer leads inexorably to closure. Where time becomes irrelevant or reversible, this chapter's texts suggest, contingency's alternate outcomes might indeed exist side by side, in synchronicity.

Yet while some critics have turned to *Through the Looking Glass* as an example of possible worlds, a philosophical and scientific theory born of the statistical indeterminacies of quantum physics,[4] my chapter also points to the limitations of that attempt to read mid-nineteenth-century aesthetics through the lens of twentieth-century science and philosophy. For like the nineteenth-century inventor's design for a machine or the cartographer's sketch of a network of roads, these works, whether through visual or narrative representation, emphasized the inscribed materiality and legibility of their articulated joints and outer edges. Even as they explored possibility and greater multiplicity, they also insisted on the boundaries of representation and the channeled delimitations of chance.

The Board Game's New Geographies

Those glancing at the *London Times* in the weeks leading up to Christmas in the 1840s would have found, nestled among the advertisements for digestive cures and ladies' pianos, announcements for new board games. A game was an ideal gift for the holidays, they suggested, or a worthwhile pastime for a winter's evening spent in the company of family members. One advertised "NEW GAMES for CHRISTMAS," such as the "Funnyshire Fox Game" and "The Progress of Cotton Manufacture: A Pictorial Puzzle," for six or seven shillings each, while another promoted board games as objects appropriately "combining instruction with amusement."[5] Yet another, welcoming readers to a shop called the Temple of Fancy, described its offerings as simply "Amusement for Long Evenings," while the purveyors at the "Noah's Ark Toy Warehouse" suggested that new board games were particularly "suitable to this season of the year."[6]

The promotion and distribution of games for middle-class audiences can be understood as one component in the broader history of print culture's transformation during the early decades of the nineteenth century. Technologies like steam power and lithography revolutionized the mass-market publishing industry in the 1830s and 40s, enabling more efficient, less expensive modes of printing and distribution, and the concomitant growth of a class of well-off consumers fed the expansion of a marketplace for both novelty and educational materials.[7] But through their changing themes and designs, early nineteenth-century children's board games trace another history, one of epistemological transformation in popular understandings of chance and contingency. Like Darwin's evolutionary tree diagram but for a much broader audience, these games exemplify the spatial and visual dimensions of the period's experiments with narrative; in them, the metaphorical nodes and branchings found in prose take immediate, legible, and material form on the board's surface.

Critics have argued that games performed important cultural work in nineteenth-century Britain, that they promoted national ideals and more specifically, a respect for rules, a spirit of competition, and a sense of mastery over both natural and colonial worlds.[8] Siobhan Carroll, for example, examines the ways in which these entertainments highlighted "mobility" and "the interlocking pathways of global trade," and I extend her conception of the "spatial agency" players and literary characters exerted over the represented geographies of the game board.[9] But the present chapter is particularly interested in the ways these games transposed formal principles across genres and contexts, and especially in the narrative epistemologies and practices their layouts exemplified. I investigate the kinds of temporal and spatial operations the designs of these boards enabled and the ways in which those operations were adapted in other genres and media. How did publishers give the temporal progress conveyed in literature—where the common eighteenth-century metaphor or conceit of the journey was used to describe narrative progress—spatial expression on the surface of a game board? How did authors transpose the logic of movement across that surface into printed lines of prose? These translations suggest that the board game, while perhaps alluding to the "ludic multiplicity" and "endless variability" to which Kaiser refers, nonetheless maintained some of the formal and operational conventions found in cartographic and literary representation. In treating these visual and narrative spaces as abstractions, less as referential geographies than as arenas of formal possibility, I trace a shift from earlier games, which adhered closely to a structure modeled after the unilinear, directional narratives of eighteenth-century morality tales, to mid-nineteenth-century games, which conveyed more complex, multidirectional visions of mobility and progress.

Borrowing the design of the eighteenth-century French "game of the goose," or "Jeu de L'Oie," early nineteenth-century English "race games" led players along a spiraling track, which usually began at the board's outer edges and moved inward, typically on a path of moral or historical progress, toward a central goal. In games such as *The Mansion of Bliss* (1822),[10] for instance, landing on a square labeled with a virtue allowed players to advance while landing on one labeled with a vice caused them to retreat or lose a turn (Figure 3.1), as they proceeded on a journey whose endpoint and culmination was a state of predictable moral perfection. In *The Mirror of Truth* (1811), a very similar game that "exhibit[ed] a variety of biographical anecdotes and moral essays calculated to inspire a love of virtue and abhorrence of vice," players encountered a series of exemplary moral episodes or conditions through play, and upon landing on one square or another, players were to read aloud or even recite the explanation that accompanied the illustrated virtue in the game's booklet. The square labeled "Courage," for instance, depicted Christians bravely volunteering to withstand torture at the hands of a Japanese ruler (and subsequently winning his respect and admiration for their courage), while "Justice" was embodied by Sir Thomas More counseling a young person. (These stories only accompanied virtues; vices were labeled simply by name, as if illustrating or narrating them might tempt rather than dissuade.)

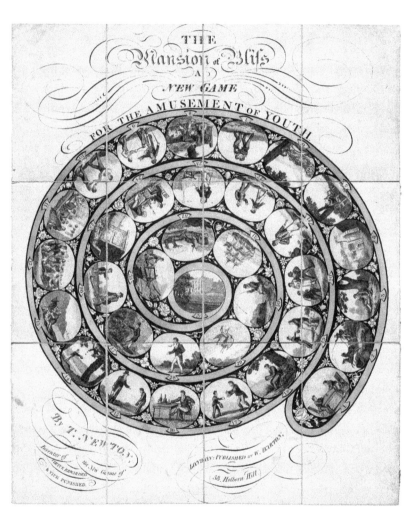

FIGURE 3.1 The Mansion of Bliss (London: W. Darton, 1822). Hand-colored engraving. Courtesy of the Yale Center for British Art, Gift of Ellen and Arthur Liman, Yale JD 1957.

Movement in such games proceeded along a single, discernible track, emphasizing the clear directionality of one's moral path. These were, in effect, the visual counterparts of a work like John Bunyan's *Pilgrim's Progress*, in which contingency took the same form in episode after episode: a binary choice between faith and temptation. So, too, the moral stakes of these games situated players between "a love of virtue and abhorrence of vice," and for them, as for Bunyan's protagonist, the moral journey necessarily follows a single, identifiable route. While the images and specific lessons might have varied from board to board, the game's visual layout was used again and again and would have been recognizable even to the youngest of players.

Caroline Goodfellow observes that such simple morality games declined in popularity by the middle of the nineteenth century, as games featuring historical or geographical themes gained ascendancy.[11] Some of these, such as *Wallis's Locomotive Game of Railroad Adventures* (1838), adapted earlier designs to updated themes; here, players also traveled along a spiraling path, starting in the rural outskirts and ending triumphantly in London. Progress in this game was as much technological as it was geographical, as players moved from a state of impeded simplicity (the unhitched oxcart) and toward a state of commercial and industrial development (signified by the smoky rooftops and spires of the city). Yet in spite of the obvious similarities in design to their moral forerunners, these transportation or travel games situated players in a world where one's fate was no longer determined by moral or providential considerations. To be sure, even earlier morality games bore mixed messages, as Siobhan Carroll and Margaret Kolb have observed, since progress always depended—ironically—upon chance, success or failure on the spin of a teetotum, or wheel, that advanced players to squares labeled "Courage" or "Idleness," and not on their own moral qualities. As Kolb puts it, "coincidental victories seem to demand an account of what value victory might have."[12] But by dispensing with the pretense of moralizing altogether, these later games largely sidestepped the question. Incorporating chance and accident as part of the explicit thematics of play, they made chance the accepted determinant of success or failure. In a game like *Wallis's*, for example, progress was shaped by a series of morally neutral events, from the quotidian (a meal taken at a station) to the disastrous (a flood or derailment).

Other games, departing not only from the moral thematics of earlier games but also from the predictable geometry of the eighteenth-century spiral altogether, often looked to a different visual referent for inspiration: the map. Eighteenth-century advances in mapping technologies and early nineteenth-century technologies for printing and distribution expanded both the availability of and consumer demand for maps, particularly those with educational, aesthetic, touristic, or entertainment value. Schools began to incorporate geography as a standard subject for study;[13] groups like the Society for the Diffusion of Useful Knowledge (SDUK) marketed high-quality one-shilling maps to the public starting in the 1830s;[14] and weekly publications like the *Illustrated London News* used free maps and geographical views as promotional items to tempt new subscribers in the 1840s.[15]

Board games, typically priced between six and ten shillings each, would have appealed to a similar group of middle-class readers and consumers. Indeed, many of the makers and distributors of the period's board games—successful London-based publishers like William Sallis, Edward Wallis, and William Spooner—also issued more traditional geographical materials such as maps and guides for children; Spooner's 1844 *Zoological Map of the World Showing the Geographical Distribution of Animals* and Wallis's 1841 *Guide for Strangers Through London*, for example, adapted existing modes of geographical representation to educational and touristic purposes.[16] But the period's board games also drew on the visual conventions of maps to reconfigure the possibilities for spatial movement, inviting players to "travel" across virtual spaces and lands.[17] Their surfaces often represented recognizable local and foreign geographies, and even when featuring a fictional landscape, adopted the recognizable conventions of cartographic practice: contrasting colors to indicate boundaries, gridlines, decorative compasses, and cartouches.

Some early versions of geographical games adapted elements of popular mapping to the logic of the race game, retaining the latter's single track and linear model of progress. Thus the 1809 *Geographical Recreation; or a Voyage Round the Habitable World,* offered a variation on the spiral structure found in *The Mansion of Bliss,* as it led players through the four quadrants of the British empire. Its surface, while circular in design, does not correspond to a flattened projection of the globe; instead, the board incorporates maps only as small insets, for reference, and geography is instead conveyed primarily through exemplary images or vignettes, each depicting an experience loosely associated with a particular geographical region. Reading or reciting the corresponding explanatory narratives from the paired booklet lent an educational element to play, but these, too, adhered to a more traditional emphasis on moral hierarchies; setbacks in this game occurred through encounters with violent natives or supposedly heathenish customs, such as when travelers see the stone "idols" at Easter Island. But other geographical games, such as the 1770 *Royal Geographical Pastime: Exhibiting a Complete Tour Round the World,* with its gridlines and decorative edges, and the 1787 *A New Royal Geographical Pastime for England and Wales,*[18] which marked the boundaries between counties with contrasting pastels, relied on the readily recognizable visual rhetoric of the period's popular cartography. Where the gently curving lines of the former suggested maritime navigation (as did its extended title, Passages into the South Sea), the network of lines in the latter, which join one city to the next in geometric array, evoked the trigonometric mapping practices that Britain had recently adopted for use in its ordnance survey projects (Figure 3.2).[19]

FIGURE 3.2 A New Royal Geographical Pastime for England and Wales (London: Robert Sayer, 1787). © Victoria and Albert Museum, London.

Still, while such games might have helped to encourage tourism, players traced often far-flung and arbitrary paths across the board, leaping from number to number, rather than developing itineraries that might approximate actual routes of travel.[20] Play tended to cultivate knowledge of place names and facts—how quickly could one find the location of Chester or identify the main exports of Leeds?—and in this sense supported one of the period's educational goals: the committing to memory of a "catalogue of the towns, rivers, mountains, animals, and vegetables of the different countries of the earth" in a demonstration of the kinds of national and imperial knowledge Megan Norcia describes.[21]

But a later generation of games emphasized a different set of geographical lessons, as they presented the surface of the board (and by extension, its geographical or fictional referent) as a space available for less arbitrary and ordered, more experiential forms of travel, where any number of itineraries might be possible. Precursors to these games had harnessed cartographic conventions to moral lessons, such as Darton and Harvey's 1794 *Map of the Various Paths of Life*, while others offered similar "geographies" for love and marriage.[22] But Wallis's 1844 *New Game of Wanderers in the Wilderness* (Figure 3.3), unmooring geography from moral anchors, used its vividly represented two-dimensional cartographic space to simulate the experiential qualities of a three-dimensional journey. That the board lacks labels (though players with basic geographical knowledge would surely have recognized South America) but depicts trees, villages, and animals suggests the relative importance of a contextualized geographical knowledge over the types of rote learning tested by the 1787 *Royal Geographical* game; and its secular, amoral landscape reflects its departure from the kinds of lessons offered by Darton and Harvey's "map."

Wanderers in the Wilderness educated young players about foreign spaces, and especially, as Norcia tells us, about how to evaluate them from a colonizing perspective—to assess resources, economic opportunities, and hazards. It thus encouraged players to interact with the board in a way that differed from the way other, more traditional race games invited them to, as it directed them along itineraries that bore a plausible resemblance to the kinds of paths that actual travelers to the Continent might have followed. Players would begin at the upper coastline around the port city of Georgetown, Guyana, where,

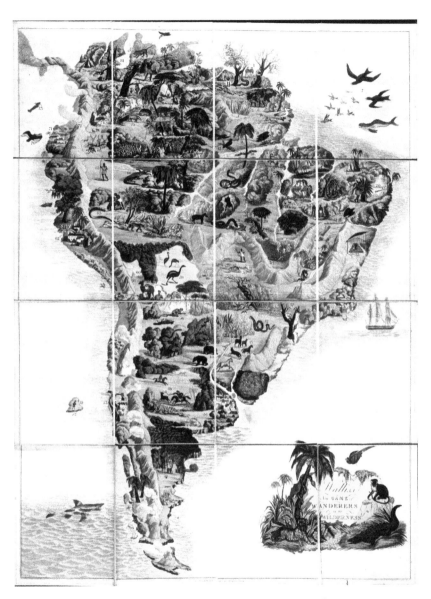

FIGURE 3.3 New Game of Wanderers in the Wilderness (London: Edward Wallis, 1844). Courtesy of Toronto Public Library.

accompanied by a local estate owner, they would move inland along the banks of the Amazon, then southward and eventually back north along the Andes. Its layout trained players in the strategic use of maps, in the process of thinking about the alignments between cartographic representation and geographic space, and about the shaping of routes of travel. In this sense, *Wanderers in the Wilderness* exercised in simplified form the kind of knowledge cultivated by the period's maritime maps; in them, the spaces beyond Britain, according to Luciana de Lima Martins, were often depicted not as fluid and continuous but as a network of strategically linked points, such as convenient ports, landmarks, trading and repair stations.[23] Similarly, *Wanderers in the Wilderness* permitted young players to appreciate the whole of the mapped surface while also encouraging them to visualize a foreign geography in a selective, systematic way, in terms of the sequential stops and routes required for its successful navigation.

Where Siobhan Carroll and Norcia have emphasized the relevance of geographical games to a period of international travel and colonial expansion, Wallis's game also joined these political lessons to more abstract, epistemological ones. For the space of engagement in *Wanderers in the Wilderness* removed players from the ordered world of geometry to the less ordered world of geography, and the game's thematics likewise removed play from the more predictable space of nineteenth-century morality to the disorder of an accidental world, where mountain ranges, bodies of water, and mechanical failures might present secular impediments to one's progress. And although Wallis's game still effectively limited play to movement backwards and forwards along a single path, others used cartography to amplify those lessons about a contingent world through the spatial organization of the board. By introducing multiple tracks traversing a mapped geographical surface, across which players might move in accordance with the directions of the compass, they invited more spatially complex and open-ended forms of movement. Play in these games—such as Spooner's 1836 *A Voyage of Discovery; or, The Five Navigators*; his 1847 *The Pirate and Traders of the West Indies*; and his 1849 *The Travellers of Europe* (Figure 3.4)—transformed the grids of cartographic longitudes and latitudes into squares for play and allowed for the tracing of a less predictable narrative.

FIGURE 3.4 The Travellers of Europe (London: William Spooner, 1849). © Victoria and Albert Museum, London.

Siobhan Carroll emphasizes that Spooner's games fostered a sense of "spatial agency" in players, even as the rules permitted only "a limited degree of control."[24] Indeed, in allowing each player to begin at a unique starting point on the board and to travel by a unique route, these games, like their cartographical equivalents, suggested that there might be multiple, equally viable itineraries toward the goal. Still, direction of movement was determined by the spin of a wheel,[25] and the boards, with their clearly marked starting and ending points, still presented players with teleological, predetermined conceptions of progress. Moreover, winning was, as ever, an achievement defined in Victorian terms, albeit now in a more secular vocabulary of domestic happiness, financial gain, and imperial success. In this respect, mid-century geographical games maintained an important link to moralizing forerunners like *The Mansion of Bliss*, as they emphasized the rewards achievable through incremental forms of progress, which could be understood as not only in geographical but in narrative terms as well.

Two of Spooner's games, *The Journey, or Crossroads to Conqueror's Castle* (1845)[26] and *The Cottage of Content or Right Roads and Wrong Ways* (1848) (Figure 3.5)—each very similar in design to the other—turned from recognizable geographies to explicitly fictional ones. And they suggested some of the ways in which narrative might be transposed into spatial, and spatial into narrative modes of representation, a connection Spooner develops in other, visually innovative genres I discuss in this chapter.[27]

Although the surfaces of *The Journey* and *The Cottage* resemble children's maps, the spaces they depict have no real-world referent, as they also dispense with the imperial, moral, and historical lessons of other games. Rather, their cartoon-like representations of people and places focus attention on the board's imaginary network of possible routes, its series of encounters and adventures, and an array of intersecting and overlapping itineraries. But what seems to matter most in both design and play is not the quality of particular paths; their names—"Shuttlecock Walk," "Holiday Road," or "Chance Road"—reflect the very absence of meaningful experiential content to be found there. Instead, interest, suspense, and momentum coalesce in the circular nodes, the points of contingency where paths intersect and diverge. The spin of the wheel still determines whether one moves forwards or backwards, left or right, but these new games encourage a fundamentally different approach to play. Almost every move brings players to a crossroads, a moment in which decisive directional shifts might occur and send them along other paths. Appropriately then, where earlier games made the endpoint the literal and figurative centerpiece of play—the "mansion of bliss" or "temple of happiness" occupying the center of the board and lending the game its title—at the center of these games lay multiple intersecting paths for movement. Hence "the journey" is effectively synonymous with the many "cross roads" through which players pass during the course of play.

While these versions of multidirectional play stopped short of offering players choice,[28] they nonetheless transformed every move into a threshold, an explicit engagement with chance. Moreover, the introduction of cartographic conventions into the board's design opened the space of the board in

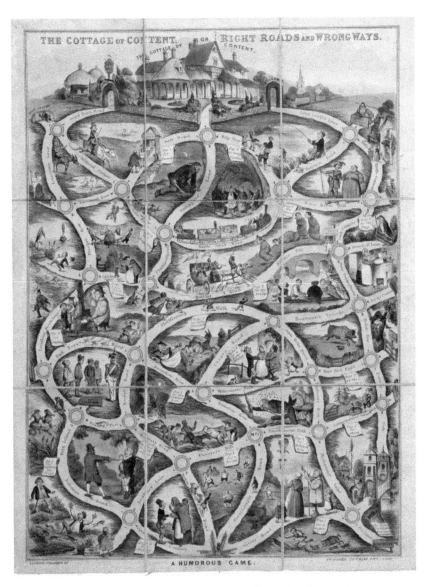

FIGURE 3.5 The Cottage of Content or Right Roads and Wrong Ways
(London: William Spooner, 1848). Courtesy of Toronto Public Library.

imagination if not fully in practice to the availability of multiple, undetermined itineraries: It invited players to visualize the alternate outcomes that lay before them, to trace the hypothetical moves and paths that might lead to success, and to see fellow players on those alternate paths during the course of the game. Thus where earlier games represented and enacted inevitability—everyone would reach the "mansion of bliss" eventually—these later games eschewed narrative certainty in favor of combinatorial possibility and probabilistic contemplation. The spin of the wheel, with its multiple directions, mirrored the play of chance at each of the game's circular nodes and in the multiple, unpredictable itineraries that would follow. While play probably felt repetitive in practice, each iteration of the game, whose paths were traceable and legible, had the effect of being unique, one among a seemingly countless number available to its players.

Spooner's Multiplots

Though little known today, William Spooner was, as Siobhan Carroll tells us, a pivotal figure in the design and publishing history of board games.[29] But in the first half of the nineteenth century he was also known for a range of other visual entertainments, through many of which he reimagined the conventions of prose fiction and of historical representation.[30] For if his board games adapted the elements of story, of picaresque adventure and the unexpected turnings of plot, to the visually oriented surface of play, he also seemed interested in the ways in which children's stories might be reimagined by adapting the spatial contingencies of the board game—with its possibilities for synchronous and parallel movement, intersection, and divergence—to narrative. Two of his publications, illustrated works for children, *The Wanderings of Mrs. Pipe & Family to View the Crystal Palace* and "Whittington and His Cat," explore the ways in which the printed page, through innovative arrangements of text and image, might express contingency's formal properties. Both transform an otherwise predictable literary genre, tales for children, into daring investigations into the temporal and causal parameters of narrative.

Wanderings, a children's book with line drawings by Percy Cruikshank, was sold in both black-and-white and color editions. Appearing within a week after the opening of the Great Exhibition in London in 1851, it relates the comic story of the Pipe family as they make plans to visit the exhibition. *Wanderings* opens with two pages of prose, but on the third page, it shifts to narration primarily through images, and explanatory text is relegated to secondary status in the form of brief figure legends.[31] Significantly, the moment of transition between text and image occurs as signs of diverging perspectives and plans emerge among the characters. The prose reveals a split between husband and wife on page 2, when Mrs. Pipe explains her desire to visit the Crystal Palace, while Mr. Pipe objects that "it would take a fortun' for all our family to see this here bit o' glass."[32] But that disjunction receives a more dramatic treatment on the facing page, where their exchange is presented in triptych (Figure 3.6). Where the prose narrative detailing their conversation takes up three columns of text spread over two pages, the illustration brings this interaction onto a single page, giving their diverging opinions the effect of simultaneity: as Mrs. Pipe presides over her dinner table, Mr. Pipe stands apart looking astonished, while the final panel focuses on the cupboard, on an unused teapot in which Mrs. Pipe has saved funds for the excursion.[33]

The emotional divergence between them anticipates the physical separation that occurs in the ensuing sets of juxtaposed images, as Mrs. Pipe and two of her children take an omnibus while Mr. Pipe proceeds by foot and boat. While the last paragraph of prose describes these divergent modes of transportation, the images show what the text cannot: the side-by-side, "meanwhile" qualities of the narrative. As Mrs. Pipe "looks for her family in every direction" at the designated meeting point, we see that Mr. Pipe, unbeknownst to her, has stopped for a drink (Figure 3.7).[34] The succeeding pages trace the characters' separate journeys, each shaped by the Dickensian contingencies of everyday life, the circumstances that take each one's intention "to view the Crystal Palace" off track: missed meetings, forgotten agreements, unlucky decisions. After a series of these adventures, and as if to emphasize the dysteleological quality of both their plot and their journey, the final scene takes place not at the exhibition but at home, where a relieved Mr. and Mrs. Pipe are reunited at their hearth, surrounded by their children.

Jonathan Grossman has delineated the ways in which the period's rapidly expanding modes of public transport—omnibus, railway, stagecoach, foot—often served as both plot device and narrative mechanism for representing the word "china" always alarmed, in connexion with an individual wearing a very long tail,—which little allegory was always repeated to him when he declined retiring to rest. Mrs. P. seized the infant, and cramming his mouth with sugar, called her now quieted husband a brute, for naming that horrid place when Billy was a good boy. Peace being restored, Mrs. P. returned to the attack.

"In respect of money, I've took good care of that: why, bless you, I've been saving for these three months!"

"Oh!" said Mr. P., indulging in a long whistle,—his custom when he thought he had discovered anything,—"that accounts for our short commons. Mrs. P.! Mrs. P.! you 're a werry hartful 'oman; why, you've been a persuading me every day, as so much meat only made me heavy. Heavy, indeed! I feels light enough now!"

"Well, never mind," was Mrs. P.'s reply; "you can make up for it when we goes our trip:" and she seated herself, smoothed down her apron and her jolly face. "Bless your hart, I've laid all my plans. We shall take all the children, and Charley Hopkins,—that, to please our Sally. As to the eatables, I shall take something filling, on account of the boys." A wink passed between her young gentlemen, expressive of their ready approval. "But I won't tease you any more, if you will promise to go without fuss; say you will, to please me, for once!"

After a little more coaxing, and bargaining he shouldn't ride in an omnibus, Mr. P., who was a good-natured man, consented to go. It was agreed he should get to the Tunnel Pier, and go by the boat to Hungerford Bridge, and then walk the rest of the way. And Mrs. P. set about preparing for the following day with a hearty goodwill.

FIGURE 3.6 From *The Wanderings of Mrs. Pipe & Family to View the Crystal Palace*, illustrated by Percy Cruikshank, page 2 and image page 1 (London: William Spooner, 1851). Courtesy of the Beinecke Rare Book and Manuscript Library, Yale University.

simultaneously unfolding trajectories in Dickens's fiction,[35] and Spooner and Cruikshank's *Wanderings* plays with that alignment between transportation and narrative, unveiling noticeably divergent paths as the Pipe family members begin their separate journeys. But the juxtaposed routings of *Wanderings* also recall the design of Spooner's own board games. For where the traditionally one-dimensional realm of prose representation promotes a linear reading process in which the eye travels across the page, left to right, and from one page to the next along a predictable, ordered path, the two-dimensional surface of the game necessarily makes all possible routes visible at once, even if only one or two paths are in play at any given moment.[36] *Wanderings* effectively flattens the game's divergent itineraries back onto the page, where the eye might take in, at a glance, a pair or triad of narrative routes in the form of images. The book thus propels readers into a kind of multiplot, but one markedly different

M.ʳˢ Pipe announces her intention of visiting the Crystal Palace, attended by her family.   M.ʳ Pipe expresses his astonishment at such unlooked for gaiety, & wishes to know where the money's to come from.   M.ʳˢ P points to her domestic "Savings Bank" on the top shelf

from that found in more traditional works of fiction, where, as Grossman puts it, "the knowledge of separate simultaneous happenings does not actually get produced in the moment of its simultaneity" but rather through "the sequencing of retrospective narratives."[37] Whereas a novel like *Bleak House* allows readers to immerse themselves in one developing narrative at a time, such that a recognition that numerous other narratives are unfolding in temporal (if not narratorial) simultaneity comes only in retrospect, the side-by-side placement of panels in *Wanderings* does not allow for immersion or much plot development but does permit juxtaposition and simultaneity in representing the separate but equivalent tracks upon which the characters' journeys run. In this sense, the work doesn't recall a Dickens novel so much as Darwin's diagram of speciation (discussed in Chapter 2), which merged two forms of temporal representation into a single image: historical process along the

M.ʳ P. being intrusted with
the liquids departs on his
Journey.

M.ʳˢ P. arrived at the place of meeting
looks for her family in every direction,
but, as usual on such occasions without
success.

Which is not very strange as regards M.ʳ P. who being taken rather faint has
sat down to refresh himself & lighten his
load suddenly he recognises a friend, at
least he thinks so by his costume.

FIGURE 3.7. From *The Wanderings of Mrs. Pipe & Family to View the Crystal Palace*,
illustrated by Percy Cruikshank, image page 3 (London: William Spooner, 1851).
Courtesy of the Beinecke Rare Book and Manuscript Library, Yale University.

vertical axis and the diversity of species at any given moment on the horizontal
axis. So, too, *Wanderings* invites readers to register a linear, diachronic process
as they proceed from page to page, and, at the same time, a lateral, synchronic
one as they view all three images on a single page. Like the players of one of
Spooner's board games, readers can see at a glance the multiple routes that
other characters have taken, and as in the game, they learn that the story is not
so much about the endpoint—Mrs. Pipe's family never reaches the intended
destination after all—but about the network of intersecting and diverging
"wanderings" at their center.

If *Wanderings* constituted one kind of experiment in representing simultaneously unfolding narratives, then Spooner's broadside illustration, "Whittington
and His Cat," published circa 1840, is another. Spooner's choice of subject,
Dick Whittington, was a canny one. A celebrated figure in English folklore
since the sixteenth century, Whittington famously rose from his position as
a friendless orphan to become Lord Mayor of London. For mid-Victorians,

he was a popular and familiar figure (as one contemporaneous essayist put it, "Who is there that has not heard of the renowned Sir Richard Whittington, the thrice lord mayor of London . . . ? His name is a household word; we learned to lisp it with the imperfect accents of early childhood"),[38] yet one about whom there seems to have been little consensus. The multiple versions in circulation between the 1820s and 1870s, as well as contemporaneous articles about his history, suggest a remarkable lack of agreement over key elements of his story. One writer, for example, objected that Dick "never could have been a poor bare-legged boy" since his father was a knight, while another asserted that the whole story is "enveloped in doubt" and that the hero's given name was, in fact, Matthew.[39] Even as, or perhaps because, Whittington's story had been retold countless times—in poems, ballads, plays, novelistic prose, and illustrations—several competing variants were available by the middle of the nineteenth century.[40] In the absence of a definitive narrative, Spooner's broadside version encompasses multiple possible readings, allowing not only for the simultaneity of multiplot but also for the simultaneities of alternate competing accounts available to nineteenth-century readers.

Among the popular versions in circulation, the chief episodes and characters tended to remain constant, while their order of appearance and causal relation differed considerably. Most agree that Whittington was taken in as an orphan by a kindly merchant, named Fitzwarren, but mistreated by one of Fitzwarren's servants, a cook. From this point, however, accounts diverge. Versions like that found in the circa 1820 *The History of Dick Whittington, Lord Mayor of London*, the 1859 *Home Treasury of Old Story Books*, and the 1860 *Nursery Tales for Good Little Boys* attribute his rise to his volunteering his cat, which he had adopted as a companion in his rat-infested garret, for one of Fitzwarren's shipping ventures. Unhappy, Whittington runs away, but turns back when he hears the bells of a London church calling to him; meanwhile, the cat has rid a royal court in Africa of its vermin and becomes the means by which Whittington wins his fortune. Two other versions elaborate on Whittington's motives; in one he had used the cat to protect the merchant's wares rather than himself, and in the other the cat is merely a loving companion;[41] in both, his running away is prompted by sadness at the cat's departure.[42] Yet other variants place the episode of running away earlier, a direct result of the cook's abuse, and well before any mention of the cat or shipping voyage.[43] And while another version omits the cat altogether, asserting that it was included only because "the common people did not care" for Whittington otherwise,[44] Eliza Cook's verse retelling focuses only on the hearing of the bells.[45] The *Holiday Album* version avoids committing to any sequence, stating simply that a "little ragged boy became Lord Mayor of London. He was Dick Whittington, and he had a pet cat," before adding (perhaps not without a touch of impatience), "Do you not know the story?"[46]

Spooner's broadside offers the viewer a montage of these familiar scenes as a collection of vignettes: Dick in a rat-infested garret, the abusive cook, the bells, the African king, Dick made Lord Mayor (Figure 3.8). The broadside, like many of the contemporaneous text versions, seems to assume some foreknowledge of the story, and like the *Holiday Album* account, puts the familiar elements of that story before readers—the "ragged boy," "the "Lord Mayor," the "pet cat"—but then places the generation of a continuous, coherent narrative into their hands. In some ways, it resembles one of Spooner's other productions, a puzzle version of "Little Red Riding Hood," whose successful reassembly depended not only on an awareness of shapes and spaces, but also presumably on some knowledge of the original story. But in "Red Riding Hood" the narrative through line is much clearer, with a continuous, left-to-right reading trajectory and a defined horizontal channel (or, to borrow the language of comics scholars, "gutter") separating the top from bottom panel. Indeed, the genre of the puzzle suggests the existence of a correct solution, a right order into which the pieces and story must fall. "Whittington and His Cat" eludes this more positivist approach to narrative reassembly: Its layout makes it unclear whether the reader should follow a horizontal or vertical path through the image, and the accompanying bits of prose (e.g., "Dick tormented by Rats & mice running across his bed" and "Dick is found by Mr. Fitzwarren at his doorstep") are descriptive rather than causally or temporally propulsive;[47] they do little to indicate sequence. Instead, Spooner's "Whittington" is ambiguous and, I argue, strategically so—a reflection of the absence of a definitive narrative, as it directs attention rather to the alternate tellings a single history itself might encompass, the multiple courses that might coexist within an understanding of the past.

For a theory of how Victorians might have read a work that was more image than prose, more montage than conventional narrative, we might turn to recent

FIGURE 3.8 "Whittington and His Cat" (London: William Spooner [c. 1840]). Image © London Metropolitan Archives (City of London).

narratological studies of graphic novels and comics. Indeed, through innovative layouts and use of images, Spooner's works advance a version of what recent critics like Thierry Groensteen and Jason Dittmer, in their analyses of twentieth- and twenty-first-century comic books, have called "plurivectorial narration," a representational strategy that encourages readers to trace a narrative along multiple axes. In bringing this critical approach to bear on works from the 1840s, my goal is not to challenge an accepted critical timeline for the emergence of comics and graphic novels,[48] but rather to point to the ways in which our readings of these experimental texts, with their innovative handling of spatial, causal, and temporal relationships, might benefit from a methodology that reaches beyond the modes of analysis generally applied to nineteenth-century works. For both Dittmer and Groensteen, comics demand "viewer participation," a kind of active reading practice that, they insist, is not relegated to "strange little experiments" (as Scott McCloud deemed them) found only in esoteric and "exotic" graphic works.[49] Dittmer in particular draws attention to the "openness of montage" that characterizes the contemporary comic.[50] Here, he explains, the layout allows for both narration and reading to take multiple courses, practices that might differ from moment to moment, from reader to reader; and Thomas A. Bredehoft concurs, noting that the layout of the page "allows comics narration to break the linearity of a time-sequenced narrative line."[51]

Bredehoft chooses the term "architecture" to describe this montage-like layout (a term particularly apt for the subject of his own analysis, the lived spaces of Chris Ware's characters), but Dittmer's metaphor, "geographies," feels better suited to Spooner's work.[52] A word that conjures the ways in which contemporaneous cartographic forms informed the design of Spooner's board games, "geographies" also alludes to the more complex navigational practices of reading that mapped surfaces required of readers. Indeed, as in his geographical games, in Spooner's "Whittington" the starting point (Dick beginning his journey, at the upper left) and ending point (Dick's "arrival," receiving his title from the king, at lower right) are intuitively clear from both a spatial and narrative perspective, but the remaining surface of the broadside, like that of the map or the board game, invites multiple possible directions of stepwise travel.

Following the usual conventions of Western reading, a viewer might proceed across the top, left to right, such that Dick's misery is adequately conveyed by the rats on his bed; no reference to the cruel cook (at lower left) is necessary to make sense of the story's trajectory. Alternately, one might read "down" the left-hand column, which emphasizes Dick's mistreatment by the cruel cook, itself a sufficient rationale for the subsequent panel to the right, which shows that after having run away from home, he hears the bells, as recounted in the *Merry Rhymes* and 1880 *Merry Ballads* versions.[53]

These two linear itineraries, as well as any number of others, exist in simultaneity, alongside a multiplot version, as related in the 1859 *Home Treasury* and 1860 *Nursery Tales* texts, in which the reader is given to understand that the African king's delight and Dick's hearing of the bells, though geographically and causally distinct, occur in simultaneity.[54] The image has, in effect, distilled Dick's story to a set of seemingly decisive moments, but the task of locating those moments within a causal sequence—of situating contingency with relation to causality—lies not with the artist or the object, but rather with the viewer. At once narrative game and puzzle, "Whittington and His Cat" exemplifies the transformation of a single document into a vehicle for plurivectorial narration and reading. Just as Spooner adapted cartographic conventions to the game board, so, too, he mobilized them within the space of a familiar narrative. In "Whittington" he generated a kind of map that invited alternate reading practices and narratives, and through which readers might trace multiple causal and chronological itineraries.

Word Play in Wonderland

Where Spooner's games turned away from the moralizing lessons of earlier board games, Lewis Carroll's *Alice* books even more emphatically refused the didactic, religious quality of their predecessors in favor of what critics have described as a more "modern" sensibility.[55] Although for some, Carroll's work is significant for the ways in which it anticipated twentieth-century intellectual concerns,[56] others have looked to Carroll's immersion in the scientific and transmedial cultures of his time. For example, Helen Groth argues that, in aligning his fiction with experiential technologies such as "photography, phonography, and the cinematograph," he rejected the "heavy-handed truisms" of earlier children's literature, and similarly, Cristopher Hollingsworth points to the influence of the period's "mixed media, collage, and assemblage" on his writing.[57] Others, including Gillian Beer and Rose Lovell-Smith, have read in the *Alice* books engagements with an array of contemporaneous mathematical, evolutionary, political, and imperial concerns.[58]

Extending the work of these historicized approaches, this chapter treats the concept of play in Lewis Carroll's fiction as a practice shaped around a controlled engagement with contingency and chance. In this sense, play shares key similarities with the legal and mathematical contexts identified in his work by other critics, in that all three reflect a productive tension between possibility and constraint, between agency and system. But a focus on play also invites us to think about *Alice's Adventures* with relation to the narrative experiments performed by the period's other popular genres, such as the board games discussed earlier. For if those games shifted the nature of play from a predictable linearity and toward a multiplicity and multi-directionality of mapped spaces by the 1840s and 50s, then the *Alice* books, too, moved away from the additive, linear logic of traditional children's literature ("This is the House that Jack built. / This is the Malt, that lay in the House that Jack built. / This is the Rat, that ate the Malt, that lay in the House that Jack built."[59]) and toward the potential for multilinearity and proliferation.

Although critical attention has often focused on Carroll's use of chess, of its moves and pieces as a metaphor in *Through the Looking-Glass*,[60] Beer cautions that while the "*Alice* books call on playing cards and chess for some of their structures . . . they do not remain within the domain of those systems."[61] Gilles Deleuze, too, turns the focus away from particularized, literal referents and toward the gamelike logic, what he calls the "rotation of the roulette and the rolling ball," expressed in Carroll's work.[62] But if the roulette wheel symbolizes the open-ended operations of chance, Deleuze acknowledges that in *Alice's Adventures* "chance is fixed at certain points, such that, for example, there are only two "alternative[s] . . . two possible means of drying."[63] And indeed the engagement with chance in these books resembles that on offer in the board game, whose spatialized logic allows for movement through series of clearly articulated alternatives.[64] For if the conventions of popular cartography were key to the development of the board game, so they may have been for these works, too, whose author was fascinated by the period's mapping practices. One of Lewis Carroll's first works was *La Guida di Bragia*, a comic operetta about Bradshaw's railway guides and maps,[65] while his 1893 *Sylvie and Bruno Concluded* parodies a map whose impossible scale of "*a mile to the mile!*" makes it unusable.[66] His *Alice* books share the cartographic logic of Spooner's games, in that discrete nodes of intersection and divergence are what allow movement and progress. For instance, Alice reasons that, "[i]f I eat one of these cakes, . . . as it can't possibly make me larger, it must make me smaller," and similarly, the Caterpillar advises her that eating one side of the mushroom "will make you grow taller, and the other side will make you grow shorter."[67] Alternatives such as these effectively constitute and motivate the plot, sending Alice, not unlike a player of Spooner's Cottage and Journey games, hurtling down one narrative path or another.

Still, those alternatives have few lasting consequences. Reflections such as, "I'm sure I'm not Ada . . . for her hair goes in such long ringlets, and mine doesn't go in ringlets at all; and I'm sure I can't be Mabel, for I know all sorts of things, and she, oh! she knows such a very little!" or, "I didn't know I was to have a party at all . . . but if there is to be one, I think *I* ought to invite the guests,"[68] appear in the optative mode, a formulation upon which, Andrew H. Miller argues, nineteenth-century realist fiction relied. Yet here Alice reenacts its rhetoric but without the weighty ramifications Eliot's and Dickens's characters have to bear.[69] For where the power of the optative derives, in part, from the awareness of being committed to a particular life path, of the "irrevocable" quality of one's narrative journey,[70] the characteristic of Wonderland as a space of play is precisely its sense of revocability. Alice's "handsome pig" might yet become an "ugly child," a process whose reversibility Carroll emphasized in a later invention, the palm-sized "Wonderland Postage-Stamp Case," in which the outer case depicted the pig and on the back side the Cheshire Cat, while the inner folder revealed the baby and the Cat's smile; for the owner of the stamp case, the action of removing and replacing the folder into its case enacted a now-you-see-it-now-you-don't visual play, whose bidirectionality reflected the play of words so central to the books. In Wonderland, Alice's too-largeness might be reversed to become a too-smallness, and even her adventure can start over, such that, like a player of a board game, she passes again through the first square: "Once more she found herself in the long hall, and close to the little glass table. 'Now I'll manage better this time,' she said to herself, and began by taking the little golden key, and unlocking the door that led into the garden."[71] The thresholds of divergence that fill the *Alice* books, between one path and another, between one identity and another, are recurrent and constant. Rather than the preludes to self-actualization, they are the stuff of inconsequence, even absurdity.

Still, if this is play, it's no free-for-all. Indeed, these moments describe, to comic effect, a decidedly Victorian tension between the possibilities on offer and their containment by a stringent logic, a visible network of explicitly defined alternatives. Wonderland takes the counterfictional's spectral alternative—the hypothetical outcome that can exist only in the reader's or character's imagination in *Adam Bede*, for example—and makes it both articulable and legible, a divergent possibility given material, synchronic existence. What's more, these alternatives multiply possibility rather than bringing Alice any closer to an endpoint: Carroll's narrative is a game without a clear goal, play for the sake of play.[72] The either-or logic, a mockery of the suppositions of serious philosophy, assumes the embodied form and voice of Tweedledum and Tweedledee in the world of the Looking-Glass—"If you think we're wax-works . . . you ought to pay" and "Contrariwise, . . . if you think we're alive, you ought to speak"[73]—and yet this leads nowhere, as it were, except back into the game.

If Spooner's two-dimensional game boards suggested, through the process of play, the twists and turns of narrative, Carroll's fiction conjures in Wonderland a playable, mappable narrative domain, whose spatial boundaries are repeatedly defined by the available alternatives: "'In *that* direction,' the Cat said, waving its right paw round, 'lives a Hatter: and in *that* direction,' waving the other paw, 'lives a March Hare.'"[74] The Cat, as if to insist on the meaninglessness of that ostensible choice, adds, "Visit either you like: they're both mad."[75] In one sense, Wonderland's logic resembles that of chess, where each "move" has a strictly defined limit and direction, but it lacks chess's directional, purposeful qualities, where skill and strategy are central to play. In Wonderland, as in the period's children's games, there is only the pretense of choice. Indeed, in spite of the explicit allusions to chess in *Through the Looking-Glass*, Wonderland's realm of play often bears a closer resemblance to something like The *Cottage of Content*, where "spatial agency" is nominal.

For in this world where the alternatives on offer lack meaning or consequence, the choices Alice makes at any given moment come to have the effect of chance. While Spooner's games do ultimately lead to a predefined conclusion, Alice's movements—whether determined by repetition, a sense of resolution, a willed choice, or simply chance—seem to lead nowhere but back into the narrative's system of proliferating alternatives. At the same time, however, if "chance is fixed at certain points," as Deleuze writes, the play of the system at these nodes of contingency is also delimited. While Wonderland is a space of multiplying outcomes—"her eye fell upon a little bottle that stood near the looking-glass. . . . 'I know *something* interesting is sure to happen . . . so I'll just see what this bottle does'"[76]—both Alice and we comprehend that the "*something* interesting" is also circumscribed in its range; it exists within a finite realm of possibility, of predetermined alternatives: larger or smaller, left or right, pig or baby.

Carroll's games and puns express a similar interest in the possibility of translating a spatial into a textual logic, and in the balance between chance and constraint. Play in these examples is not free play, but a navigation of what such constraints and degrees of movement might allow. Even Charles Dodgson's choice of pseudonym adheres to Wonderland's principle of linked alternatives. As Beer explains, "Lewis Carroll" was "composed with considerable sleight-of-hand out of his own family name Charles Lutwidge Dodgson: Charles = Latin: Carrolus, becomes Carroll, and Lutwidge, less obviously, becomes Lewis."[77] And the many forms of word play in which the *Alice* books themselves famously abound adhere to a similar logic of alternatives. Like the etymological hinges that operate in his pen name, these puns focus attention on the points of divergence between two outcomes, whether for homophones like "tale" and "tail," or "not" and "knot"; not-quite-homophones like "purpose" and "porpoise"; or alternate meanings, as in the mouse's "dry" English history that promises to "dry" off a nearly drowned Alice.[78] Deleuze identifies in these word games a radical severing of the link between signifier and meaning, a "dismissal of depth" and a "deployment of language" along a more superficial plane,[79] and to be sure the flattened relationships expressed by these puns, like the fictional lanes and locations in Spooner's *Journey*, turn away from the referential and approach (as Deleuze's metaphors imply) the surface. But at the same time, I want to resist the postmodern inflection in Deleuze's and others' approach, for the surface along which Carroll "deploy[s]" these words nonetheless operates in what I would call a mid-nineteenth-century fashion, as a finite space with a defined logic of linked alternatives, of options tethered to each other at shared nodes of contingent divergence. Like the bigger-smaller, Tweedledum-Tweedledee alternatives embedded in the plot, these alternatives spring from a single hinge, and even as they invite readers to reflect on the rules governing their existence, they also seem to ask how far that divergence might take them. Here, as in Darwin's *Origin*, the authorial presence is palpable in the transformative, even deformative, exertions that press against the formal principles—of a limb, of a word—that give such transformations meaning.

Like his contemporary at Oxford, German philologist and family friend Müller, Carroll was interested in the "demands of literary form over the semantic principles of communication," in the unlikely relationships among words as things.[80] For Müller, the relationships between cognates could be traced back over the course of millennia and over geographical expanses as well, to Gothic or Sanskrit origins.[81] But where Müller's interest, like Darwin's, was primarily historical, even archaeological, Carroll's puns eschew historical depth or diachronicity. Indeed, Andrea Henderson affirms that Carroll's vision of language demonstrates not a historical but a mathematical principle, where formulations like "I see what I eat, I eat what I see" express the "commutative property" of "a mathematical law rather than an oratorical flourish."[82] His puns thus revel not in origins but in the generative variety that might result from such divergences, and his word plays are as likely to depend on related etymological origins (as in the case, for example, of "dry") as on aural and orthographical likeness (as with "purpose" and "porpoise").

In this sense Carroll's word games also explore what we might call the formal properties of transformation, the varied itineraries by which one thing—a word, an image, an identity—might become another. This principle is perhaps best illustrated by a game he composed some years later, "Word-Links."[83] How, Carroll challenged players, could a "Hare" be made into "Soup," a "Mine" be made to generate "Coal," a "Grub" become a "Moth," or "Bread" become "Toast"?[84] The solution lay not in regarding those words as signifiers corresponding to physical objects, but instead as objects in themselves, such that one word might be transformed into another through a series of single-letter, orthographical substitutions. In a diagram illustrating how "Head" becomes "Tail," he provides an example of this process of transformation:

Head	Heal	*Teal*	*Tell*
Hear			Tall
Heir	Hair	Hail	*Tail*[85]

Stepwise moves take the originating word through a process of evolution, as it were, and along two different itineraries, along which, by the rules of the game, all of the intermediate words must have their own viable existence independent of the "chain."[86] And regardless of any qualms he may have had about Darwinian evolution, Carroll confirmed that an "ape" might well become a "man" by these means:

APE ARE   ERE   ERR   EAR   MAR   MAN[87]

These games effectively recreate the missing links about which Darwin fantasized: "[T]he most wonderfully diverse forms are still tied together by a long, but broken, chain of affinities.... [I]f every form which has ever lived on this earth were suddenly to reappear, ... all would blend together by steps as fine as those between the finest existing varieties."[88] Unlike the developmental transformation of a tadpole into a frog, or the evolutionary transformation of a lost ancestor into its present-day descendant, though, these word games, in transforming "Head" to "Tail" or "Ape" to "Man," do not extinguish or absorb previous incarnations, but conjure those intermediate forms into life, each bearing, in shape or sound, the trace of its ancestor. While they depend on a teleology that Darwin consistently sought to distance himself from—for him, part of the "wonder" associated with natural processes lay in the variety produced by nature's undirected modulations of form—Carroll's games also refuse to reduce transformative processes to an isolated or irreversible itinerary. They effectively restore the links to Darwin's "long, but broken, chains" of existence, making those "most wonderfully diverse forms" legible elements in the process of transformation.

If Carroll's word plays "mathematize" language, as Henderson contends,[89] these play-by-play transformations suggest that, in rewriting temporally and causally meaningful narratives as itineraries that traverse the surface of the page, he also gamified language, such that the orthographical properties of words become the means for achieving something like geographical movement or evolutionary development across the planes of the English language. In an examination of another version of this game Fred Madden proposes that these links—in which, Carroll suggested, "QUEEN" could alternately be made "WHITE" or "ALICE"—are central to the "direction of ... [emplotted] movement" in the *Alice* books, which should be understood at the level of language rather than of causal event.[90] For as these works move us forward in pages and words, they also upend the directional movement understood to exist in conventional narrative. Although Alice insists to the Caterpillar that he will "have to turn into a chrysalis ... and then after that into a butterfly," she also undetermines her own developmental ends, declaring, "That'll be a comfort ... never to be an old woman."[91] The word-link, too, exemplifies the bidirectional, revocable properties of these narrative transformations. Players might trace multiple itineraries from "Head" to "Tail," "Bread" to "Toast," but those itineraries are not only reversible, but can also be made to start and stop at different points. The property illustrated here might be a mathematical one, but where the "commutative" expression Henderson locates in Carroll's syntax ultimately promises an almost algebraic reduction of terms, the word play in his games, as in his books, propels narrative through an incremental (though not temporal or causal) process achieved through juxtaposition and multiplication, in which seemingly equivalent terms like "dry" and "dry," "tale" and "tail" diverge and find lives of their own.

Critics have sometimes interpreted the appearance of Dodo at the Caucus-race in *Alice's Adventures* as a commentary about the fact of extinction,[92] but we might also read it as a zoological version of the word game, as Carroll's invitation to speculation: What if processes of transformation operated, as Darwin suggested they sometimes did, not through erasure but through proliferation, such that alternatives might come to exist side by side in simultaneity? Where Beer characterizes the Dodo's existence as a "cheering riposte" to the facts of natural selection, its presence is not just Carroll's refutation but his invitation to counterfactual speculation: What if evolutionary history could be retold such that, in the Dodo's own words, "*Everybody* has won, and *all* must have prizes"?[93]

Darwin had enacted his own, somewhat infamous move-by-move version of this form of play in chapter 6 of his 1859 *Origin of Species*, where he ruminated that, "if the supply of insects were constant, and if better adapted competitors did not already exist in the country, I can see no difficulty in a race of bears being rendered, by natural selection, more and more aquatic in their structure and habits, with larger and larger mouths, till a creature was produced as monstrous as a whale"—a supposition he retracted in the 1860 edition, but one nonetheless provocative, where bear and whale, like pig and baby, might simply be two alternate products of a single point of divergence, with no distinction drawn between extinct and extant, past and present.[94] In Wonderland transformation regularly results not in extinction but in population, simultaneity, coexistence, variety. In the absence of selection, natural or otherwise, divergence yields a wondrously synchronic multiplicity. Indeed, from this perspective, Wonderland looks remarkably like a fantastic fulfillment of Darwin's "endless forms most beautiful and most wonderful,"[95] its crowded images and laden pages the meeting place for species both imaginable and unimaginable, actual and hypothetical, where we find the "purpose" and the "porpoise," the monkey and the Dodo, the gryphon and the speaking flamingo, all present and alive, inhabiting the same landscape and moment.

Contingency in William Spooner's Protean Views

In a city saturated with visual experience—from ubiquitous broadsides, advertising, and window displays, to large-scale dioramas, theatrical events, and exhibitions both grand and Great[96]—Spooner's successes as a publisher and seller cut across genres, encompassing not only children's books and board games, but also puzzles and other kinds of paper-based visual toys, such as perspective and protean views. And his storefronts—first at 259 Regent Street in London in the 1830s, then at 377 on the Strand in the 1840s, and eventually at 379 by the early 1850s—literally traversed an urban geography of commercialized leisure and visual entertainment centered around Leicester Square. On nearby Piccadilly, for example, at William Bullock's Egyptian Hall, Napoleonic memorabilia and archaeological artifacts thrilled the public, and a short walk away on the Strand, fellow printmakers and map publishers—such as Rudolph Ackermann at 96, Charles Smith at 172, James Reynolds at 174, and G. & J. Cary at 181— tempted passersby with items for purchase. These sat only a few blocks from established cartographer Edward Mogg at Covent Garden in one direction and from the popular map store run by geographer James Wyld at Charing Cross in another, as well as from Wyld's own Great Globe spectacle at Leicester Square.[97] Consumerism, education, pleasure, and politics converged in these spaces, where Britons could purchase Morrison's Pills down the street at 368 Strand and, at 372, attend a religious or philanthropic lecture at the massive Exeter Hall, the same venue where Prince Albert delivered an oration against slavery in 1840 and Godfrey Ablewhite would, later in that decade, draw throngs of adoring charity workers in Wilkie Collins's *The Moonstone*.

Just as Spooner's innovations in board game design drew inspiration from the period's taste for cartographic display, so his other publications participated in the dynamic culture of exhibition and visual spectacle that surrounded him in the metropolis. Alongside other London-based publishers and print sellers—such as Darton and Son, Ackermann, and G. S. Tregear—Spooner produced illustrated broadsides in the wake of important events like the fire at the Parliament buildings on 16 October 1834. His one- and two-shilling versions appeared beside images offered by his competitors, all of which, in spite of differences in the use of color and perspective, some showing the fire from land and others from the Thames,[98] have a great deal in common. The almost formulaic quality of these depictions seems intended to have made them immediately recognizable to those browsing a newsstand or shop window: The burning buildings were given dramatic effect by the night sky, and signature architectural elements were depicted in a state of ruin. Likewise Spooner's images of Queen Victoria's coronation in Westminster Abbey in 1838 and of Victoria and Albert's wedding procession through St. James's Palace in 1840 joined a marketplace filled with illustrations of those same events for public consumption. Appearing for sale within weeks—and in the case of the coronation, within two days—of the events they depicted, these visual clichés likely filled multiple roles for their purchasers: as images to supplement text-based journalism, as keepsakes of an event of historical importance, as objects of aesthetic or educational value.

But Spooner was also interested in the ways new visual technologies could enhance the experiential quality of his images. His "Perspective View of the Great Exhibition," for instance, published a few months after the official opening in 1851, adopted a popular mode of representation used for other monumental scenes, such as the opening of the Thames Tunnel. Like an analogue version of the stereoscope that would become popular later in the decade, Spooner's accordion-like contraption invited viewers to look through a peephole, where a layered series of two-dimensional images of the Crystal Palace gave the effect of a three-dimensional scene.

In the 1830s and 40s Spooner experimented with another visual genre, known as the protean or transforming view: a visual toy whose ancestors included a number of eighteenth-century art forms used to depict transformations. Some of those earlier artists placed static images in a side-by-side, comparative view, a practice that Rebecca N. Mitchell traces to Hogarth's graphic sequences (with their contrast between the "industrious" and "idle" apprentice, for example).[99] Eighteenth-century landscape architect Humphry

Repton issued a popular series of before-and-after views to advertise the effects of his "improvements" on gardens and parks,[100] and in the nineteenth century, the architect Augustus Pugin achieved a similar effect when he presented in diptych an English city in both medieval and industrial eras.[101] Still others used prose to conjure in the imagination the "architectural spectres" and other "hidden and dormant" pasts that, according to Kate Flint, nineteenth-century Britons regularly discerned beneath modern-day ruins and archaeological sites.[102]

The protean view achieved a similar effect by employing various forms of trickery involving paper (and later glass), such as transparent tissue overlays, heat-sensitive ink, or a hinged window that could rise and fall. But unlike the technologies of the diorama and the magic-lantern show—in which a static image was sometimes given the quality of a dynamic one by means of manual or mechanical intervention, through movement or the alteration of lighting effects[103]—Spooner's protean views propelled the transformation of past into present and distilled possibility into a single, pivotal moment of historical or temporal contingency, in which he invited viewers to immerse themselves. Ephemerist Maurice Rickards notes that the Victorian genre of protean views had some eighteenth-century antecedents, but that these earlier examples tended to employ the overlay to achieve differences in lighting and scenery, something like the effect of changing backdrops in a theater. Reviving that "dormant" genre, Spooner produced around ninety different designs whose more dramatic narrative effects, Rickards tells us, "not merely enhanced but transformed" the image altogether before the viewer's eyes.[104]

While Spooner's protean view was a reinvention of an existing contrivance, the subjects he chose suggest a more immediate source of inspiration: the panoramas, dioramas, phantasmagorias, and other visual spectacles of the type that had appeared starting decades earlier in pleasure gardens like Vauxhall, but which, by the 1830s, had migrated into Leicester Square and its environs, at strolling distance from Spooner's Regent Street and Strand shops. While many of these popular entertainments, as Ralph O'Connor explains, used the larger-than-life theatrics of panoramic display to depict theological subjects, such as biblical or Miltonic scenes, to apocalyptic effect, others lent sublimity to secular ones.[105] Popular themes included scenes drawn from early nineteenth-century natural histories, of ancient reptiles dominating the land-scape or earthquakes devastating surrounding areas, as well as contemporane-ous political events, such as coronations and battles. Collectively these served, Richard Altick observes, not only as the "newsreels of the Napoleonic era" but also as the communal displays to which even for decades afterward the "public repaired to visualize what it read about" in the dailies and weeklies.[106] Among them, volcanic eruptions that were "second only to sea storms in popularity" and Napoleonic battles were perennial favorites, both featuring not only in these London spectacles but also in Spooner's protean views.[107]

Spooner's views appealed to consumers surrounded by and likely im-mersed in the period's multiple forms of visual culture, and like many of the spectacles on show at venues near his storefronts, his objects favored secular rather than religious subjects. Still, in other key ways, his protean views differed from their Leicester Square and Covent Garden counterparts. For while the effect of the panorama depended in large measure on its scale—one painted scene at Vauxhall unfurled to a length of 900 feet, and Robert Barker's famous Leicester Square rotunda displayed a scene several stories high, a trompe l'oeil of sublime proportions[108]—the protean view was intended as a private object and offered an experience scaled to the drawing room. With an image about the size of an adult hand, it was meant to be viewed by no more than two or perhaps three persons at once. Moreover, while the panorama tended to rely on atmospheric effects, like changes to sound, image size, or lighting to simulate the sensations conjured by a momentous event,[109] the protean view invited the viewer to experience a single shift in time, and sometimes also in geography or causality, from one scene to another.

One of Spooner's early subjects for protean representation was Queen Victoria's visit to the City of London in 1837, a popular choice among artists and publishers. While Edward Mogg and others issued static versions of this scene, Spooner overlaid a primary image of an empty Temple Bar in early evening, depicted on a fine layer of paper, onto a secondary one of the Queen at Guildhall, which became visible through the overlay when held to a strong light. The shift produced was both temporal and spatial, from evening to day, from the entrance to the City at Temple Bar to the Queen's ultimate destina-tion at Guildhall several streets away, though the first image arguably bears no causal link to the second except by reference to contemporaneous narrative accounts of the Queen's journey into London.

Yet some of Spooner's other views, by focusing on a single location or event, insisted upon a clearer relationship between before and after. The 1838 "The Royal Exchange, London, with a View of Its Destruction by Fire," for example, and the 1839 "The New Houses of Parliament Which Seem to Rise from the Ruins of the Conflagration of the Old Buildings," both appeared soon after the depicted events, and like their more conventional, static counterparts, could have served as a supplement to print journalism's reportage. But unlike those static images, Spooner's protean views invited observers to inhabit the pivotal moment, the historical point of contingency, and specifically, to reproduce the process by which an event transformed a familiar element of London's cityscape. The appeal of these objects depended on known outcomes, but what they offered was not a contemplation of *faits accomplis*; rather, they drew viewers into a reenactment of the temporal and causal sequences shaping a particular moment. While Kern associates Victorian narrative with a linear determinism, in marked contrast to the "nonlinear narrative form" of twentieth-century modernism where he finds (and here he quotes David Lodge) a more "complex or fluid handling of time, involving much cross-reference back and forward,"[110] these works point to the ways in which middle-class Victorian audiences understood and engaged with the temporal and causal plasticity of historical narrative, the ways in which they participated in forms of narrative, temporal, and historiographical play.

Some of these protean views focused not on recent or local events, but on historical ones. The eruption of Vesuvius and the destruction of Pompeii, for example, had acquired a familiar, even formulaic quality by the time Spooner's series appeared, an effect reinforced, perhaps, by the volcano's continued eruptions in the 1820s and 30s. It inspired a range of popular spectacles, including a fifteen-minute show at Covent Garden in the late eighteenth century, which involved "transparencies, 'machinery,' and the sound of rumbling underground convulsions and peals of thunder," as well as "an eighty-foot-high scene of the Bay of Naples" that "erupted nightly" at Vauxhall in the nineteenth.[111] But Vesuvius was also a topic for much serious discussion among the period's archaeologists, geologists, and historians, as well as for artistic depiction in dozens of late eighteenth- and early nineteenth-century paintings. Virtual tours of Pompeii delighted those who visited the panoramas on display at Leicester Square in 1824, and the eruption served as the backdrop for Edward Bulwer Lytton's 1834 historical novel (which itself inspired a series of theatrical adaptations), and as the main event for the well-attended reenactments at Surrey Zoological Park. Indeed, the iconic moment of Vesuvian eruption was, as Isobel Armstrong characterizes it, a "compulsive image . . . a deep, insistent obsession of the era."[112] According to Martin Rudwick, the historic scene, "with its catastrophic human effects at Herculaneum and Pompeii," served as "a vivid reminder of ineluctable contingency" in the century's early decades, and similarly, Nicholas Daly, linking the period's fascination with volcanic eruptions to a contemporaneous sense of political contingency in 1830s, argues that "readerly pleasure in the vivid detail" of these representations "is always predicated on our knowledge" of what is about to occur.[113] Spooner published at least two protean views of Vesuvius (as well as one of the Surrey reenactment), each of which contrasted a first scene of a dormant volcano, a populated, active town at its foot, with a second, dramatic image of fiery lava engulfing all (Figures 3.9 and 3.10).

Some scholars have treated protean views as technological forerunners of film, and indeed, the technology of cinema effectively combined a long series of such frame-by-frame transformations to generate the effect of movement.[114] In this genealogy, the protean view is a less promising and certainly less glamorous cousin to other visual entertainments of the early nineteenth century, like the thaumatrope and the phenakistiscope, fast-moving technologies that displayed a sequence of images using a spinning wheel or quickly flipped pages to create an effect of animation. These "philosophical toys," as Tom Gunning calls them, were meant not only to entertain but also, according to Jonathan Crary, to illustrate the physiological principles behind the illusion of fluid visual transformation.[115] In that the "classic thaumatrope's composite images (a bird and a cage; a vase and flowers; a horse and a rider; a bald man [or woman] and a wig)" were designed to enable the "merging [of] two separate pictures into a new unity,"[116] these devices, like film, achieved their effects by erasing both the moment of transition and the mechanism by which the substitution occurred. By comparison, even as the protean view may have allowed the viewer insight into the new temporal sensations of "transience" and "obsolescence" that, according to Crary, characterized the period and animated these other toys, it did

FIGURE 3.9 Unlit view of "Mount Vesuvius." *Spooner's Protean Views* (London: William Spooner, c. 1840). Courtesy of The Bill Douglas Cinema Museum, University of Exeter.

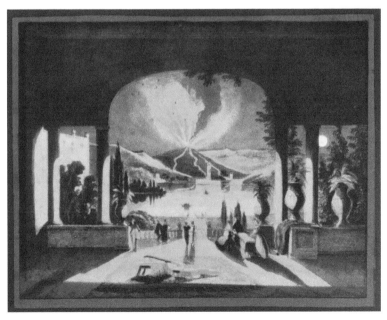

FIGURE 3.10 Lit view of "Mount Vesuvius." *Spooner's Protean Views* (London: William Spooner, c. 1840). Courtesy of The Bill Douglas Cinema Museum, University of Exeter.

so by means of a clumsy, rudimentary mechanism. What's more, the cardboard frame around these images—Spooner's views of Vesuvius doubly framed by the proscenium-like portico in the foreground—linked them visually to their theatrical antecedents, where the intradiegetic spectators standing in the foreground mirror the viewers' own anticipation of the inevitable outcome. Writing about the genre of "dissolving views" to which the protean view belongs, Isobel Armstrong explains that, "[t]ransition was their essence.... Transition between two states was central to the image," and as such, they emphasized "binary reversals . . . a latent duality" in the represented scene.[117] And indeed, far from eliding the moment of transformation, the protean view, for all its limitations, drew attention to what Armstrong calls "the pause" between the two images.[118]

Armstrong's interest lies in the aesthetic, sensory experience made available to the viewer in the liminal interval, in the transformation between environmental binaries of "day to night, summer to winter, calm to storm," and in the material form the process of "becoming" assumes, and her reading encompasses the effects of both earlier protean views and of contemporaneous panoramic displays.[119] But more than the aesthetics of transformation, Spooner's views attend to the historical and narrative contingencies indexed in that moment of "becoming." Like the scene at Pompeii, Spooner's two views of London fires—the Royal Exchange before and after burning, and the destroyed and rebuilt Parliament buildings—refer to known events with a clear temporal and narrative directionality. Yet the very technology of the protean view, with its manipulation of opacity and light, imposed its own (not always consistent) directionality on these scenes. Thus both his "Destruction of a Swiss Village by an Avalanche" and his very similar "A Village Destroyed by an Avalanche" show, in their default, unlit states an alpine scene with a mound of snow filling a valley;[120] it's only upon holding these views to a light source that the village is restored to the foot of the mountain, its rooftops and windows illuminated by hearths within and a glowing moon without. The two views of London fires that are effectively mirror images of each other—one a destruction by fire as the other is a restoration from it—likewise point to the possibility of reversing time and causality, of rearranging events within a historical narrative.

The ability to make and unmake a transformation at will, which Carroll's "Wonderland Postage-Stamp Case" would decades later allow, where the pig-to-baby became as readily available as the baby-to-pig transformation with a movement of the wrist, was what Spooner's protean views of the 1830s and 40s also enabled. Historical events might be undone, the Royal Exchange first destroyed by fire, for example, and then with the removal of a light source, miraculously "restored" to its original, intact state. In this sense, too, the protean view—more so than other, more mechanically driven visual technologies of the nineteenth century, like the lantern show and zoetrope—communicated with its viewer in a way not unlike the comic, where meaning is, as Dittmer and Groensteen assert, a product not only of narratorial but also of viewerly agency.[121]

Many of Spooner's other views depicted scenes so familiar that, like the image of Vesuvius, they held the status of something approaching visual cliché. Between 1838 and 1840, for example, he produced at least three views featuring Napoleon: "Napoleon Powerful and Napoleon Powerless" showed the emperor first facing his troops and then alone on a beach (Figures 3.11 and 3.12); the "Tomb of Napoleon at St. Helena" had as its alternate an image of him surrounded by supporters; and "Napoleon at the Battle of Wagram, Changing to the Conflagration of Moscow" offered a view of the emperor's victory over Austria in 1809, and then his entrance into Moscow in 1812. As Martin Meisel explains, Napoleon and Napoleonic battle scenes were popular subjects for artistic and theatrical representation on both sides of the Channel in the years following his defeat.[122] Napoleon seemed to be everywhere: at a 420-square-foot model of the Battle of Waterloo put on display at London's Egyptian Hall in 1838; as the central figure in J. M. W. Turner's painting *War. The Exile and the Rock Limpet*, exhibited at the Royal Academy in 1842; and even at the chaotic stagings of the Trojan War at Astley's Amphitheatre.[123] But this interest went beyond a mere desire to see remembered events reflected in the period's art forms. Like the Vesuvian eruption, Napoleon seems to have functioned as a kind of visual shorthand for historical contingency, an occasion for setting historical foreknowledge aside and for revisiting the unrealized possibilities and pleasures of *medias res*.[124] His military endeavors, for example, served as a common focus for counterfactual thinking, while the man himself was a "familiar figure" in the emerging genre of "alternate history," and his entrance into Waterloo provided the historical backdrop for *Vanity Fair* and its author's ruminations on historical determination—whose readers were

FIGURE 3.11 Unlit view of "Napoleon Powerful and Napoleon Powerless."
Spooner's Protean Views (London: William Spooner, c. 1840). Courtesy
of The Bill Douglas Cinema Museum, University of Exeter.

FIGURE 3.12 Lit view of "Napoleon Powerful and Napoleon Powerless."
Spooner's Protean Views (London: William Spooner, c. 1840). Courtesy
of The Bill Douglas Cinema Museum, University of Exeter.

asked to think "to themselves what a specially bad time Napoleon took to come back from Elba."[125]

While some buyers might have wished to educate and entertain their children with these views, their familiar, well-publicized subjects also suggest a practiced audience, one far from surprised by the revealed outcome. The viewer's experience, in other words, would have been impelled not only by suspense but also by expectation, a feeling that the formulaic quality of these images could only have reinforced. These views affirmed cultural consensus around historical knowledge and the inexorable outcomes constituting it: In each case, the historical consequences represented in the second image, like the second half of a published chapter, would always be there, a reminder of what was to come. At the same time, these objects enabled the possibility of dwelling in the illusion of history's undetermination, of remaining suspended in that moment before "history" took one course rather than another. Just as Eliot's *Adam Bede* slowed and expanded the instant in which contingency operates (just before Arthur appears in Hetty's sight, just before Adam discovers her locket), Spooner's views amplified and solidified the moment in an image, its duration and direction now at the whim or will of the viewer.

These protean views, like the contemporaneous public reenactments elaborately staged on a grand scale outdoors, allowed audiences to inhabit the historical pause, to suspend themselves on the threshold of a historical event with an outcome at once known and as-yet unknown. But these images also reshaped the experience of historical transformation from a life-sized spectacle to a private, cabinet curiosity. The sublime nature of the depicted event—the viewer's sense of being overwhelmed by a transformative, apocalyptic moment when captured on large canvases, panoramas, or in live reenactments—necessarily assumed a different quality in the case of the hand-held protean view. Unlike those large-scale, public spectacles—unlike even the magic-lantern shows that, in separating projectionist from spectator, might be viewed as "instruments of control," both directing the gaze and enforcing epistemological order through a predetermined arrangement of images[126]—the protean view was a personal entertainment that made the viewer into the agent of transformation. More than the board games Spooner produced and the *Alice* books by Carroll, both of which offered the illusion of almost frictionless transitions from one point to the next, the protean view enforced a temporal pause between frames, even when the viewer knew what outcome the next frame would contain. It demanded decision and deliberate participation of its viewers, as they raised or lowered the overlay, or moved the image to the light to look again. If the board game allowed for the play of chance under the guise of choice, the protean view, with its mechanization of contingency, remade an often chance historical event into an act of personal will or choice. As viewers immersed themselves in the tiny scene before their eyes, the protean view conjured a moment not so much of aesthetic as of technological sublimity. For the power it represented inhered to an extent in the depicted scene—the volcano, the battle, the fire—but also, and perhaps even more, in the power the object's mechanism transferred to viewers themselves. Through a single action of the wrist, a literal, slightly awkward sleight-of-hand, they could make and unmake a historical event.

If the pause is, as Isobel Armstrong contends, an interval of sensory passage, an aesthetic metamorphosis, it is also, as Spooner's views reveal, a revisiting of contingency, in which a clumsy, deliberate technology enables the viewer to intervene in a narrative leading to an otherwise foregone conclusion. Indeed, it recalls the similarly deliberate intervention that opens chapter 28 of Thackeray's *Vanity Fair*, when the narrator calls upon those who "like to lay down the History-book, and to speculate upon what MIGHT have happened in the world."[127] The pause between images situates viewers at a like moment of historical contingency, making them the causal pivot in the unfolding of a historical narrative. As I discussed in Chapter 2, engagement with such moments was central to the period's historical fiction, military training, and geological writing, all of which strategically situated readers on the brink of a decisive historical event and invited speculation about alternate outcomes. Protean views transformed that moment by means of technology into a visual trick: narrative rendered into mechanism. Yet where Thackeray's (or Lyell's, or Darwin's) prose speculations, with their layered and complex conditionals, had an open-ended quality, as objects these protean views bespoke the physical limitations of the static image and the hinge, through which they expressed something closer to the shunting logic and predetermined array of alternatives of the game board.

The protean view's discrete, fixed images; its use of juxtaposition to imply temporal, causal, or metonymic relation between them; and the role of the viewer in generating a coherent narrative all suggest that we might read in the formal qualities of this early genre something more closely aligned with the twentieth-century comic than with the magic-lantern show or with cinema. Indeed, recent critical work on comics by Groensteen, Dittmer, and others supplies a theory for analyzing and understanding the experimental qualities in these views. Meaning emerges not only through a linear, unidirectional reading of images and text, but also through the potentialities of the plurivectorial narrative, where telling and reading alike move forward but also backward temporally and causally, to include what Groensteen calls "retroactive determination."[128] Whereas cinematic and pre-cinematic technologies register the "uni-directional and irreversible" passage of time,[129] the comic allows, in Dittmer's words, a "shuffle back and forth across the page," a bidirectional practice of narration and reading.[130]

The protean view offers the possibility of a similarly reversible reading process, where each image has a meaning informed by its temporal, causal other, lying just in its shadow. The image of the standing Royal Exchange thus gains significance through a knowledge of its eventual destruction, just as the act of seeing the new Parliament building acquires meaning through remembering the destruction of its predecessor. The joining of the two, not only through the temporal and causal processes of narrative, but also through the imaginative processes of anticipation and remembrance, is reinforced by the imperfect nature of the protean view, its visual trick depending on an overlay that is, by necessity, only semi-opaque. The view of the Royal Exchange, even unlit, is effectively haunted by the inexorability of its eventual conflagration in the future, just as the view of Parliament (Figure 3.13) is haunted by the memory of its ever-present past—as Spooner's legend tells us, it "seems to rise from the Ruins & Conflagration of the Old Buildings." Like the back-and-forth between pig and baby made possible by the "Wonderland Postage-Stamp Case," the protean view focuses attention on the moment of contingency, on the play between then and now, presence and absence, fires and avalanches and eruptions, all dissolving and resolving like the flickering smile of the Cheshire Cat before Alice's eyes.

FIGURE 3.13 Half-lit view of "The New Houses of Parliament."
Spooner's Protean Views (London: William Spooner, c. 1840). Courtesy
of The Bill Douglas Cinema Museum, University of Exeter.

Where readers like Babbage and Lyell sifted through piles of newspaper clippings and geological layers to identify moments of contingency in the fragmentary histories they studied, the works discussed in this chapter—the
geographical board game, the protean view, *Wanderings* and "Whittington,"
and Carroll's *Alice* books—extended that work, effectively distilling narrative
down to its moments of contingency, the articulated hinges where transition
or divergence might occur. They transformed story into a kind of mechanism,
a space within which contingencies and possibilities could not only be anticipated but also mapped out and given visible, operable form. Rather than the
modern or postmodern forerunners some critics have located in these forms
of nineteenth-century play, then, Spooner's vision, like Carroll's, is decidedly
Victorian, a near cousin to the London Underground, Joseph Balzagette's
sewerage system, and Babbage's own Analytical Engine. Theirs was not the
free-flowing "chaos" Deleuze and Félix Guattari identify with a rhizomatic

system, nor was it built on what they call the "classical" form of the "root book,"[131] but constituted another genre of experiment. As playful engagements with the secular contingencies animating other types of Victorian narrative, from insurance documents to historical fictions, they remade the hypothetical into the material, the divergent into the synchronic, but always with a mathematical precision around moment and multiple—and with an awareness of the limits of the system, and of its beginning and end.

These examples also shed light on more recent interpretations of the twentieth-century theory of "many worlds," a philosophical extension of quantum mechanics advanced by Hugh Everett III and others.[132] While some of the probabilistic and physical models that enabled its development will be discussed in the next chapter, recent discussions of possible worlds have, especially among narratological interpreters, been less interested in the abstractions of quantum physics than in the field of outcomes defined by narrative representability. For them, as for these Victorian examples, chance takes material and mathematically calculable form, operating through the binary (or, as in the case of Spooner's board games, trinary or quaternary) nodal logic found in the either-or puns of Carroll's *Alice* books as well as in the period's historical fiction. The next chapter turns to an alternate vision of these divergent narratives, located in the writings of James Clerk Maxwell and Eliot's *Daniel Deronda*, where a return to the language of probability accommodates the impossibility of finite representation.

CHAPTER 4

Two Experiments in Probabilistic Thinking

Maxwell's "Demon" and Eliot's Daniel Deronda

IN NOVEMBER 1875, just before the first monthly part of *Daniel Deronda* was scheduled to appear in February 1876, Eliot's editor, John Blackwood, wrote the author to express concern about the manuscript's opening lines. His worry was not its depiction of gambling nor its representation of the heroine in a compromising circumstance, but rather, as he put it in his letter, because "I remember pausing at the use of the word dynamic in the very first sentence and I am not quite sure about it yet as it is a *dictionary* word to so many people."[1] As readers know, Eliot chose to retain the questionable word for her opening, but neither it nor any of its variants appear again in her massive novel.

This final chapter, too, pauses at Eliot's word, now common but then—as both she and Blackwood understood—one whose use was almost entirely limited to scientific circles.[2] How the author arrived at her choice is unclear, but the word had begun to surface more regularly in materials with which she was familiar. Physicist James Clerk Maxwell had first introduced his revolutionary "dynamical theory of gases" only a few years before when, in an 1866 lecture (which appeared in print the following year), he set out to oppose what he viewed as a more traditional "statical theory" according to which bodies were presumed to be "homogeneous" and "uniform"; the latter state, he claimed, could only exist as a theoretical premise, an assumption whose purpose was to make the mathematics more manageable for physicists.[3] In fact, he argued there, "[t]he dynamical theory supposes that the molecules of solid bodies oscillate" and are constantly "in motion."[4] Revisiting these key points in an 1870 address to the British Association for the Advancement of Science, Maxwell referred multiple times to a "dynamical" explanation for molecular behavior, and after his lecture was reprinted later that year in *Nature*,[5] Eliot transcribed portions of it into the notebook she was keeping for the composition of her final novel. Revealing there her interest in the "dynamic," the excerpts she selected detail the "whirling" and "evanescent" molecular motions encompassed by the period's new "hydro-dynamical theorems," and the distinctions between a Continental theory of "molecular action . . . formed by investing the molecule with an arbitrary system of central forces" and a British theory that posits "nothing but matter & motion."[6]

The sentence that prompted Blackwood's misgivings, "Was she beautiful or not beautiful? and what was the secret of form or expression which gave the dynamic quality to her glance?" hints at the emotional dynamism in Gwendolen Harleth's labile feelings, the rapid shifting just beneath her visible surfaces.[7] But the narrator implies that this quality belongs not just to the object being observed, but to a mode of observation as well, a process that demands something new both of the observer and of narrative itself. For these opening lines of free indirect discourse—encompassing rather than exact, a series of open-ended interrogatives rather than focused declaratives—reflect the principles governing the act of perception. To be sure, they conjure something like a Paterian sensibility, the "whirlpool" of "thought and feeling" available at any given instant of contemplation, the fleeting sensory "impressions" that touch the viewer from moment to moment.[8] But just as Eliot's repeated allusions to the "web" in *Middlemarch* reflect the ways in which she mobilizes a vocabulary of tissues and textiles as defining analogies in that work, her insistence on the word "dynamic" ("in the very first sentence" no less) suggests that the epistemological model she adopted for her last novel was drawn as much from the world of physics as from that of aesthetics.

Christopher Herbert contends that in the last decades of the century a wide range of intellectuals began to question the value of absolute knowledge, and Peter Garratt agrees, demonstrating that mid-century Victorians were acutely aware that "knowledge of any kind" was necessarily "relational" and "situated."[9]

Maxwell and Eliot understood the limitations of individual perception, and they pressed beyond empiricism to unsettle more traditional scientific and narrative practices. In the 1860s and 70s, their writings shifted attention away from conceptions of statistics that dominated in the earlier part of the century, when studies of populations and frequentist data lent themselves to deterministic conclusions of the kind parodied as "facts" in Dickens's *Hard Times*; they turned instead to the new modes of probabilistic understanding their investigations into molecular and emotional dynamics, respectively, demanded. Indeed, their work proposed that a condition of uncertainty, a state of not knowing, could become the basis for a different way of knowing. For them, statistical probabilities were the key to this alternate sphere of knowledge, a means of populating a field of possibilities rather than designating absolutes. In place of the verifiable figures that described populations or frequencies over extended periods, that is, both Eliot and Maxwell suggested that probabilities, imprecise and indeterminate though they might be in any specific application, could provide a way of approaching the particular, not of knowing it directly through empirical observation or measurement but rather through the process of generating a fertile realm of possibility around it. Contingency gave probabilistic knowledge narrative dimension in their writings and provided an instrument for representing the conditions that might define the range of the possible and the outcomes that might fall within it.

A number of recent critics have examined the relationships between an earlier emphasis within the statistical sciences on populations and averages, and the probabilistic approach that characterized the work of Maxwell and others.[10] For George Levine, Eliot's *Daniel Deronda* exemplifies a departure from the "objective" epistemologies of frequentist statistics as it forges a "new epistemology" and ethical sensibility by joining a "passionate participation of the self" to a kind of self-forgetting, a combination of "emotional" and more "rational" forms of knowing.[11] My own reading of Maxwell's and Eliot's work is likewise interested in the alignments between "rational" and "emotional" epistemologies, but it shows how both writers situated those modes of understanding with relation to, rather than outside, statistical methodologies. With its emphasis on indeterminacy rather than certainty, variations rather than means, distributions rather than averages, the statistics of the 1860s and

70s provided an alternate space for the reconciliation of passion and objectivity. In Maxwell's writings of this period and in Eliot's 1876 *Daniel Deronda*, the indeterminate nature of the object engaged the imaginative faculties, inviting the viewer to adopt a new stance, one that would test both the capaciousness and the limits of the probable; both required an acknowledgment of possibility's many fields and a consideration of the outer limits of both objectively and subjectively determined probabilities, as the spaces where numerical calculability and personal desire might converge.

This chapter looks first to efforts by scientists in Britain—especially by Maxwell and his contemporary, physicist John Tyndall—to investigate the realm of submicroscopic particles in the 1860s and 70s. They advised readers not to expect direct empirical knowledge about their subject and, in the case of Maxwell in particular, initiated them into a probabilistic epistemology that provided one way of knowing in the face of indeterminacy. These pages then turn to his thought experiment, commonly known as Maxwell's "demon," which offered a means of accommodating, if only in the imagination, a desire for material evidence of the indeterminate and invisible. But rather than focusing on the agency of the "demon," I argue that the premise of the two-chambered vessel and the doorkeeper made visible an otherwise abstract statistical principle that the law of large numbers and an emphasis on averages tended to occlude: the contingencies encompassed by a dynamical theory of molecular movement. In a similar turn away from omniscience, even from determinability, Eliot extends her exploration of the "dynamic quality" of her subject in *Daniel Deronda*, proffering what we might call a probabilistic narrative mode of approximating knowledge about human feelings and events. Contingency serves a critical narrative function here, not only as a way of acknowledging uncertainty but also, in her own novelistic version of Maxwell's thought experiment, as a way of tracing the trajectories that lie beyond the average, where the exceptional outcome becomes, if not expected, nonetheless available to the imagination.

Knowing the Molecule

In an 1873 *Nature* article, Maxwell introduced lay readers to the molecule, about which little had heretofore been known. "Every substance . . . has its own molecule," he explained methodically in his opening remarks, and every molecule a characteristic mass and composition.[12] Yet there were significant limitations to the investigator's knowledge, he admitted, in spite of the period's many advances in the physical and thermodynamic sciences. Even in the article's first paragraph, he declares that "[n]o one has ever seen or handled a single molecule," and characterizes his own work as "deal[ing] with things invisible and imperceptible by our senses, and which cannot be subjected to direct experiment."[13] After devoting several pages to an explanation of the principles of molecular velocity and diffusion, he returns in his concluding paragraphs to the more fundamental methodological problem with which the article began, the problem of seeing and knowing, and notes that despite these obstacles to traditional scientific methods, molecular research compensated by "develop[ing] a method of its own, and it has also opened up new views of nature."[14]

Rather than naming this revolutionary new "method" at once, however, the article embarks on a long digression, turning first to the assertion by Lucretius, the ancient Roman philosopher and poet, that the "complicated motion of the invisible atoms" might be understood through mediated effects, such as the movement of dust particles rendered visible in shafts of light, and then quoting Tennyson's 1868 poem, "Lucretius," with its vivid description of "flaring atom-streams / And torrents of her myriad universe."[15] Only after these two examples of the ways in which the invisible might imaginatively be rendered visible does his article return to and identify the new "method" mentioned earlier: statistics.

As Daniel Brown, Barri J. Gold, and Michael Tondre have shown, Maxwell had an abiding interest in Lucretius and other poets, and also enjoyed composing poems of his own; and here he draws on that knowledge to point to the correspondences between poetic and scientific approaches and to the continuities between traditional and newer methodologies.[16] Like Lucretius and Tennyson, nineteenth-century physicists can, he implies, only speculate about their objects of study. But Maxwell also makes clear that by "statistics" he does not mean the approach most would associate with a "report of the Census": those averages and frequencies that emerge from historical data about populations. This more common notion of statistics he contrasts with the new "statistical method" afforded by probability theory, one suited to representing the dynamic movements of the individual molecules that make up those Tennysonian "streams" and "torrents." Scientists cannot know "the actual motion of any one of these molecules," he explains, and their "experiments can never give . . . anything more than statistical information"—averages, likelihoods, a range of chances and possibilities—impressionistic data beyond which finer examination yields only imprecision and uncertainty.[17] In place of empirical knowledge drawn from direct observation and measurement, statistics offers a speculative, imperfect vision of its object. The molecule itself, imperceptible and unfixable, is a "mental representation" in Maxwell's words, something generated by and resident in the imagination.[18] Like poetry's visions of illuminated particles of dust, statistics, with its probabilities and indeterminacies, provides what can only be, as he puts it, a "probable conjecture" about the molecule.[19]

For chemists and physicists of the mid- and late nineteenth century, these seemingly abstruse contemplations about epistemology and the role of the imagination registered concerns they grappled with on a regular basis, both in the laboratory and in the pages of professional journals. As the thermodynamic sciences, in particular, turned their attention to the realm of unseen atoms and molecules, new questions arose about the very nature of scientific inquiry: What kind of knowledge could be considered legitimate, or even possible, about this invisible and largely imperceptible world of molecules? What constituted knowledge in the absence of direct empirical evidence about one's subject?

The larger epistemological questions implicit here reached beyond the limits of the laboratory, as Maxwell's *Nature* article suggested, and touched upon concerns both theological and aesthetic. How scientists responded often had to do with their national affiliation.[20] As the leading German physicists of the period, men like Carl Friedrich Gauss and Wilhelm Weber, were turning away from the Romantic language of affinity, inclination, faith, and desire that had suffused an earlier generation of scientific research, and toward mathematical precision and certainty,[21] their British counterparts began to champion the power of imaginative speculation and uncertainty. By the 1850s, Weber was directing his efforts to the mathematical description of forces through the calculation of distance and potential energy between particles. Yet British scientists like chemist Michael Faraday, the director of the Royal Institution and the first to describe electromagnetic induction, as well as prominent mathematician and energy physicist William Thomson (later Lord Kelvin), among others, resisted such Continental attempts at mathematical determinations. Indeed, Maxwell complained that Weber's mathematical solution, what he called "action at a distance," reduced molecular phenomena to little more than "a system of points" and overlooked "the perseverance of matter."[22] For Maxwell and his colleagues, particles were not mathematical abstractions, but material bodies, albeit invisible ones, whose actions needed to be explained according to the laws of mechanics and physical causalities. These arguments extended as well as to the spaces between molecules, such that Maxwell, Faraday, and others posited the existence of "aether" as a material, and possibly even mechanical, substrate that could mediate and transmit effects among molecules across space,[23] but knowledge about the ether also lay beyond the scope of scientific certainty, and scientists ventured hypotheses based on speculation and analogy.[24]

Tyndall, an experimental physicist who had succeeded Faraday to the directorship of the Royal Institution in 1867, considered this difficulty in his 1870 address to the British Association for the Advancement of Science. He focused primarily on the microscopic but, he asserted, once scientists moved beyond the microscope's limits and toward the molecular, "the speculative faculty" necessarily compensated in "regions where the hope of certainty would seem to be entirely shut out . . . beyond the present outposts of microscopic inquiry lies an immense field for the exercise of the imagination."[25] Citing the work of his contemporary Lord Kelvin, as an example, Tyndall observed that "[w]hen William Thomson tries to place the ultimate particles of matter [molecules] between his compass points, and to apply to them a scale of millimeters, it is an exercise of the imagination."[26] Beyond the limits of the visible, more speculative forms of knowledge necessarily took the place of epistemological certainty and empirical knowledge. Maxwell and Tyndall maintained an otherwise adversarial relationship, a result of their disagreement about the relevance of religion to science, but in giving an account of the role of the imagination to the British Association that year, they expressed a degree of cordial agreement in public, Maxwell even praising "the penetrating insight and forcible expression of Dr. Tyndall" in his remarks.[27] But Maxwell also pressed further beyond Tyndall's claims, to consider what new epistemologies might be available to the scientist. Knowledge about the molecule, as he put it, lay in "the still more hidden and dimmer region where Thought weds Fact," a region in which "molecules . . . in their true relation" might be apprehended only through a combination of empirical and theoretical study.[28] As he concluded, "the way to [the molecule]" passes not through the scientific laboratory or the mathematician's notebook, but rather "through the very den of the metaphysician."[29]

The difficulty in obtaining information about the individual molecule was due in part to the technical limitations of available instruments; even the highest resolution offered by microscopes did not allow scientists to visualize the particles they studied. But as Maxwell's dynamical theory posited, the very nature of the particle and its motions also rendered imaging and measurement impossible. Never a "single hard body" whose contours and motions could be perceived with mathematical accuracy, the molecule was a site of "vibration" internally as well as externally, engaged in what he evocatively described as a "dance" with other molecular bodies.[30] Thus a scientist might state with assurance that particles in air travel at an average velocity of "1505 feet per second" and experience an average of "8,077,200,000 collisions per second,"[31] and while such figures might well strike the uninitiated reader as communicating empirical knowledge, these data were, as Maxwell emphasized elsewhere, "of an essentially statistical nature, because no one has yet discovered any practical method of tracing the path of a molecule, or of identifying it at different times."[32] The ramifications of drawing this distinction between two categories of knowledge—the empirical and the statistical—in effect, "between two methods for studying natural phenomena," were, Bernard Lightman emphasizes, "staggering."[33] Maxwell himself underscored the scientific and epistemological significance of his claim: "This is a step the philosophical importance of which cannot be overestimated. It is the equivalent to the change from absolute certainty to high probability."[34]

But even this assessment too easily skims over the steps his theory was taking beyond empiricism, an observational methodology that belonged to what Lightman calls an "old Newtonian notion of science."[35] For Maxwell sought not only to replace empirical with statistical data, but also to turn away from the statistical averages and assumptions of earlier decades in favor of a new, probabilistic statistics. This shift in "statistical method" aligns with a broader cultural shift over the course of the century, as traced by Lorraine Daston, Ian Hacking, Theodore Porter, and others. Gaining influence in both professional and popular discourse in the 1830s and 40s with the founding of a statistical section of the British Association for the Advancement of Science in 1833, the contemporaneous creation of statistical societies in London and Manchester, and the open support of political economists like Thomas Malthus and social reformers like James Phillips Kay, early statistical methods acquired legitimacy not only in scientific circles but in political ones as well.[36] The creation of the General Register Office in 1837, which was tasked with collecting comprehensive population statistics for all of Britain, and the establishment of the *Journal of the Statistical Society* the following year gave these professional efforts a more public voice. By the middle of the century, proportions and percentages were referred to as matters of common parlance.

Yet as readers of these reports and tables came to realize, there were two seemingly divergent phenomena that emerged from this widespread application of the statistical sciences to insurance policies, social reform, public health planning, and political economy. On the one hand, statistics illustrated the mathematical regularity with which events (e.g., death, crime, sickness, fire) occurred when measured in large populations and over long stretches of time. This law of large numbers lent such incidents an effect of determinacy and certainty. Although one might not be able to predict their time or location, the fact of their occurrence gave statisticians and laypersons the impression of a world governed, if no longer by providence, then by a secular principle at once consistent and transcendent in its application. But on the other, statistics spoke through the language of uncertainty. Its percentages and proportions might have calculated the chances and risks of an event's occurrence, but particulars— where, when, who—were left to the imagination and the future. Recent scholarship has tended to focus on the former, on the containment and control represented by statistical regularities, and particularly on the role of numbers and averages in reinforcing the middle class's normalizing agendas.[37] But the uncertainties conjured by statistics, while not exactly liberatory, nonetheless moved beyond predictability and determinism and instead encouraged readers to think in terms of probabilities and possibilities. As Lewis Carroll (using terms that conjured the mid-century geographical game) explained in his 1888 *Curiosa Mathematica*, "the whole region of certainty and probability may be roughly mapped out into three districts—an out-lying district of certainty in *one* direction, a similar one of certainty in the *opposite* direction, and a middle district of probability."[38]

By the 1850s and 60s, as the language of statistics extended beyond the specialized report and became all but commonplace, some lay writers wrestled with the disjunction between large-scale certainties, the law of large numbers that might describe populations, and the vagaries and indeterminacies associated with the individual. One anonymous essayist, for instance, complained that public health statistics, rather than providing certainty, left the individual ever in doubt: for "the one death that must come . . . the time is to him personally—in spite of libraries full of statistics—utterly unknown and uncertain."[39] More typical, perhaps, was Dickens's treatment of statistics in his 1854 novel *Hard Times*, which criticized the period's proliferation of numbers and tables for their overdetermined, dehumanizing qualities, for how little they concerned themselves with the individuals they claimed to represent. The character Sissy Jupe, for example, learns that in a population of "a million of inhabitants . . . only five-and-twenty are starved to death in the streets, in the course of a year."[40] For the novel's characters, the statistical focus on populations is wrongheaded, at odds with the lives and experiences of individuals. From this perspective, the incontrovertible, unfeeling "fact" was synonymous with statistics.

In explicating the way probabilistic knowledge might be applied to the molecule, Maxwell referred to the large-scale data, the frequencies and averages, that many readers would have equated with the statistical sciences. As he observed on a number of occasions, what one could know about individual molecules, like what one could know about individual persons, was different from what one could know about a group.[41] He resorted to this analogy between molecules and populations, for instance, in his 1873 *Nature* article, explaining that just as surveys by "registrars and tabulators" differed in fundamental ways from the more individualized "study of human nature by parents and schoolmasters," so by extension, "the smallest portion of matter which we can subject to experiment consists of millions of molecules, not one of which ever becomes individually sensible to us. We cannot, therefore, ascertain the actual motion of any one of these molecules, so that we are obliged . . . to adopt the statistical method."[42] Offering a similar comparison in his letter to social scientist Herbert Spencer that same year, he declared that our knowledge of the molecule—of its rotations, which "var[y] at every encounter with another molecule," and of its velocity—can be "*statistical* only—there is nothing definite in any other sense than the death-rate of a city is definite."[43] Statistics in its traditional form, with its focus on averages and frequencies, was, he acknowledged, fundamentally constrained as a tool. In another lecture that year, this time to the Eranus Society,[44] he directed particular attention to the limitations of the statistical method for the thermodynamic sciences; turning to his now familiar analogy with population studies, he explained that to rely on statistics for knowledge of humans was to "confess . . . that we are unable to follow the details of each individual case" and to draw conclusions based instead on the "propensities of an imaginary being called the Mean Man."[45] The "Mean Man," of course, was an absurd fiction, a mathematical convenience that revealed nothing about individual variances; as Maxwell cautioned, "the regularity of averages . . . which when we are dealing with millions of millions of individuals is so unvarying that we are almost in danger of confounding it with absolute uniformity."[46]

The distinction between the frequencies observed in populations and the behavior of individuals, which most readers of the 1870s would have comprehended, thus provided a ready language through which Maxwell could explicate a more abstruse distinction, between the gaseous mass and the single molecule. But the "statistical method" Maxwell advocated in the late 1860s and 70s also moved beyond the sense of helpless resignation expressed by the *All the Year Round* essayist who lamented not knowing the date of "the one death that must come." For Maxwell, uncertainty, whether around the person or molecule, was not a debilitating condition but an epistemologically generative one.[47]

The "Demon": An Experiment in Improbable Belief

While the move from empirical to probabilistic knowledge might now seem an inevitable and self-evident foundation for the thermodynamic sciences, German physicist Rudolf Clausius, who had formulated the second law of thermodynamics in 1850 and whose work had dominated the professional conversation since, was interested in statistical averages rather than in deviations, which he dismissed as "accidental inequalities."[48] Other leading physicists, including James Joule, relied on similar assumptions about the uniformity of particle movements, whether for reasons of mathematical convenience or otherwise.[49] But for Maxwell, the average was of limited value to the physicist. As Porter writes, he deserves "credit for first introducing the explicit consideration of probability distributions into physics,"[50] and indeed he viewed the statistical distribution as a key instrument, a tool for providing greater resolution without implying greater certainty in this new methodological arena. Reflecting that the problem of studying the velocity of individual molecules within a volume of gas might henceforth be addressed by "distributing the molecules into groups according to their velocities," Maxwell posited that "the impossible task of following every individual molecule through all its encounters" was now the more manageable one of "registering the increase or decrease of the number of molecules in the different groups."[51] The range encompassed by the distribution, he knew, included not only those velocities close to the mean but also what Clausius would have called "accidental" outliers, those particles whose movements were, by chance, especially fast or slow. Unlike his predecessor's preferred averages, then, Maxwell's distribution foregrounded variation, one of the central principles of the dynamical theory of gases. It demonstrated, he explained elsewhere, "that the velocities range through all values, being distributed according to the same law which prevails in the distribution of errors of observation."[52]

His arguments about the importance of the statistical distribution also served as the foundation for what is now famously known as Maxwell's "demon," a thought experiment he first developed in December 1867 and then published as a mere two-page entry under the modest heading "Limitation of the Second Law of Thermodynamics" in the closing section of his 1871 textbook *Theory of Heat*.[53] Maxwell himself avoided the term "demon," describing that entity alternately as a "doorkeeper, very intelligent and exceedingly quick, with microscopic eyes" or as a "pointsman on a railway with perfectly acting switches who should send the express along one line and the goods along another."[54] Standing guard over a two-chambered vessel filled with molecules moving at different speeds, the imaginary doorkeeper allowed fast-moving molecules through a small aperture in the dividing wall while excluding slow-moving ones. The result was a velocity—and hence, heat—differential across the two chambers, even as the average velocity for the whole remained unchanged. Maxwell posited that the act of selection producing that differential was intellectual and perceptual rather than physical, and that the doorkeeper therefore performed no work.[55] The proposition that such a differential might exist at all was, as Maxwell knew, a provocation, a violation of what he called "[o]ne of the best established facts in thermodynamics,"[56] the second law of thermodynamics, whose formulation by Sadi Carnot and Clausius held that the energy within a system would always dissipate (or put another way, that entropy or disorder would always increase). The law, Porter explains, had until that point been understood in terms of measurable quantities like heat and temperature, as a purely thermodynamic, as opposed to probabilistic, principle based on averages. By that interpretation, molecules both fast and slow should be evenly and randomly scattered across both chambers of the hypothetical vessel.[57] But as Maxwell countered, this was "true as long as we can deal with bodies only in mass"; but with "a being whose faculties are so sharpened" to discern variations in velocity and thereby generate a differential across the two chambers without violating natural law, the experiment demonstrated that the second law's predicted distribution was no more than a statistical probability.[58]

Much critical attention has been devoted to the symbolic significance of the "doorkeeper" or "demon." Matthew Stanley and others have discussed the philosophical implications of the doorkeeper as a sign of Maxwell's insistence on the power of free will or of human intellect in a world governed by natural laws, or as a figure for an unachievable ideal of perfect perception.[59] Brown and Gold recognize that the experiment was rather a way of addressing a statistical principle, a reminder that "particular molecules can act unpredictably."[60] As Gold explains, it demonstrated that "entropic decay was not so much inevitable as really *really* likely," though her analysis nonetheless frames the demon with respect to other fictional, ordering agencies of the period—Dr. Jekyll, Dorian Gray, Dracula—and Tondre extends this literary reading, likening the demon's agency to that of the Victorian narrator, "a detached observer of multiple individuals."[61] By contrast, P. M. Heimann insists that Maxwell's primary purpose was simply to "provid[e] an illustration of a fundamental feature of nature.... he was not speculating as to whether a being could operate in such a way."[62]

The critical and historical focus on the demon, both in Maxwell's time and more recently, has threatened to eclipse the statistical principles at the experiment's core.[63] To be sure, Maxwell's first public articulation of his thought experiment, in *Theory of Heat*, itself directs attention to the selective agent. His reference to "one who can perceive and handle the individual molecules which we deal with only in large masses" would seem to encourage speculation about superhuman capacities rather than serve the more abstract statistical principle he had in mind; elsewhere, his engagement with questions of free will and his rumination that Lucretius "attempted to burst the bonds of Fate by making his atoms deviate from their courses at quite uncertain times and places" suggest that if the demon was a hypothesis concerning thermodynamics it was also an exploration of the means by which some form of agency might overcome its laws.[64]

Still, I want to look at Maxwell's thought experiment in a way that aligns more closely with Heimann's reading—and, I suggest, in a way that Maxwell elsewhere encouraged others to understand it—such that the doorkeeper recedes in importance, becomes merely a premise, a way of approaching an understanding of statistical distributions. For just as the distribution offered a theoretical means of sorting molecules into "different groups" for explanatory purposes, we might consider the two-chambered vessel of his thought experiment a virtual expression of the statistical distribution. While the histogram was not yet in regular use as a way of illustrating distributions, Maxwell's experiment, with each "box" populated by molecules of distinct characteristics, conjures an approximation of one. He would have known that in imagining how a distribution might apply to a group of molecules, he was not (contrary to appearances) engaging in a descriptive process of a physical reality but in a directive act of "distributing the molecules into groups" according to a given hypothesis. For he, like the demon in the experiment, was the agent who assigned molecules to "different groups" in a statistical distribution, who exercised his sorting powers to produce an equation or table on the page, just as his hypothetical counterpart might use those powers to produce a heat differential within a vessel. Yet, at the same time, the experiment enjoins us to imagine a distribution, even an unlikely, non-normal distribution, occurring without authorial agency. The demon's posited existence, in other words, was simply a means of affirming that, as Maxwell wrote to fellow physicist Peter

G. Tait some years later, "the 2nd law of Thermodynamics has only a statistical certainty," before adding, with perhaps a touch of exasperation at the way in which Thomson's metaphor had assumed a life of its own, "Call him no more a demon but a valve."[65] As a premise, whether doorkeeper or valve, his experiment invites us to consider an improbable, though still statistically possible, state—one in which the combined average velocity of all the vessel's molecules might approximate an average figure at the center of a statistical distribution but in which, at the same time, a sharp differential in velocities might happen to exist across the two chambers.

Maxwell's experiment may have unsettled earlier understandings of thermodynamics, but it also complicates recent historical accounts of the statistical sciences, and specifically, of the relationship between Enlightenment and Victorian conceptions of probability. Eighteenth-century conceptions of probability emphasized an ideal of individual rationality, such that, as Daston puts it, "probabilists regarded expectation as a mathematical rendering of pragmatic rationality. The calculus of probabilities reflected the thought and practice of a small elite of perspicacious individuals who exemplified . . . the virtue of reasonableness"; similarly, Porter characterizes this early probabilistic approach as centered in an "imaginary being" with "perfect vision and unlimited powers of calculation."[66] This probability designated "degrees of belief" as a function of the rational observer, what prominent mathematician and logician Augustus De Morgan called a "feeling of the mind, not the inherent property of a set of circumstances."[67]

Both Porter and Daston suggest that by the early decades of the nineteenth century, this conception of probability as a personal judgment of likelihood receded in the sciences, and in its place the "mathematical theory of risk had triumphed, and . . . whole classes of phenomena previously taken to be the very model of the unpredictable, from hail storms to suicides," came to be regarded as "governed by statistical regularities."[68] By the early 1840s, according to Porter, a range of prominent intellectuals like John Stuart Mill and A. A. Cournot were championing this frequentist position, where events like the aforementioned storms and suicides came to seem subjectively predictable.[69] As facts, they seemed to obey Poisson's law of large numbers, the "mathematical expression of the uniformity of nature," in which occurrences take place with calculable frequency when enumerated over long periods and large populations.[70] In other words, rational "expectation" no longer served as the foundation for probability, but what Laplace (in a furthering of Condorcet's philosophy) called *possibilité*, an objectively conceptualized probability, based in "actual ratios of events."[71]

Still, Porter cautions, it was not the case "that the frequency interpretation immediately—or ever—eclipsed completely the subjective interpretation,"[72] and Maxwell's thought experiment exemplifies the messiness of the relationship between the two. If, following Heimann's assertion, we think of the experiment not as posing an ontological question about the doorkeeper (Could such a being exist?), but rather a layered, epistemological one about distributions (Could we conceive of a state that might seem subjectively improbable while also accepting that it falls within the range of an objective statistical probability, of a Laplacean *possibilité*?), then Maxwell's two-chambered vessel represents the convergence of these two forms of probabilistic thinking in a single experiment. The analogy Maxwell used to explain the experiment in a letter to John William Strutt (who would, after Maxwell's death, succeed him as the Cavendish Professor of Physics at Cambridge), illuminates this point: "The 2nd law of Thermodynamics has the same degree of truth as the statement that if you throw a tumblerful of water into the sea you cannot get the same tumblerful of water out again."[73] He knows that the idea of getting the same "tumblerful of water" back strains not only the laws of statistical averages but also rational judgment, whose subjective force he foregrounds by making "you" the agent of the experiment. By juxtaposing a moment of contingency against an assessment of likelihoods, Maxwell's analogy draws attention to the tendency of both the statistical distribution and our own sense of probable outcomes to revert to the average, in a convergence between these two conceptions of probability. Yet the "truth" to which he refers, the law of averages, is not absolute, but has "degree[s]": Under what circumstances could "you" imagine getting that "same tumblerful" back? What if you could imagine a "doorkeeper" who kept the fast molecules from escaping and slow ones from entering, or a "demon" who, through a similar sort of action, ensured that every molecule of water that left your tumbler later reentered it? However improbable a rational observer might judge it, Maxwell suggests that the outcome—whether the spontaneous emergence of an energy differential or the retrieving of the same glass of water from the ocean—still falls within a sufficiently capacious range of what is statistically possible.

By dramatizing a confrontation between personal belief and statistical possibility through these thought experiments, Maxwell seems to be elaborating on an issue that interested him years before, in his university days, when he wrote to his friend, classics scholar Lewis Campbell:

> What is believing? When the probability . . . in a man's mind of a certain proposition being true is greater than that of its being false, he believes it with a proportion of faith corresponding to the probability. . . . This is faith in general.[74]

The immediate inspiration for this musing was almost certainly John Herschel's review of Quetelet's work, which had just appeared in an 1850 issue of the *Edinburgh Review*.[75] Significantly, Herschel himself makes no clear distinction between the two forms of probability; his review glides from one to the other and back again. He begins his discussion by framing probability as a matter of subjective, personal understanding, a sense of "expectation" occupying the "contemplating mind," but later shifts to a frequentist definition, where "Probabilities become certainties when the number of trials is infinite, and approach to practical certainty when very numerous."[76] For Herschel, these two conceptions intersect where the categories of the statistically possible and the subjectively improbable overlap: In the exceptional occurrence, the aberration. As he queries, "[w]e are thus led to the important and somewhat delicate question,—What we are to consider as reasonable limits, in such determinations—beyond which, if deviations from the central type be recorded, they are either to be referred to exaggeration, or regarded as monstrosities?" and his response consists of an extended contemplation, in the essay's middle section, of figures like the "dwarf Bébé, king of Poland" and "the Philistine, whose stature is expressly stated at six cubits and a span (11 ft. 5 in.)," as well as of "thirteen instances of coincidence between the direction of circular polarization in rock crystal, with that of certain oblique faces in its crystalline form. . . . The chances against such a coincidence happening thirteen times in succession by mere accident are more than 8000 to 1."[77] Herschel's essay, that is, investigates the limits of both statistical possibility and subjective belief by pointing to the contingencies generating outcomes that lie beyond the average, just as Maxwell's thought experiment would do in a more scientifically rigorous fashion two decades later. The rational reader might dismiss any of the named events as an "exaggeration" or "monstrosit[y]," a test of the limits of rational belief, but Herschel's essay knowingly reframes what an earlier epistemology might have treated as freak or miracle within the scope and vocabulary of the new statistical sciences. He gestures, as Maxwell will, too, to the existence of another limit, the calculable limit of statistical possibility.

Maxwell draws on Herschel's description of belief as a quantity subject to mathematical solution, where "higher or lower degrees of expectation or belief" might be "susceptible of numerical subdivision into fractional parts,"[78] mathematically calculable increments along a single continuum. But where Herschel was drawn to the regions of the continuum where statistical and subjective probabilities might approach a point of divergence, in the improbable "deviations" that strained credulity, Maxwell in his letter to Campbell contemplates the point at which they might converge in "faith." Just as probability, for the scientist, was the quantifiable likelihood of a hypothesis holding true, so too was faith a matter of ever-increasing probabilities, of an asymptotic, not identical, relation to truth. To be sure, faith held a particular meaning for Maxwell, who in his early 20s, just a few years after his letter to Campbell, would convert from the more conventional Anglicanism of his childhood to the "fierce evangelical faith" he would profess for the rest of his life; indeed, it marked the beginning of a lasting personal commitment to Christianity, exemplified by regular references to the Bible in his correspondence with his wife as well as by his role as a church elder in Scotland.[79] But elsewhere, insisting on a necessary division between scientific practice and religious belief, he wrote, "the results which each man arrives at in his attempts to harmonize his science with his Christianity ought not to be regarded as having any significance except to the man himself."[80] Moreover, even as Maxwell sought to limit the doorkeeper's power, noting that he is "still an essentially finite being,"[81] historians have been tempted to view the demon, if not as an exact proxy for God, then as a "scientific and religious entity" nonetheless, as Maxwell's way of thinking about the relationship between the mortal capacity for free will and the immutable, divine framework encompassing it, or as a kind of figure for divine agency.[82]

But the influence of Herschel's publication, legible in Maxwell's letter to Campbell and in his famous thought experiment nearly twenty years later,[83] suggests another, more abstract way in which the idea of faith might have informed Maxwell's vision of the second law. Not only does the experiment challenge readers to believe in an entity whose powers transcend both the capacities of ordinary human perception and definitions of agency (For what species of being could sort molecules without doing work?), but it also asks them to believe in an extraordinary condition (the miracle, the monstrosity) as a statistically possible occurrence. Whether understood in theological or secular terms, it invites a suspension of rational—subjective, but also statistical—belief, pressing belief beyond the average and toward the "deviation," the unlikely outer edges of the distribution. Exploring the personal and mathematical limits of probability, Maxwell seems to posit, thus operates as another version of faith, a willing and willed act of acceptance analogous to that of the Christian believer, in a realm beyond empirical proofs.

Feeling, Faith, and Eliot's Improbable States

Around the time that Maxwell was elaborating on the meaning of his thought experiment, Eliot was developing her own in the form of her final novel. From its allusion to the "dynamic" theory of gases in its first sentence to its use of scientific metaphor throughout, the novel demonstrates an awareness of the ways in which both the language and the principles of the contemporaneous sciences could animate novelistic representations of emotional complexity. In turning away from certainty as an epistemological ideal, Eliot's last novel proffers its own theories concerning the value of indeterminacy and probability. The novel begins with Gwendolen being viewed across a smoke-filled room, an apt figure for the epistemological haze that occludes her feelings from Daniel's studying gaze as she sits at the gambling table. The roulette game—like the accidents that occur throughout: the Harleth family's financial crises, Daniel's chance encounters with Ezra Cohen and with Mirah Lapidoth, Henleigh Mallinger Grandcourt's drowning—reminds readers that these characters inhabit a secular rather than a providential world, filled with events whose causes are often indeterminable and in which the traditional certainties of empirical knowledge, religious belief, or even narratorial omniscience have little hold. Perhaps for this reason, when faith does emerge in the novel, Eliot represents it in a form that would have been foreign to most of her Victorian readers. Rather than a nostalgic turn toward the assurances of a traditional, familiar theology, Daniel's Judaism represents, both for him and for the majority of Eliot's nineteenth-century readers, a step toward the unknown.

For Eliot, a modern world unguided by Christian or narrative providence was not necessarily an unfeeling or unsympathetic one. As critics have demonstrated, this novel is, like the rest of her fictional oeuvre, deeply concerned with the potential for human sympathy. But in this last work, she suggests that feeling and sympathy might require for their generation and sustenance new modes of understanding, guided by probabilistic thinking and approximation. Acknowledging the limitations of one's vision—the hindrances to seeing or knowing with certainty, as the narrator herself does when she admits how little the empirical evidence of the physical world tells us—becomes the prerequisite for a new form of knowledge.

Maxwell, too, understood that the value of a probabilistic approach extended beyond the sciences. After all, he asserted, there was little difference between "a physicist" like himself, "disarmed" of the "weapons" of empirical and experimental data, and a metaphysician who contemplated human motives and behaviors.[84] The contingencies of human affairs, he explained, were not unlike those found in the natural world, where "the rock loosed by frost and balanced on a singular point of the mountain-side, the little spark which kindles the great forest, . . . the little spore which blights all the potatoes," might be described retroactively, but otherwise elude the forecasting impulses suggested by the average; by analogy, the individual was more like the dynamic molecule than his statistical avatar, the "Mean Man," for "in our own nature there are more singular points" than ever, he emphasized, making any act of "prediction . . . impossible."[85] Throughout her final novel Eliot likewise reminds us that her characters are, like Maxwell's scientist, "disarmed," denied omniscience or assurances of perfect understanding. References to scientific experiment recur in *Daniel Deronda*, though not as metaphors for the power of empirical understanding but rather for its failures and limitations. Sympathetic knowing functions in its pages not unlike scientific observation in an era of probabilistic knowledge, where both move toward but never reach a point of epistemological resolution.

Eliot's interest in the period's sciences encompassed natural history and medicine—and spanned the length of her career as a novelist.[86] A number of other Victorian novelists shared her interest in promoting contemporaneous scientific discoveries and theories, such as Charles Dickens, who was fascinated by the period's physical chemistry, and Charles Kingsley, who championed sanitary and hygienic reform in his fiction. But as Sally Shuttleworth explains, Eliot maintained a depth of engagement in and "knowledge of contemporary social and scientific theory [that was] unmatched by any of her peers."[87] Her expertise was enforced by personal connections, such as her acquaintance with Tyndall through her companion, editor George Henry Lewes, for example, and her lifelong friendship with Spencer, as well as by scholarly application and investigation. Like Maxwell, she had absorbed Herschel's 1850 *Edinburgh Review* essay, and she read Tyndall's and Maxwell's published work and assiduously transcribed excerpts from their two 1870 British Association lectures into her working notebooks in preparation for writing *Daniel Deronda*.[88]

A consideration of Eliot's accomplishments as a whole, however, belies any suggestion that her literary experiments were merely derivative of contemporaneous scientific ones. Her earlier writings had explored versions of these same questions about the limits of knowledge and of belief, both from a theological perspective, through the translations of key Christian philosophical texts that were among her first publications in the 1840s and 50s, and from a secular stance, through novels that asked readers to consider the difficulties inherent in the processes of seeing and knowing. The narrator of *Middlemarch*, for example, famously encourages readers to turn a critical eye to the limitations of vision and perspective, as the novel sheds light on the difficult process by which characters might know each other or, as in the case of her well-meaning but myopic hero, Dr. Tertius Lydgate, might know themselves. But when she adapted the language of new scientific methodologies to these epistemological questions in her 1876 *Daniel Deronda*, she turned away from what Shuttleworth identifies as the "empiricism" of early natural history and toward an increasingly "creative, experimental" approach to her subject.[89] Yet while Shuttleworth emphasizes Eliot's extension of the "more radical theory of scientific method" developed by Darwin and French physiologist Claude Bernard to contemporaneous social concerns,[90] in this chapter I turn to the common ground she identified between her own literary investigations and recent developments in the physical and thermodynamic sciences, especially in the questions they posed about the possibility of empirical knowledge and the meaning of incalculability.

Those interested in the intersections between science and literature in Eliot's work have typically looked to *Middlemarch* as a critical case study. *Daniel Deronda*, which traces the intertwined histories of two young English-persons confronting unsettling circumstances—Daniel, a wealthy gentleman who discovers and ultimately embraces his Jewish ancestry, and Gwendo-len, a woman who attempts to resolve her personal and financial difficulties through marriage to the aristocratic Henleigh Grandcourt—has tended to attract critical attention to the thematics of social identity, especially to the place of Jews and of women in Victorian London. Unlike *Middlemarch*, with its doctor protagonist and its focus on the rise of the medical profession, sci-ence plays no explicit role at the level of theme or character in *Deronda*. But given Eliot's preparatory research into Maxwell's and Tyndall's writing, we might read *Deronda* as another "scientific" novel, and indeed, as a number of critics have noted, this last novel investigates epistemological questions about the relationship between scientific and sympathetic, and between objective and subjective, ways of knowing.[91] Indeed, like *Middlemarch*, with its recur-rent turns to the language of light and microscopy as figures for perception, *Deronda* makes science, and probability theory in particular, central to its nar-rative and epistemological strategy. It provides one way of responding to the question, How can one know something about the unknowable? For Eliot's characters, religious faith (in this case, Judaism) offers one viable response to the problem of arriving at such knowledge. But scientific investigation and understanding, and, specifically, the ways scientists like Tyndall and Maxwell handled the broader epistemological challenges of studying an invisible world, provide another way for Eliot's narrator to reflect on the limits of knowing. Their approaches serve as a useful model, and sometimes a useful metaphor, for describing experiments in narrative, where omniscience gives way to specu-lation, certitude to productive doubt.

The novel's opening scene situates characters and readers within multiple levels and forms of unknowability: around Gwendolen's character and motives, around Daniel's fascination with her, around the possible outcomes, both moral and financial, of her gambling. As the novel progresses, its plot continues to defy any expectation that often-crucial questions will find ready answers: how and why Grandcourt dies, whether Daniel will reach Palestine and succeed in founding a Jewish state, how or whether Gwendolen will remake her life as a young widow. The novel declines to resolve these matters, but it suggests, even from its opening scenes, how we might begin to address them.

Like Eliot's other works of fiction, *Deronda* offers multiple lessons in reading and knowing others, its narrator repeatedly instructing us in the distinctions between appearances and emotions, generalities and particulars, types and individuals.[92] Where the narrator of *Adam Bede* made similar moves, warning us against assumptions based on typology—not to rest on assurances that Arthur Donnithorne is "'a good fellow'" or that no more needs to be said about Hetty Sorrel than that "her cheek was like a rose-petal" (even while advancing other typologies to take their place)[93]—the narrator of *Deronda* dwells on the epistemological difficulty in placing our trust in an empirical data set, in observations, averages, and categorical findings. Introducing Grandcourt, for instance, she lingers for a moment on the surface of this "correct Englishman," on his "faded fairness" and "long grey eyes," then cautions us about coming to any conclusions about him as an individual based on certitudes about "correct Englishmen" as a population.[94] Where in other works this dismissal of generalizations often leads to an invitation to see the individual character with clearer eyes and greater resolution, her last novel denies even that possibility. Indeed, pressing further, she exclaims,

> Attempts at description are stupid: who can all at once describe a human being? even when he is presented to us we only begin that knowledge of his appearance which must be completed by innumerable impressions under differing circumstances.[95]

With this emphasis on the dynamic, ephemeral Paterian impression rather than on stable empirical perception, the narrator pronounces the supposedly legible surfaces of the body only the beginning of epistemological difficulty, where we encounter the limits to our understanding. Empiricism is a weak instrument, and the resulting data set consists of no more than an assemblage of fleeting observations, scattered points delineating a field of possibility, rather than communicating facts or certainties. From a narrative perspective, this stance represents a striking difference from the nineteenth century's typical literary omniscience, in which authoritative third-person narrators implicitly know, even if they do not reveal, all. Here, such knowing is a delusion, based on generalizations or assumptions about types or averages. As the chapter's epigraph admonishes, "The beginning of an acquaintance whether with persons or things is to get a definite outline for our ignorance."[96]

To be sure, the difficulty of knowing, particularly when bridging the distance between characters or between readers and characters, is central to Eliot's oeuvre as a whole, and numerous critics have ably explored both the significance and challenge of sympathetic feeling in Eliot's work.[97] Where Rae Greiner cautions us against the notion that sympathy in Eliot's work is coterminous with omniscience or any kind of identificatory fullness of knowledge, she nonetheless observes that sympathy is about thinking more than feeling, "a mental exercise but not an emotion."[98] Other critics likewise frame sympathy in Eliot's fiction as presenting an epistemological rather than emotional problem; according to Forest Pyle, for instance, Eliot's discourse of sympathy extends the Romantic emphasis on the imagination, but where the latter expanded the purview of the self, sympathy is more directed in its ends, "promis[ing] to bridge the epistemological and ethical gap between self and world."[99] For George Levine, characters' confrontations with the national, cultural, and religious differences that thread throughout *Deronda* express the "working through of an adequate epistemology of otherness."[100] The epistemological difficulty in sympathetic processes arises not only from the limitations of the viewer's or reader's perceptive abilities, however, but also from the nature of the perceived object. As implied through her selection of the word "dynamic" to describe Gwendolen, Eliot was interested not in fixing her subject under Daniel's or her own gaze, but in portraying the ever-shifting contingencies of feeling and action that constitute the individual, the emotional equivalent of the "dance" Maxwell posited for the molecule. In *Deronda*, what the narrator calls an "iridescence of character—the play of various, nay, contrary tendencies,"[101] is what gives characters and scenes psychological depth and complexity.

Where *Middlemarch* provides a space for the certainties of empirical observation ("it is demonstrable that the scratches are going everywhere impartially" in "your pier-glass," the narrator famously tells readers[102]), *Deronda* employs the language of experiment to reflect rather on the limitations of scientific methods. Science does not stand apart as a category of knowledge but serves as a figure for other modes of uncertain knowledge: religious faith in a time of secular rationalism, emotional attachment to a particular vision of one's future, sensitivity to what others feel but cannot express. For example, when Thomas Lush, Grandcourt's assistant, considers the possibility of a union between his employer and Gwendolen, he launches into a series of hypotheses:

> What was the probable effect that the news of [Gwendolen's] family misfortunes would have on Grandcourt's fitful obstinacy he felt to be quite incalculable. So far as the girl's poverty might be an argument that she would accept an offer from him now in spite of any previous coyness, it might remove that bitter objection to risk a repulse which Lush divined to be one of Grandcourt's determining motives; on the other hand, the certainty of acceptance was just "the sort of thing" to make him lapse hither and thither with no more apparent will than a moth. Lush had had his patron under close observation for many years, and knew him perhaps better than he knew any other subject; but to know Grandcourt was to doubt what he would do in any particular case. . . . Lush had some general certainties about Grandcourt. . . . Of what use, however, is a general certainty that an insect will not walk with his head hindmost, when what you need to know is the play of inward stimulus that sends him hither and thither in a network of possible paths?[103]

More than the content of Lush's insights, this passage reveals their limitations. The first half of the passage inhabits Lush's limited perspective through indirect discourse, then turns away to the narrator's point of view, a third-person commentary on Lush's reflections. Yet if we expected omniscience in the passage's second half (beginning with "Lush had had his patron"), the narrator disappoints us. In place of insight we receive an exposition on the necessarily imperfect state of Lush's knowledge as well as, by extension, our own. Moreover, that imperfection is hardly particular to Lush; as the narrator suggests, it is as fundamental to observation of a creature like Grandcourt, as it is to any act of scientific observation of a moth or other insect. Like the traditional scientist, Lush is familiar with generalities, average behaviors deduced from "close observation for many years," but that knowledge has no predictive force for any one case, including the case that interests him most.

As the narrator pauses over the divide between Lush and Grandcourt, her subject is not Grandcourt himself but rather the difficulty that characters like Lush or Gwendolen, or even we as readers, face in ascertaining Grandcourt's feelings and motivations. That space of intersubjectivity—of emotions, inclinations, and influences between individuals—can only, Eliot's novel suggests, be accessed through speculative and imaginative effort.[104] The condition of uncertainty Lush experiences applies to other characters as well, as indeed Daniel discovers when he observes Gwendolen in the novel's opening pages. While the epistemological challenge of intersubjective knowing is central to many of Eliot's writings, what distinguishes this last novel from her earlier work is the degree of certainty residing in such moments between characters. Much is left unarticulated in *Middlemarch*, for example, but this earlier novel nonetheless leaves us with the sense that the characters had reached a deeper understanding with one another and we as readers with them. In a novel where, as Beer tells us, "everything is presented finally as knowable and explicable,"[105] the primary characters find themselves joined in moments of mutual insight by its final chapters; through descriptions of the sympathetic touch of hands and meeting of eyes, the narrator reassures us that such secular communion of feelings between persons can exist.

But in *Daniel Deronda*, Eliot invites us to explore the indeterminability of the interpersonal, while she also denies us the certainties offered by her earlier novel. The uncharacteristic certainty with which she resolves the lingering question of Daniel's parentage aside,[106] the realms of faith, emotion, attachment, and motivation remain in the shadow of uncertainty. *Deronda*'s characters approach each other, but the sympathetic resolutions that take place in *Middlemarch* are elusive in this last novel, whose final pages evoke something more like the suspended, incomplete narratives Babbage had pasted into his scrapbook. The widowed Gwendolen sends one last letter to Daniel, and

Daniel, inspired by the dying Ezra's religious fervor, sails off to Palestine, leaving the characters and us as readers in a state of emotional irresolution: What effect does Gwendolen's last letter have on Daniel? Will Gwendolen carry out Daniel's encouragement to become "one of the best of women"? Will Daniel fulfill the dying Ezra's final, prophetic wish?

An awareness of this fundamental indeterminability informs Lush's own insecurities, as he knows that he cannot rely on what the narrator calls "general certainties," a probabilistic calculus based on some knowledge of Grandcourt's past actions combined with a sense of average behaviors. In this state of uncertainty Lush resorts to generating alternative hypotheses, much as the novel itself proliferates "possibility and prediction" to the point that, as Beer concludes, "we are more jostled by possibilities than invited to select."[107] This act of multiplying "possibilities" engages characters like Gwendolen and Daniel, as well, as they generate a field of hypotheses for the characters and events around them. In this sense the model of sympathy Eliot advances here aligns with that of Adam Smith, who, as Greiner reminds us, encouraged a "'situating' [of] the other in an imaginative narrative temporality made up of every circumstance 'that can possibly occur' (not those that demonstrably *have*)."[108] But Eliot's narrator locates this imaginative process with relation to a contemporaneous scientific epistemology and experimental practice. By describing characters in terms of "dynamic qualit[ies]" and "iridescence" (another word that still retained a primarily technical meaning even as it had slipped into colloquial, figurative usage over the course of the century),[109] she refers us to an epistemological problematic at the center of the period's sciences, where the challenge lies not only in the moment of perception, in the distance between observer and observed, but in the nature of the object itself.

Hence she presents Gwendolen, for example, as she contemplates Grandcourt's offer of marriage and speculates on the relationship between husband and wife:

> For what could not a woman do when she was married, if she knew how to assert herself? Here all was constructive imagination. Gwendolen had about as accurate a conception of marriage—that is to say, of the mutual influences, demands, duties of man and woman in the state of matrimony—as she had of magnetic currents and the law of storms.[110]

This might read at first like a deprecation of Gwendolen's ignorance of both married life and science, but the narrator's comparison with phenomena that can only be described as "dynamic"—subject to invisible and shifting forces, circumstances, and influences—hints at an epistemological difficulty that is general rather than specific to her alone. The feelings of one's husband, like the behavior of masses of air or of atoms, are largely resistant to more traditional, empirical modes of study, and Gwendolen's challenge lies as much in her own limited powers of perception as in the shifting, dynamic quality of her subject of study. She might indeed be ignorant, the novel seems to say, but so too was the trained meteorologist, whose knowledge of "storms" at this time was, as Katharine Anderson tells us, necessarily a "tension between observation and speculation,"[111] and the physicist, whose understanding of "magnetic currents," as Maxwell himself had admitted, was necessarily probabilistic. Any semblance of certainty could be no more than an extrapolation from limited data, an effect of the "constructive imagination."

Indeed, to insist on certainty is to fail in understanding, the narrator tells us, comparing Grandcourt to a "terrier" who apprehends his wife's feelings "in dog fashion, . . . with the narrow correctness which leaves a world of unknown feeling behind."[112] To know in "human fashion" is to acknowledge uncertainty, to admit that there is no such thing as an empirical transmission of knowledge. Instead, occasions for intersubjective contemplation often come in the form of a dense series of speculations, and these moments are more present, often even more potent, than what's actualized and realized. Take, for example, these reflections of the young artist Hans Meyrick on the romantic inclinations of Mirah, Daniel, and Gwendolen:

> Suppose Mirah's heart were entirely preoccupied with Deronda in another character than that of her own and her brother's benefactor: the supposition was attended in Hans's mind with anxieties which, to do him justice, were not altogether selfish. He had a strong persuasion, which only direct evidence to the contrary could have dissipated, that there was a serious attachment between Deronda and Mrs Grandcourt; he had pieced together many fragments of observation . . . which convinced him not only that Mrs Grandcourt had a passion for Deronda, but also, notwithstanding his friend's austere self-repression, that Deronda's susceptibility about her was the sign of concealed

love. Some men, having such a conviction, would have avoided allusions that could have roused that susceptibility; but Hans's talk naturally fluttered towards mischief, and he was given to a form of experiment on live animals which consisted in irritating his friends playfully. His experiments had ended in satisfying him that what he thought likely was true.[113]

The contingencies associated with the dynamics of each character's internal state as well as the dynamic interrelationships among them—what Hans knows about Mirah's emotional state, what Mirah might feel for Daniel, what Daniel and Gwendolen feel for each other—occupy the center of this long passage. Following the pattern used in tracing Lush's reflections, the narrator first mediates Hans's thoughts in indirect discourse, only to intercede without warning, as the narrator shifts from Hans's limited knowledge of his friends to her own commentary on Hans. Like Lush, Hans is compared to a scientist, and yet here, too, science represents not the power of comprehensive knowledge but rather its limitation. Hans, like the scientific observer, draws what conclusions he can about what he can neither see nor measure, and these limited data lead Hans, as both he and we discover, to incorrect judgments. For the narrator's analogy reveals that in place of empirical conclusiveness, Hans manages to accumulate only "fragments of observation" and "sign[s]." What he knows is an uneven patchwork based on his assessment of subjective probabilities ("what he thought likely"), his wishes (his own romantic inclinations), and his attempts to hazard a guess about the objective limits of possibility, signaled by the tentative "supposition" with which the passage opens. In his vision of this otherwise inaccessible realm of felt feelings and unexpressed desires, knowledge can only ever be an approximation, a good guess about the object of study. The very nature of that space is probabilistic, a space of potential rather than of resolution, of all those things that might be rather than the one thing that is.

Science itself is not at fault, the novel suggests, but rather the inadequacy of traditional scientific methods of observation and experimentation. If Eliot seems to concur with Maxwell in promoting probabilistic thinking as a more productive approach to the object of study, then Daniel is, at least in the narrator's eyes, a model of the new scientist, whose practice of not seeking empirical certainty about others serves as the foundation for an alternative mode of understanding. Daniel, according to the novel, seems to reside in a state of indeterminate irresolution, an acceptance of his own and others' "iridescence"; rather than seeking vainly after "valid evidence," he "regard[s] his uncertainty as a condition to be cherished."[114] This "uncertainty," the novel makes clear, is not the same as a wholesale refusal of knowledge. Rather, he consistently situates those he encounters within a capacious field of possibilities, an intersubjective equivalent of Maxwell's statistical distributions. Hence when Daniel contemplates Gwendolen's marriage, the narrator tells us that "his mind had perhaps never been so active in weaving probabilities," and indeed, his feeling for her is conveyed not by any single insight but through a series of rapidly proliferated, open-ended possibilities:

[What] caused her to shrink from [marriage]—a shrinking finally overcome by the urgence of poverty? . . . Was [she,] under all her determined show of satisfaction, gnawed by a double, a treble-headed grief—self-reproach, disappointment, jealousy?[115]

Similarly, his attachment to Mirah begins when he sees her by the river, and "fell again and again to speculating on the probable romance that lay behind that loneliness and look of desolation."[116]

This condition of not knowing, far from being futile or passive, is instead what enables the sympathetic imagination. It demands the capacity to thread through multiple contingencies, to generate an imaginative field of possibility around the feelings and experiences of others, and to actively populate the indeterminate spaces between the necessary and the impossible. Again, two chapters later, when thinking back on his discovery of Mirah, Daniel "saw and heard everything as clearly as before—saw not only the actual events of two hours, but possibilities of what had been and what might be which those events were enough to feed with the warm blood of passionate hope and fear,"[117] followed by several paragraphs of speculation: about Mirah's past and about her future, about the true character of her lost relatives. In similar fashion, Gwendolen's connections to other characters will never achieve the resolution she longs for. Her emotional isolation, a result of her marriage to the domineering Grandcourt, "caused her to live through [conversations with others] many times beforehand, imagining how they would take place and what she would say."[118] The emotional rewards of social interaction come not from actualized conversations, which are too often kept in check by social or physical barriers, but from a conjuring of that intersubjective realm, in the time spent envisioning the many directions these conversations might take. Speculation acts as a positive, generative force, filling the unknowable, unspeakable space that divides observer from observed, empirically available "actual events" from the unavailable emotions of lived experience, with a multiplicity of narratives, which reach out toward its object like so many benevolent tentacles of potential understanding. Indeed, Eliot's novel proposes that this sensitivity to qualities "which can never be written or even spoken—only divined by each of us" in "our neighbours' lives," a capacity that Daniel clearly possesses, constitutes a kind of "genius" of sympathetic knowing.[119]

This process of "weaving probabilities," in effect generating a field of possibilities, a statistical distribution of potential narrative outcomes, also provides a model for readers. In describing Daniel's thought processes, the narrator makes a now familiar move— first inhabiting Daniel's speculations about Gwendolen through indirect discourse, then turning her third-person gaze onto Daniel himself:

> Was she seeing the whole event—her own acts included—through an exaggerating medium of excitement and horror? Was she in a state of delirium into which there entered a sense of concealment and necessity for self-repression? Such thoughts glanced through Deronda as a sort of hope. But imagine the conflict of feeling that kept him silent.[120]

Here the narrator departs from the pattern set in the earlier examples. Rather than offering a generalizing commentary about speculative knowledge, she shifts our attention from the intersubjective space between Daniel and Gwendolen to the intersubjective space between Daniel and the novel's readers. Moreover, rather than filling that space with the certainties of her own omniscient knowledge, she issues an invitation to speculate ("imagine the conflict of feeling"), to generate our own field of narratives and to approximate through their multiplicity something like a statistical distribution of emotional states within which Daniel's own might, for an instant, reside.

In this sense, Eliot's last novel seems to pick up where her 1871–72 *Middlemarch* leaves off, with its contemplation, in its final paragraph, of a single person's "incalculably diffusive" influence on others, a phrase that hints at the author's thermodynamic interests as she finished one novel and embarked on the next.[121] Where the preceding chapters of this earlier novel had affirmed that mutual understanding was possible—whether between Lydgate and Dorothea Brooke, between Dorothea and Rosamond Vincy, even between Will Ladislaw and James Chettam, characters divided by temperament and social class and where any residual perceptual limitations were usually offset by the narrator's own transcendent vision—its last lines dwell on the value of a subjective experience that cannot be calculated or perceived. *Daniel Deronda* commences with and elaborates on precisely the "incalculably diffusive" in intersubjective experience, a kind of "ether" of unconfirmed influence and emotion—where Ezra's feeling for Daniel, Daniel's feeling for Gwendolen, even Daniel's feeling for God—elude description, observation, or calculation. While readers might identify in the emotional complexity of these vicissitudes an anticipation of Modernism's refusal of omniscience in favor of a more nuanced exploration of feeling, Eliot's articulation of that uncertain terrain very much belongs to the late Victorian era, with its shift from empirical to probabilistic modes of understanding. Still, her valuation of uncertainty also departs in important ways from that found in Maxwell's work. His thought experiment revealed a willingness to conceive, at least theoretically, of the possibility of perfect perception, of an ability to know the velocities and paths of individual molecules with certainty. Indeed, as he mused in that 1870 address, "we may hope that . . . our means of experimental inquiry [will] become more accurate," and that as a result, knowledge of any given "molecule will become more definite, so that we may be able at no distant period to estimate its weight."[122] Eliot's novel, while emphasizing the power of social context—a congested and circumscribing space of social codes and rituals that reinforce the opacity of individuals—suggests that an ethical and sympathetic understanding of others—their desires, impulses, and temptations—must always retain something of the inaccurate and indefinite.

But if the novel allowed for a wide field of uncertainty in the understanding of persons, it applied a somewhat different, though still experimental, calculus to the representation of events. Like Maxwell's thought experiment, which was, in effect, a way of reimagining through the new statistical sciences what might, in earlier times, have been deemed the work of divine miracle, *Deronda* as a novelistic experiment offers an intervention into the traditional apparatus of plot: How do we plausibly arrive at a result that seems subjectively unlikely or unexpected? Even as her novel accepts some of the conventions of narrative resolution and closure, it rejects the arbitrary mechanisms that figured so prominently in the English literary tradition, in works like *Tom Jones* and *Oliver Twist* (as well as in later, providential incarnations in novels like *Jane Eyre* and even *Adam Bede*). If, as Marie-Laure Ryan argues, coincidence is "a phenomenon of low probability," one that, in some fundamental sense, fiction depends on but for which "our tolerance . . . has grown lower through the ages,"[123] then Eliot reframes those novelistic coincidences using the contemporaneous language of probability and contingency, remaking them into versions of Maxwell's thought experiment. Even as she remobilizes some of the most time-worn conventions of eighteenth-century plot—the chance meetings, the orphan who discovers his parentage (though here, not in the local squire, but in a foreign princess)—she transforms the novel into an experiment in secular causation, statistical distributions, and the probability of outcomes. Like Maxwell's, her experiment knowingly thwarts assumptions about outcomes based on averages and tests the limits where subjective belief and statistical distributions might align. The novel directs us to the improbable-yet-still-possible outer edges of the distribution, to the narrative equivalent of a dual-chambered vessel within which a heat differential has come to exist, and it invites us, as did Maxwell's experiment, to suspend our disbelief when Daniel turns out to be Jewish, when he falls in love not with the more typical heroine, Gwendolen, but with the atypical one, Mirah.

"Weaving probabilities" thus functions not only as a means of achieving sympathetic understanding with others but also as a mode of being in an uncertain world, in which one navigates a wide range of statistical possibilities as well as the breadth of one's own belief. The field of possibilities must not be so circumscribed that it allows only average outcomes, but neither can it encompass the supernatural in its account of causalities, and *Deronda's* characters repeatedly map the topography and boundaries of that field for themselves. In their rehearsing of what counts as probable and improbable, possible and impossible, they delineate something like a scatterplot distribution of possible outcomes. The novel repeatedly presses them toward an awareness of their own place within that range, and where it metes out moral judgments, it often does so here, revealing when they have calibrated their expectations incorrectly. Gwendolen, for example, straining against the "girlish average" she perceives in others, strives to learn whether she might be exceptional in some way, might "achieve more than mediocrity" as a singer or "live to be one of the best of women"; still, as Herr Klesmer reminds her, one must allow for "probabilities," an ambivalent statement that nonetheless serves as a caution both to her and us that the greater part of probability still rests in the unexceptional average.[124] But in other cases, the failure lies in not imagining the exceptional outcome, as when the Arrowpoints learn that their own daughter Catherine is engaged to the eccentric musician, an unhappy "possibility" that for them lay well outside the realm of understood likelihoods.[125] Likewise Mirah, now resident in London, is haunted by the fear that when "turning at the corner of a street I may meet my father"; even when Daniel reassures her that "[i]t is surely not very probable," he admits to himself that he "wish[es] that it were less so."[126] Collectively, these examples support what we might call the novel's statistical realism, as they also enforce the lesson that wishes bear no weight. To believe otherwise, as Gwendolen does in the first chapter, entertaining "visions" of herself as a "goddess of luck," can be no more than self-delusion.[127]

We might say that the novel as a whole, much like Maxwell's statistical re-thinking of Clausius's thermodynamics, is concerned with distributions—and less with the averages that fall in the middle of those distributions than with the deviations that might lie at their far reaches. In this sense Eliot's last novel indeed exemplifies what Ryan has described as fiction's abiding interest in "low probability" occurrences, as it also seeks out the non-normative potential that Tondre identifies with the late Victorian probabilistic sciences. Her narrator attends to the ways in which characters depart from the average, reminding us, for example, that Daniel's "circumstances, indeed, had been exceptional."[128] Musing further on the relationship between the average and the exceptional, the narrator describes Daniel in his rowing gear and declares, "Such types meet us here and there among average conditions," but then shifts course, return-ing to the suggestion that in fact, far from "average," Daniel's "appearance was of a kind to draw attention."[129] That statement serves as a fitting prelude not only to the distinctly un-average episode about to unfold on the next page, in which he saves Mirah, but also to the revelation of his exceptional ancestry, his Jewishness, many chapters later. Like Maxwell's thought experiment, these and other moments invite characters and readers to confront both the objective and subjective limits of probabilistic thinking. Accustomed to reverting to the average, we mistake subjective assessments of probability for statistical likelihoods, and in this, too, our judgment is at risk of delineating too narrow a scope of possibility. *Deronda* challenges readers to consider what seemingly unlikely events might still fall within the realm of statistical possibility. As one of the chapter epigraphs, in which Eliot translates the language of Aristotle's *Poetics* into the vocabulary of mid-Victorian statistics, reminds them, "This, too, is probable, according to that saying of Agathon: 'It is a part of probability that many improbable things will happen.'"[130]

By repeatedly reflecting on the exceptional event as exceptional, *Daniel Deronda* reframes those engines of eighteenth- and early nineteenth-century plot: coincidence and providence. Eliot leans away from their handling of contrived outcomes, where the revelation that the orphan's savior turns out to be his aunt or that the working-class heroine turns out to be an heiress signals a providential, moralizing presence. Instead, she recasts our assessment of events that might be statistically possible yet strike us as unlikely in probabilistic terms. In part, *Deronda* accomplishes this through explicit references to the play of contingency, through which the novel suggests that outcomes are not authorially determined but arise rather through chance and its wholly possible degrees of freedom.[131]

That language enters into the characters' own reflections about outcomes. When, for example, Daniel contemplates his meeting with the newly widowed Gwendolen, he admits "that if all this had happened little more than a year ago, . . . the impetuous determining impulse which would have moved him would have been to save her from sorrow, to shelter her life for evermore from the dangers of loneliness."[132] And similarly, Gwendolen frames her romantic involvement with Grandcourt in the language of contingency, noting that its outcome was to be "one of two likelihoods that presented themselves alternately, . . . as if they were two sides of a boundary-line, and she did not know on which she should fall," a comparison that transforms her, at least in her own mind for the moment, into a wheel spun or a die thrown.[133]

But beyond these reminders that the novel's characters knowingly inhabit a world replete with contingency, the narrator, too, participates in resituating such revelations and occurrences for us within a framework of statistical understanding, locating them within a space in which "objective" and "subjective" forms of probability overlap. Where Dickens, for example, typically incorporated exceptional events without narratorial commentary,[134] Eliot refuses to pass the extraordinary moment off as merely another effect of plot, another demand for the suspension of disbelief. After having saved Mirah from death, the novel shows us Daniel's reflection on this moment: "To save an unhappy Jewess from drowning herself, would not have seemed a startling variation among police reports; but to discover in her so rare a creature as Mirah, was an exceptional event."[135] Questions of believability—whether anyone would believe that this unhappy woman was, in fact, a worthy "creature," or whether we can believe, as we are later asked to do, that Daniel turns out to be Jewish, too—come to the fore in this novel as questions to be assessed through a combination of personal belief (what might seem "startling" to the observer) and a calculus of averages, distributions, and deviations. For even exceptional events, the novel reminds us, as unlikely as they might seem, can still be encompassed by statistical probability. Where the nineteenth-century reader might deem Mirah's qualities implausible—given that nearly drowned women, all too common in "police reports," tend to fall closer to a more dismal average—the novel's acknowledgment that this is an "exceptional event" implicitly grants that outcome a place within the distribution of statistical possibility.

Eliot's novel foregrounds these intersections between personal and statistical assessments of probability in a number of key episodes that serve, I suggest, as her own versions of Maxwell's "tumblerful of water." When Daniel, for example, seeks Mirah's long-lost relatives in London's Jewish quarter, he comes upon a shop sign emblazoned with the name of her brother, Ezra Cohen. Dreading the discovery that Mirah's brother might turn out to be no more than what Daniel would describe as an average Jew, he consoles himself with the thought that "There might be a hundred Ezra Cohens lettered above shop-windows."[136] Jesse Rosenthal reads this line as reflection on "the providence which trails Deronda throughout the novel—what are the odds?" a recognition of the way the law of large numbers enforces an older vision of novelistic coincidence.[137] But I suggest that the line speaks to a different alignment, between statistical knowledge and the agency of desire: In this moment, Daniel's awareness of the objective fact of population (there might indeed be many Ezra Cohens in London) converges with his subjective desire that *this* shopowner Ezra Cohen might not, in fact, be Mirah's brother. To reflect that "There might be a hundred Ezra Cohens" is implicitly to recognize that the capaciousness of the statistical distribution might in fact serve as a kind of reassurance. If only imagined broadly enough, it seems to say, that distribution might also encompass desire, might serve as a kind of proxy for agency: With enough Ezra Cohens, Daniel can reasonably envision that there might be one Ezra Cohen who lies far from the average, someone "rare" like Mirah. The novel dwells on the distinction between the exception and the average here, as it considers where to place him in that imagined distribution. At first it positions this Ezra as an outlier, at least nominally, calling him a "most unpoetic Jew," but it soon enforces his commonness, his troubling "vulgarity of soul."[138] And the novel ultimately affirms Daniel's desire for that exceptional Jew. When he finally meets the right Ezra Cohen, he describes him as "certainly something out of the common way."[139] If the novel does not exactly endorse the idea that the uncertain power of wishing might conjure the longed-for exceptional outcome into existence, it does suggest that wishing can exercise the probabilistic faculties, pressing them even beyond the limits of prejudices and cultural assumptions.

But *Deronda* later revives and entertains the notion that wishing might have the power to shape outcomes, especially those that lie beyond the average. The narrator elsewhere disavows the idea that characters' wishes might be able to shape the future, and here the narrator confides, "I confess, he particularly desired that Ezra Cohen should not keep a shop. Wishes are held to be ominous, according to which belief the order of the world is so arranged that if you have an impious objection to a squint, your offspring is the more likely to be born with one," an effect the narrator describes as consistent with a "desponding view of probability."[140] Even if the narrator doesn't share that "desponding view," neither does her satirical intervention provide reassurance about any positive alignment between wishes and outcomes. But in the section entitled "Revelations," whose title aptly hints at the truths both religious and secular disclosed therein, the novel gives more serious attention to the power of wishes. Specifically, as Daniel contemplates Ezra's surprising insistence that he is destined to serve as Ezra's own "executive self," to fulfill his spiritual desires, he considers the shape and limits of belief, in the form of Ezra's highly personal wish as well as of religious faith more generally.[141] Having not yet discovered his Jewish parentage, Daniel inhabits Sir Hugo's secular skepticism as though it were his own, deeming Ezra's apparent fanaticism something "exceptional in its form" yet nonetheless "not rare."[142] Such faith, in other words, might occur at the outer regions of a population distribution, a kind of standard deviation within the realm of possibility.[143] Yet those deviations have also been the home to greatness, Daniel admits, where men like Copernicus, Galileo, and James Watt, in remaining "immovably convinced in the face of hissing incredulity," might be accused of an enthusiasm resembling prophetic fervor more than scientific detachment.[144]

Does Ezra's wish have a "spiritual force . . . a determining effect on a white-handed gentleman" like himself, the book asks—does it, in effect, have the power to make Daniel Jewish? Such passion, he reasons, might not be so distinct from "strictly-measuring science," whose "forecasting ardour . . . feels the agitations of discovery beforehand, and has a faith in its preconception that surmounts many failures of experiment."[145] The inclinations of religion might be driven forward by belief, but so too are the operations of scientific research. Moreover, Ezra is not alone in his speculative fanaticism, as Daniel acknowledges that Ezra's wish competes with his own long-held belief (what he, borrowing scientific language again, terms a "hypothesis") transformed into near assertion, that he is Sir Hugo's biological son.[146]

The questions raised in these scenes anticipate those that emerge for Gwendolen as well. When she speculates about her possible marriage to Grandcourt, the narrator tells us that she thinks of him as "a handsome lizard of a hitherto unknown species. . . . But Gwendolen knew hardly any thing about lizards, and ignorance gives one a large range of probabilities."[147] The conclusions she ultimately draws are wrong ones, as both the narrator and the eventualities of her own plot make clear. Yet the state of not knowing and the probabilistic stance it produces are not in themselves to be faulted but rather, the novel suggests, Gwendolen's inexperience, which leads her to allow her own desires to play too great a role in delineating that "range of probabilities."

But as the novel advances toward one of the climactic moments in her plot, we see that her probabilistic faculties have sharpened. Several chapters before Grandcourt's drowning, Lush presses Grandcourt's will upon her, revealing that, in anticipating the possibility of his own death, he has prepared for a range of outcomes. And when she contemplates her own unhappiness a few pages later, his methodical weighing of likelihoods, including that of his own mortality, appears to have migrated into her thoughts as well:

> What possible release could there be for her from this hated vantage-ground, which yet she dared not quit, any more than if fire had been raining outside it? What release, but death? Not her own death. Gwendolen was not a woman who could easily think of her own death as a near reality, or front for herself the dark entrance on the untried and invisible. It seemed more possible that Grandcourt should die:—and yet not likely.[148]

Gwendolen marks the increments carefully in this exercise, noting that her own death seems less "possible" than Grandcourt's, but even so his is "not likely." And similarly, just before Grandcourt drowns, the narrator tells us that "her own wishes . . . were taking shapes possible and impossible, like a cloud," language that is repeated a few pages later when Daniel learns that an accident has occurred but does not know how or to whom: "the strokes of the oars as he watched them were divided by swift visions of events, possible and impossible, which might have brought about this issue."[149]

When Grandcourt's death does come, it lands within the range of possibility she had generated. The language surrounding that sudden death maintains its probabilistic stance, in a convergence of subjective and objective assessments of likelihood—a kind of ethical meditation on the same questions Maxwell posed. Daniel deems it "an accident," the official statutory finding as well.[150] But in her anguished, "wandering confession" to Daniel, Gwendolen says that "I had cruel wishes—I fancied impossible ways of—I did not want to die myself; I was afraid of our being drowned together. . . . I knew no way of killing him there, but I did, I did kill him in my thoughts."[151] To be sure, readers are not to confuse wishful thinking for action. Throughout her fiction, as Debra Gettelman points out, Eliot is consistent in refuting the possibility of "wishfulfillment," and these scenes clearly reflect what we are meant to see as no more than a "fantasy of agency"; moreover, Beer explains, Eliot's last novel was especially interested in showing how "lateral wishes and possibilities" might happen to align with a "[d]ysteleological series of events."[152] But that "fantasy" verges on something more, for in exploring the guilt that even uncaused events can inspire, her explanation invites a set of reflections very similar to those presented by Maxwell's experiment.

What are the limits of statistical possibility? Here the novel presses beyond its gesture at the capaciousness of distributions, which might encompass both average and "rare" Ezra Cohens, and asks how an understanding of probabilities might strain against our own ostensibly rational assessments when we encounter a state that—almost *because* it aligns with desire—lies outside the realm of the subjectively likely, a "tumblerful of water" recovered from the ocean or a cruel husband drowned? Can we imagine a situation where some unnamed force that lies between the empirically demonstrable poles of absolute randomness and work, between entropy and order—a "fantasy of agency," a wish—produces that unlikely result? Maxwell's rescripting of the second law of thermodynamics itself supposes this "fantasy of agency," where a doorkeeper sorts molecules without doing any work, and one can almost sense in Maxwell's description of the tumblerful of water a desire to see that most unlikely possibility realized. *Deronda* had earlier dismissed this mode of thinking in its opening pages, when Gwendolen, hopeful for a win at the roulette table, speculates, "was it not possible? . . . With ten louis at her disposal and a return of her former luck, which seemed probable," and there the novel demonstrates what comes of counting on "agreeable consequences."[153] Still, when Grandcourt drowns, the novel asks both character and readers to reevaluate. Like Maxwell's experiment, this episode invites contemplation of the circumstances under which the imagination might produce an unlikely outcome without having performed the "work" to achieve it, as it also probes the ethical dimensions of thought or desire as a form of agency. Indeed, Gwendolen seems almost as horrified by the possibility of her own unlikely agency as by the drowning itself. Should she and we read the unlikeliness of the outcome as a ratification of that agency? Or is the fiction of agency irrelevant—as Maxwell contended, the doorkeeper might as easily be an inanimate valve—such that the unlikely, wished-for outcome and statistical possibility might align without any causal force?

George Levine reads Daniel's ruminations in "Revelations" about how "seriously" to regard "an epistemology that depends upon wish and desire" as a reflection on the role of hypothesis and speculation in scientific inquiry.[154] But I suggest that, like Gwendolen's question about Grandcourt's death, what prompts those deliberations—Ezra's wish—poses another kind of epistemological question. Both scenes press into the far reaches of the statistical distribution, where we are invited to consider whether the act of wishing can conjure the exceptional, unlikely outcome into existence, or whether such convergences of wish and outcome are no more than mere coincidence. The answer to this question and many others—about Gwendolen, about Daniel—with which the novel leaves us lies beyond empirical determinations.

In his 1850 letter to Campbell, Maxwell wrote,

> They say that Understanding ought to work by the rules of . . . Logic; but the actual science of Logic is conversant at present only with things either certain, impossible, or *entirely* doubtful, none of which (fortunately) we have to reason on. Therefore the true Logic for this world is the Calculus of Probabilities.[155]

His assertion anticipates the new epistemological model he would shape in the years to come, in which "understanding" is based not in what is "certain" or "impossible" but inhabits the realm of possibility. As his and Eliot's writings amply demonstrate, while the possible might not be empirically determinable, it lends itself to statistical evaluation, to experimentation, and to narration. By focusing on this space of potential rather than of resolution, these modes of representation offer searching meditations on the relationship between subjective assessments of likelihood and statistical probabilities, and between the agency of wishing and the distributions of chance.

The Pleasures of Undetermined Futures

MY FATHER, a professor of biostatistics and an expert in head injury outcomes at the Medical College of Virginia, liked to "stop by" the intensive care unit on the way back from lunch. As a child, I was doubtful, to say the least, about the pleasures to be had in such a morbid setting, especially when other parents seemed content to pass their time glancing through newspaper headlines or browsing the aisles of a store. I realize now that he might have wanted to check on a patient's recovery from a recent surgery or to consider how a new drug regimen was affecting care, but even so, these visits, unlike his professional evaluations of the statistically significant patterns legible in clinical data, were not necessary elements of his research. Looking back, my sense is that they were simply his preferred way of spending a spare moment. My father didn't particularly enjoy reading novels, but over the course of his intermittent visits, the spaces of the ICU must have conveyed their own stories to him. Full of suspense and anticipation, sudden plot twists, and foregone conclusions, he probably found in them pleasures approximating those on offer in the pages of fiction.

Perhaps this upbringing gave me a heightened awareness not only of the ways in which the contours and outcomes of our lives are shaped by contingency (as indeed insurance advertisements continue to emphasize), but also of the ways in which we willingly embrace it. Most of us would probably avoid unnecessary visits to actual hospital bedsides, but readers of Victorian novels are familiar with the frequency with which those works usher us into sickrooms and to bedsides, where we might perceive, mirrored in ailing characters and the bevvies of watchful relatives who surround them, our own states of anticipation and suspension. Where some who gathered at those fictional deathbeds were drawn by a sense of sympathy and care for the dying, others, like those who assembled outside Miss Havisham's door in *Great Expectations* or who called on the ailing Peter Featherstone in *Middlemarch*, did so out of a sense of self-interest, hoping that they might be rewarded with an inheritance. But these spaces of anticipated (though, in many cases, not at all imminent) demise also provided the backdrop for more mundane emotions and activity, for gossip, bickering, and flirtation, as well as for the lesser contingencies of characters' lives: a chance meeting, a card game. They were, in effect, the characters' way of spending a spare moment, and they serve as reminders that a casual aware-ness of the contingencies of life and death, much like the fact of death itself, was an essential part of the fabric of Victorian existence.

As those temporally extended contingencies played in the backgrounds of their and our reading experience, sometimes over a months-long course of chap-ters and installments, others—such as those related to romance, money, and familial tensions—unfolded in the foreground. Contingency might be an essen-tial element of any kind of story, but in nineteenth-century fiction, its presence thickened readerly engagement with otherwise familiar plots. Not far into Trol-lope's *Barchester Towers*, its narrator effectively gives away the ending by stating, "It is not destined that Eleanor shall marry Mr Slope or Bertie Stanhope," though he insists, in spite of what he has divulged, that "the story shall have lost none of its interest" for readers.[1] Carolyn Dever interprets this passage as relevant to the "*micropolitics*" of a "post-1848" landscape and of its readers' awareness of the potential for social change.[2] Yet as the preceding chapters have shown, Trollope's readers would have had a longer and broader experience maintaining the kind of "interest" his narrator expected of readers. Indeed, like those who purchased Spooner's protean views of avalanches and fires, they would have been familiar with the condition of suspending foreknowledge, even if only for a moment, and of engaging with contingency in the shadow of that "destined" outcome.

For knowing where the determinations of history or fiction would eventu-ally lead did not, in fact, extinguish pleasure, but heightened it. By creating a

space outside the forward momentum of plot, such moments allowed readers to invest in the potentialities of undetermined futures—to imagine that
Eleanor might choose Mr. Slope after all, or to envision the Jacobites not yet
defeated or the continent of Europe taking an alternate shape. Like children at
their board games with their journey's end laid before them, readers took pleasure in inhabiting the expanded narrative spaces the play of contingency made
available, revisiting (and sometimes even reversing) the causal and temporal
trajectories of plot. For nineteenth-century Britons might have devised multiple
practices and technologies for managing uncertainty, such as life insurance,
meteorological forecasts, and the kinds of statistical modeling my father would
use to evaluate medical treatments, all of these contributing to the semblance
of certainty and control with which their era has long been associated.[3] But at
the same time, as the works I have discussed show, they were drawn to vertigi-
nous experiences of uncertainty and irresolution. As though the contingencies
of their own lives were not enough, Victorians piled in alongside the virtual
deathbeds Dickens and Eliot provided, thronged to the Royal Zoological Gardens at Surrey where every "Monday, Tuesday, Wednesday, and Thursday"
they might witness the "ERUPTION of VESUVIUS, and DESTRUCTION
of HERCULANEUM and POMPEII" enacted before them,[4] and immersed
themselves in other scenes of contingency, replaying fires, floods, and battles
many times over in their leisure hours at home.

The Victorians might have multiplied forms of knowledge, as Foucault and
scholars influenced by him have cogently argued, but knowledge was not (and
is not) coterminous with certainty or closure. To imagine that it ever could
be, he might have said, is to understand it in a willfully impoverished way. Indeed, the period's scientific and narrative innovations, from Lyell's geological
history and Maxwell's thermodynamics, to Eliot's psychological realism and
nineteenth-century geographical games, all revealed through moments of contingency the many potentialities and alternate routings available in the worlds
of science, literature, and play. By experimenting with multiple, contingent, and
undetermined futures, they enriched ways of seeing and knowing, texturing
those experiences with ever-greater complexity for their readers.

Notes

Introduction

1. "Popular Illustrations," 5. The example might have been inspired by one of Hume's footnotes: "Mr. Locke divides all arguments into demonstrative and probable. In this view, we must say, that it is only probable all men must die, or that the sun will rise to-morrow" (Hume, *Enquiry*, 46). For Hume, these examples illustrate the principle by which near certainties might come to be regarded as natural laws—when, as George tells us, probability takes an event "beyond the shadow of a doubt"; see George, *Everlasting Check*, 6–7. By contrast, the *Saturday Magazine* article invites readers to consider apparent exceptions to natural law.

2. Dickens, *Bleak House*, 989. Emphasis in original. Darwin, *Origin of Species*, 318, 325, 342.

3. Darwin, "Darwin's Notebooks," 142.

4. Babbage, *Passages*, 350.

5. Implicit in this framing of contingency as mechanism or technology is what Ketabgian calls a "technocultural approach," which acknowledges the ways that machines (and a language and epistemology associated with machinery) were a central part of Victorian subjectivity, leisure activities, and literature. Ketabgian, *Lives of Machines*, 6.

6. Dickens, *Bleak House*, 989.

7. I borrow this helpfully expansive account of narrative from recent narratological work that encompasses non-prose genres and media, such as video games and computer programs. See, for example, Ryan, "Toward a Definition."

8. Grishakova, "Narrative Causality," 127. See also Richardson, *Unlikely Stories*.

9. Beer, *Darwin's Plots*, 5. Emphasis in original.

10. Daston, "Historical Epistemology," 282–289; Poovey, *Making a Social Body*, 2–3; C. Levine, *Forms*, 7.

11. Doane, *Emergence of Cinematic Time*, 11.

12. There is an impressive literature on nineteenth-century risk management across multiple disciplines. Freedgood, *Victorian Writing*, and P. Fyfe, *By Accident*, examine the literary and cultural history of accident and risk in Victorian Britain; Hacking, *Taming of Chance*, and Daston *Classical Probability*, survey transforming conceptions of probability and risk in the broader contexts of Continental science and culture; Ewald, "Insurance and Risk," and Clark, "Embracing Fatality," consider assessments of risk with relation to the history of life insurance.

13. Luhmann, *Observations on Modernity*, 45, 44. Liu, situating it in literary critical terms, grants it a yet narrower scope: "[C]ontingency is a philosophy of compromise between determination and random access" (*Local Transcendence*, 261). In contemporary general usage, the term has come to serve as a synonym for randomness, accident, or a state of precarity.

14. Rescher, *Conditionals*, 1, 76.

15. Roese and Olson, "Counterfactual Thinking," 5, 1.

16. S. Gould, *Structure of Evolutionary Theory*, 1340.

17. Kern, *Cultural History*, 13.

18. Ibid., 11, 6. Richardson, *Unlikely Stories*, 21, 29. Richardson nonetheless acknowledges that eighteenth- and nineteenth-century writers took an interest in the operations of chance. A similar dichotomy between nineteenth- and twentieth-century writings appears in Monk, *Standard Deviations*, and Vargish, *Providential Aesthetic*.

19. Doane, *Emergence of Cinematic Time*, 16, 18.

20. P. Fyfe, *By Accident*, 23.

21. Gallagher, *Telling It*, 26–43.

22. G. Levine, *Darwin and the Novelists*, 97; Tondre, *Physics of Possibility*.

23. See Gallagher, "Formalism of Military History"; Gettelman, "That Imagined 'Otherwise'"; A. Miller, "Lives Unled"; I thank Debra Gettelman for sharing the full text of her conference paper with me.

24. Gallagher, *Telling It*, 4; see also 17–18; and Luhmann, *Observations on Modernity*, 44, 46. Whereas Luhmann identifies a clearer break between these religious questions about divine prerogative and an eighteenth- and nineteenth-century philosophical and scientific tradition, Gallagher frames those secular investigations as an extension of theological ones.

25. Leibniz, *Theodicy*, 127, 128.

26. In general, the *Magazine* assumed a progressive attitude toward education and

the sciences; in its inaugural issue in 1832, it promised to deliver the most advanced of findings, to attend to "the improvements of modern times," the "wonderful things of Natural History," and the "greatest of human inventions." "Introduction," 1.

27. Whewell, ["When any one"], 228.

28. Lightman, *Origins of Agnosticism*, 3. Elsewhere Lightman explains that a historical focus on select figures like Darwin and T. H. Huxley has hindered our appreciation for the wide range of ways in which religious belief overlapped with scientific work in the nineteenth century; see Lightman, *Evolutionary Naturalism*.

29. These publications cultivated a readership for whom Christian belief was consistent with a desire for scientific knowledge. For a more extended discussion of how such works brought scientific findings into alignment with religious belief, see Lightman, *Victorian Popularizers*; Secord, *Victorian Sensation*; and Topham, "Biology," "Beyond the Common Context" and "Science."

30. Zemka, *Time*, 32; Matz, *Modernist Time Ecology*, 3–16.

31. Canales, *Tenth of a Second*, x.

32. Beer, *Darwin's Plots*, 5. As narratologists have noted, the two defining principles of narrative are temporality and causality. See Genette, *Narrative Discourse* for a foundational articulation of these principles. For more recent elaborations of this point, see Grishakova, "Narrative Causality" and Kafalenos, *Narrative Causalities*.

33. Stern, "Time Passes," 238.

34. Doane, *Emergence of Cinematic Time*, 6.

35. As economist Daniel Kahneman suggests, investigations into causality are necessarily historical in nature: "the perception of causality is a backward-looking process: It is initiated by the occurrence of an event (the consequence), which triggers a search for possible causes among recent occurrences." Kahneman, "Varieties," 376.

36. There is an extensive and excellent literature on the period's popular literacy, from works focusing on the technological dimensions of this revolution, to studies of the experiential elements of mass visual and textual culture. See, for example, Altick, *English Common Reader*; Brantlinger, *Reading Lesson*; A. Fyfe, *Steam-Powered Knowledge*; Secord, *Victorian Sensation*. Two works that analyze the period's rich visual culture, especially in the urban setting, are Daly, *Demographic Imagination*, and Nead, *Victorian Babylon*.

Chapter 1

1. Corporation of the London Assurance, *Agent's Instructions* (1843), 24.

2. For more extended treatments of the rise of the insurance industry, see Alborn, *Regulated Lives*, and Daston, *Classical Probability*, ch. 3.

3. Pocock, *Familiar Explanation*, 96; Alborn, *Regulated Lives*, 4.

4. Campbell-Kelly, "Charles Babbage," 5.

5. Campbell-Kelly provides a more extensive account of the marketplace for insurance companies during this period (though his account of the Protector's fate is largely circumstantial); "Charles Babbage," 8–9. Alborn mentions that a "Protector" Life Assurance Company was acquired by the Eagle in 1826; *Regulated Lives*, 60.

6. Babbage, *Passages*, 357–358.

7. "Review of *Assurance of Lives*," 482; [John Barrow], "Review of *Assurance of Lives*," 1.

8. Campbell-Kelly, "Charles Babbage," 5.

9. See, for example, Bromley, "Charles Babbage's Analytical Engine"; Bromley, "Evolution"; Collins, *Little Engines*, 279; Swade, "Construction."

10. G. Miller, "Charles Babbage"; Romano, "Economic Ideas"; Schaffer, "Babbage's Intelligence." See also Swade, "'It Will Not Slice'" and Uglow, "Introduction: 'Possibility'" for two other examples of works that consider the historical influences behind Babbage's inventions.

11. Campbell-Kelly, "Charles Babbage," 6.

12. Poovey, *History*, 308–309.

13. "Popular Illustrations," 5, 6.

14. In this sense, *Assurance of Lives* seemed uncertain about its intended readership, sometimes addressing industry insiders and other times potential consumers; this may have contributed to its lackluster critical and popular reception.

15. Babbage, *Assurance of Lives*, xiii.

16. Ibid., 2.

17. Babbage, *Assurance of Lives*, 4–5, 10.

18. Ibid., 15.

19. Ibid., 16.

20. A number of scholars have examined the emergence of the statistical sciences during this period, and their works provide an excellent overview of the mathematical, social, and political implications of the "law of large numbers." See Cullen, *Statistical Movement*; Hacking, *Taming of Chance*; Porter, *Rise of Statistical Thinking*.

21. Babbage, *Assurance of Lives*, 8.

22. Babbage, "Rates," 19.

23. Babbage, *Assurance of Lives*, xvi. For his discussion of variables and equations, see Appendix III, 91–92, in that same volume.

24. Clark, "Embracing Fatality"; Daston, *Classical Probability*, 163–169.

25. Daston, *Classical Probability*, 165–166.

26. Ibid., 167, 171.

27. Ibid.

28. Francis, *Annals*, 265, 263.

29. On some of the ways in which this sense of risk extended to everyday life during the nineteenth century, see Choi, "Writing the Victorian City"; Freedgood, *Victorian Writing*; and P. Fyfe, *By Accident*.

30. Daston, *Classical Probability*, 173.

31. Babbage, *Assurance of Lives*, 5.

32. Alfred Life Assurance Company, 6; Aegis Life Assurance Company, 15.

33. The Colonial Life Assurance Company, n. p.

34. Minerva Life Assurance, n. p.

35. The Edinburgh Life Assurance Company, *Prospectus and Rates*, n. p. By the 1860s companies began to market policies to a wider audience. *The People's Guide to Life Insurance* declared that insurance was "important to all classes" and sought to cultivate a working-class clientele; Grant, *People's Guide*. The Colonial Life Assurance and the India & London Life Assurance companies looked to insure Britons in the colonies; by the end of the century, companies such as Oriental Life, and London and Lancashire Life Assurance were advertising policies available for "Native Gentlemen." Oriental Life Company, 202; London and Lancashire, 216.

36. The concept of generalizable risk was also common in discussions of public health in the 1830s and 40s; see Choi, "Writing the Victorian City."

37. Prudential Insurance, n. p.

38. Babbage, *Assurance of Lives*, 21–22. As Babbage notes, there were also provisions put in place to prevent individuals from insuring the lives of others as a kind of wager, as they might have done in the eighteenth century; ibid., 86.

39. "Review of *Assurance of Lives*," 502. Emphasis in original.

40. Sharman, "Have You Insured," 5.

41. Spurr, "Contested Identity." A literary illustration of this principle occurs in *Great Expectations*, where both Herbert Pocket and Pip work temporarily as clerks before ascending to higher positions.

42. Sharman, "Have You Insured," 5.

43. Elliott, *Wax-Taper*, 2.

44. *Second Chapter*, n. p.

45. Ewald, "Insurance and Risk," 207.

46. *The Oxford English Dictionary* dates an early example of the use of "provident" with specifically financial connotations to 1802, around the time when life insurance companies were growing in popularity. *Oxford English Dictionary*, online edition, "provident," meaning 1b.

47. Prudential Mutual Assurance, n. p.

48. Edinburgh Life Assurance, cover.

49. Ewald, "Insurance and Risk," 207.

50. Catholic, Law, and General, 2.

51. The United Mutual Life Assurance Society and the Sun Fire and Life Offices also offered their own versions of decorative and useful calendars to potential clients.

52. Corporation of the London Assurance, *Agent's Instructions* (1846), n. p.; Corporation of the London Assurance, *Agent's Instructions* (1853), 54, 59, 60.

53. Legal and Commercial Life Assurance; Metropolitan Counties and General, 1.

54. Albert Life Assurance, 2.

55. Athenaeum Life Assurance, 4.

56. Catholic, Law, and General, 2. Emphasis in original.

57. Cooter and Luckin, "Accidents."

58. Babbage, *Assurance of Lives*, 3.

59. Railway Passengers' Assurance, n. p.

60. Metropolitan Counties and General, n. p.

61. Lardner, "Babbage's Calculating Engine," 132–139.

62. Sussman, *Victorian Technology*, 40–41. See also 41–43 for an explanation of the nature of the mechanism and operation of the Difference Engine.

63. Babbage, "Letter to Sir Humphry Davy," 9.

64. This formula, also known as a generator of prime numbers, was one that Babbage himself used as an example. Babbage, "Letter to Sir Humphry Davy," 9.

65. Baily, "Mr Babbage's New Machine," 45.

66. Babbage, "On the Theoretical Principles," 42.

67. Baily, "Mr Babbage's New Machine," 58.

68. Babbage, "On the Theoretical Principles," 42–43.

69. This view was consistent with the uniformitarianism that dominated early Victorian natural history—the theory that a single, consistent law could explain the whole of the natural world. See Ashworth, "Memory," 651; and Bullock, "Charles Babbage," 21–25.

70. Lardner, "Babbage's Calculating Engine," 124, 125.

71. [Babbage], "Addition," 83.

72. Schaffer sees this dispute as symptomatic of Babbage's desire to distinguish— both in his engines but also in factory labor—between mechanical action and intellectual endeavor, while Clement, a highly skilled engineer, claimed for himself some measure of ownership over the construction of the engine ("Babbage's Intelligence," 213–216).

73. Lovelace, "Sketch," 97.

74. Babbage, "Statement," 6. As Collins notes, Babbage's letter was careful not to suggest that the Analytical Engine had rendered the Difference Engine superfluous, but by 1836 he had admitted as much; Collins, *Little Engines*, 167.

75. Campbell-Kelly, "Introduction to *Passages*," 24.

76. Because many of his records are fragmentary and changed over time, our

sense of the Analytical Engine's mechanism and capabilities is necessarily incomplete. Collins writes, "it is doubtful that anyone other than Babbage has ever understood it fully," and he suggests that Babbage may never have intended to construct a working machine; Collins, *Little Engines*, 140, 279. The project has, however, been revived by twenty-first-century scientists and historians who, using Babbage's designs, are making plans to build the Analytical Engine; see Fildes, "Campaign Builds."

77. As Collins observes, Babbage had contacted scholars in Italy and Germany (including Alexander von Humboldt) to enlist support for his new project—and probably to pressure the English government into continuing funding for his research; Collins, *Little Engines*, 176.

78. There has been considerable controversy among historians and Babbage's biographers over Lovelace's role in the composition of "Sketch" and the extent to which she wrote independently.

79. Lovelace, "Sketch," 133. In his discussion of the Analytical Engine as what he calls a "full thinking machine," Sussman emphasizes its capacity for "memory," both its ability to store functions on cards and its ability to retain the results of one calculation while performing another; Sussman, *Victorian Technology*, 44, 45.

80. Collins, *Little Engines*, 138.

81. Lovelace, "Sketch," 157.

82. Ibid., 121. Emphasis in original.

83. Ibid.

84. The difference between the Difference and Analytical Engines thus also aligns with the distinction that Daston suggests emerges around this time, between work and intelligence in calculation ("Enlightenment Calculations"). Locating this distinction within the class politics of the early nineteenth century, Schaffer contends that Babbage's account of the "intelligence" of systems constitutes an assertion of social privilege over the working bodies—the engineers, calculators, machinists, and factor workers—whose labor took place within them.

85. Topham, "Science," 398.

86. The eight treatises were themselves uneven in their adherence to an earlier tradition of natural theology, however. See Topham, "Biology," especially 96–100, for an extended discussion of how each author's approach differed from Paley's *Natural Theology* as well as from the others' contributions.

87. At the same time, the cost of the volumes largely limited its readership to the wealthier classes. One exception was Whewell's 1834 *Astronomy and General Physics*, which appeared in numerous editions and by 1837 had been reissued in a cheaper version as well; Topham, "Science," 400.

88. See Topham, "Science," 397–398.

89. Campbell-Kelly reviews these opinions in his "Introduction to *Passages*," 25. See also Campbell-Kelly, "Introduction to *The Ninth Bridgewater Treatise*," 5.

90. Swade, "Charles Babbage"; Liu, *Local Transcendence*, 241–248.

91. Whewell, *Astronomy*. After the publication of Babbage's *Ninth*, Whewell reached out to Babbage, calling him a "fellow-labourer" in a friendly letter, though it seems that the feeling was not reciprocal; see Campbell-Kelly, "Introduction to *The Ninth Bridgewater Treatise*," 6.

92. Babbage, *Ninth Bridgewater Treatise*, vii.

93. See Cannon, "Problem of Miracles," 24–26, and Topham, "Biology," 109–111, for a discussion of some of the ways in which Babbage's claims overlapped with and differed from those of his contemporaries.

94. Topham, "Biology," 108.

95. Ketabgian describes the machine as a "prosthesis" that, according to Babbage, allowed humans to access "something close to a divine vision." Ketabgian, "Prosthetic Divinity," 35.

96. Babbage, *Ninth Bridgewater Treatise*, 9–10, 16.

97. Ibid., 1; W. Buckland, *Geology*, 586.

98. Babbage, *Ninth Bridgewater Treatise*, 29.

99. Ibid., 30. Emphasis in original. As Babbage notes in the appendix, his mathematical examples are "drawn from the powers of this new engine"; ibid., 68. He had previously demonstrated that the Difference Engine could be made to display a single deviation from an established pattern but not the multiple courses of which the Analytical Engine was capable; Bullock, "Charles Babbage," 23–25; Lardner, "Babbage's Calculating Engine," 167–168.

100. Campbell-Kelly, "Introduction to *Passages*," 25.

101. Babbage, *Ninth Bridgewater Treatise*, 1.

102. Ashworth, "Memory," 636.

103. It was only Robert Chambers who, in his 1843 *Vestiges of the Natural History of Creation*, adopted Babbage's analogy and extended it. See Cannon, "Problem of Miracles."

104. Babbage, *Ninth Bridgewater Treatise*, 10. Emphasis in original.

105. Liu, *Local Transcendence*, 245.

106. This is Campbell-Kelly's translation of "rien ne serait incertain pour elle [l'intelligence de Dieu], et l'avenir, comme le passé, serait present à ses yeux" in the original; Babbage, *Ninth Bridgewater Treatise*, 70–71. Ashworth emphasizes the Laplacean aspect of the Analytical Engine's operations; "Memory," 651–653. Babbage's choice of Laplace was an interesting one, given Laplace's own equivocation on the role of God in the operations of the natural world; see Hahn, *Pierre Simon Laplace*, especially ch. 4 (pp. 48–63).

107. Babbage, *Ninth Bridgewater Treatise*, xiii.

108. Ibid., 59.

109. Ewald, "Insurance and Risk," 198.

110. Babbage, "On the Mathematical Powers," 31.

111. Menabrea's original text: "la machine n'est point un être qui pense, mais un simple automate qui agit suivant les lois qu'on lui a tracées"; Menabrea, "Notions," 67. Lovelace's translation appears in Lovelace, "Sketch," 98.

112. Lovelace, "Sketch," 98. Green, "Was Babbage's Analytical Engine," 35–45, explores these differing assessments of the engine.

113. Lovelace, "Sketch," 98, 101. Among Babbage's efforts in later years was a plan to make the Analytical Engine pay for itself by marketing it as a chess-playing automaton. It would operate precisely by considering the multiple conditions and courses at every move:

1. Is the position of the men . . . consistent with the rules of the game?
2. If so, has Automaton himself already lost the game?
3. If not, then has Automaton won the game?
4. If not, can he win it at the next move? If so, make that move.
5. If not, could his adversary, if he had the move, win the game?
6. If so, Automaton must prevent him if possible.
7. If his adversary cannot win the game at his next move, Automaton must examine whether he can make such a move that, if he were allowed to have two moves in succession, he could at the second move have *two* different ways of winning the game; and each of these cases failing, Automaton must look forward to three or more successive moves.

Babbage, *Passages*, 350; emphasis in original. As Babbage elaborated, "the whole question of making an automaton play any game depended upon the possibility of the machine being able to represent all the myriads of combinations relating to it." Ibid., 351.

114. Babbage, *Assurance of Lives*, 21–22.

115. "Review of *Assurance of Lives*," 502.

116. Ryan, "Toward a Definition," 28–29.

117. Babbage, *Ninth Bridgewater Treatise*, 6.

118. Ibid., 35–39, 84–90. Babbage's interest in the persistence of sound perhaps also anticipates his later preoccupation with street noise; in later life he lodged a number of complaints against street musicians, and a chapter of his *Passages from the Life of a Philosopher* is an extended complaint against such "street nuisances"; *Passages*, 253–271.

119. Babbage, *Ninth Bridgewater Treatise*, 38.

120. Babbage also devoted energy to developing another kind of code, specifically,

a new system of mathematical notation, by which complex functions and relation-ships could be denoted using "underbars" and "overbars," for example. See Grattan-Guinness, "Charles Babbage," 34–48.

121. Babbage, *Ninth Bridgewater Treatise*, 111.

122. Ibid., 113.

123. Campbell-Kelly suggests that Babbage's work on the "Difference Engine Number 2" during this period was motivated by a desire to show the government, which had long since suspended support and funding for the first Difference Engine, that he was a man of his word; see Campbell-Kelly, "Introduction to *Passages*," 29. As noted, he had long since dismissed the Difference Engine as superseded by the Ana-lytical Engine, and his plans for "Number 2" did not include any of the improvements that he had designed for the Analytical Engine.

124. Ibid., 30.

125. Secord, "Scrapbook Science," 176. See also Helfand, *Scrapbooks*; Lutz, "Por-trait of the Writer"; Lynch, "Recycled Paper."

126. Indeed, the only handwritten traces are a few dates, and it is possible that these were added by another hand—perhaps that of a relative or archivist. Babbage, [Scrapbook]. The page references that appear here correspond to the online ver-sion, which seems to include some duplicate pages; the pages in the original text are unnumbered.

127. Carey, *Scrapbook*.

128. Babbage, [Scrapbook,] 8, 26, 34, 9, 11, 10, 140.

129. Ibid., 143, 59, 75, 59, 64, 72, 61.

130. W. Smith, *Advertise*, 127.

131. Babbage, [Scrapbook,] 129, 151.

132. Ibid., 20.

133. Ibid.

134. Ibid., 23.

135. Ibid., 22, 154.

136. Ibid., 151. Clippings taken from the *Times* [London] (27 January 1843): 1b; (5 April 1843): 1f; (16 January 1844): 1f.

137. Babbage, [Scrapbook,] 154.

138. Ibid., 152.

139. Both advertisements from the *Times* [London] (23 June 1845): 1c.

140. Cardinal, "Collecting and Collage-Making," 87, 92.

141. Babbage, *Ninth Bridgewater Treatise*, 36.

142. Babbage, "On the Mathematical Powers," 31.

143. Babbage, *Ninth Bridgewater Treatise*, 30.

144. Ibid., 5–6. Emphasis in original.

145. Bullock, "Charles Babbage," 31.

146. Indeed, this announcement appeared at least six times in the *Times* in June 1845: 16 June, p. 1c; 17 June, p. 1c; 18 June, p. 1c; 19 June, p. 1c; 20 June, p. 1c, and 21 June, p. 1b. Its sequel appeared several days later: 24 June, p. 1b; 25 June, p. 1d; 26 June, p. 1b; 27 June, p. 1d; and 28 June, p. 1b.

147. Babbage, [Scrapbook,] 98.

148. Babbage, *Ninth Bridgewater Treatise*, xiii.

Chapter 2

1. Lyell, *Principles of Geology*, I: 1.

2. Ibid. This analogy and others like it recur throughout *Principles* and serve as one of Lyell's principal modes of argument. See Griffiths's *Age of Analogy* for an extended discussion of the role of analogy more generally in nineteenth-century scientific and literary argument.

3. In this sense, Lyell also anticipates the comparisons between scientific practice and historical writing made mid-century, when historians like Henry Thomas Buckle and Lord Acton debated the place of empiricism, objectivity, and artistry in the writing of history. See Hesketh, *Science of History*, 35–54.

4. J. Smith, *Fact and Feeling*, 92.

5. Quoted in ibid.

6. Lyell, *Principles of Geology*, I: 1.

7. Ibid., I: 2.

8. Heringman attributes Lyell's attention to geological events to his lingering "debt to Plutonism," an older theory that emphasized the role of volcanic activity and lava in the earth's formation; Heringman, *Romantic Rocks*, 8.

9. Gallagher, *Telling It*, 27–43; Gallagher, "What Would Napoleon Do?"

10. Rudwick, *Worlds Before Adam*, 6. Emphasis in original.

11. See Cannon, "Problem of Miracles," for an extended treatment of the place of miracles in these debates over natural history.

12. Buckland offers a helpful and nuanced clarification of the term "uniformitarianism," whose theories did not exclude the possibility of catastrophic occurrences like earthquakes and eruptions. A. Buckland, *Novel Science*, 106–109.

13. A. Buckland, *Novel Science*, 15; Secord, *Visions of Science*, 151.

14. Indeed, in spite of the distinction A. Buckland convincingly asks us to draw between the geological sciences and natural history, this chapter rejoins them, not so much as part of a scientific but rather a narratological lineage.

15. G. Levine, *Darwin and the Novelists*, 85.

16. Rudwick, *Bursting the Limits*, 182–193.

17. Topham, "Biology," 92–94.

18. Paley, *Natural Theology*, 52.

19. Babbage, *Ninth Bridgewater Treatise*, xiii.

20. Paley, *Natural Theology*, 38. As G. Levine explains, for Paley "chance" is an "'appearance' resulting from the ignorance of the observer"; *Darwin and the Novelists*, 30.

21. Paley, *Natural Theology*, 200–201. Emphasis in original. Even so, Paley was careful to explain that "those events which depend upon the will of a free and rational agent," as well as the "exertion" of "moral agents" were not inconsistent with, but rather had their proper place within, the natural order; *Natural Theology*, 266, 270.

22. Paley, *Natural Theology*, 55, 206–207. Similar arguments about the proper relationship of parts to organic anatomical whole also found their way into discussions of novelistic aesthetics; see Dawson, "Literary Megatheriums."

23. Paley, *Natural Theology*, 114.

24. See Topham, "Biology," 96–100, for a more extensive discussion of how the *Bridgewater Treatises* departed from Paley's vision, even as many of them remained under his influence. Topham observes that Babbage's *Ninth Bridgewater Treatise*, by applying Whewell's conception of natural law to the transmutation of species, extended the latter's argument into new terrain; Topham, "Biology," 110–111.

25. See, for example, Whewell's *History of the Inductive Sciences*, book I, ch. 1, and book XVII, chs. 3, 4, and 5. This definition of hypothesis is especially common in the sciences, according to the *Oxford English Dictionary*; see Achinstein, *Particles and Waves*, and J. Smith, *Fact and Feeling*, for a discussion of its significance to nineteenth-century science in particular.

26. Whewell's volume had reached its sixth edition by 1837, and it was the only one of the eight *Bridgewater Treatises* to be issued in a cheaper six-shilling format; see Topham, "Science," 400.

27. Whewell, *Astronomy*, 24.

28. Ibid., 43.

29. Ibid., 144. Whewell's statement is an echo of Hume's contention that "there be no such thing as *Chance* in the world"; Hume, *Enquiry*, 46. Emphasis in original.

30. G. Levine, *Darwin and the Novelists*, 21, 24–25.

31. Lightman, *Origins of Agnosticism*, 153.

32. Vargish, *Providential Aesthetic*, 6.

33. G. Levine, *Darwin and the Novelists*, 19; Doane, *Emergence of Cinematic Time*, 16–18.

34. Doane, *Emergence of Cinematic Time*, 10.

35. Dannenberg, *Coincidence and Counterfactuality*, 109, 110. Emphasis in original.

36. Ibid., 137.

37. Ibid., 200. Emphasis in original.

38. Gallagher, "What Would Napoleon Do?" 323.

39. Gettelman, "That Imagined 'Otherwise'"; A. Miller, "Lives Unled."

40. Quoted in the entry for Lyell in the *Dictionary of National Biography*; see Rudwick, "Lyell."

41. Rudwick, *Bursting the Limits*, 237, 234.

42. Lyell, *Principles of Geology*, I. 15.

43. Secord, "Introduction," xiv. See also Klaver's discussion of the ways in which the public reception of earlier geological histories informed Lyell's handling of theological concerns in *Principles*; Klaver, *Geology*, 32–36, 41.

44. Rudwick, *Worlds Before Adam*, 351.

45. Secord, "Introduction," xiv.

46. O'Connor, *Earth on Show*, 306–315.

47. Daly, *Demographic Imagination*, 17–45; Rudwick, *Bursting the Limits*, 186–193.

48. Rudwick, *Bursting the Limits*, 193.

49. J. Smith, *Fact and Feeling*, 97. As Buckland observes, Lyell, "like his colleagues, was suspicious, if not of theorizing in general, then at least of its liability to excess"; A. Buckland, *Novel Science*, 25.

50. Secord, "Introduction," xxxv.

51. O'Connor, *Earth on Show*, 172.

52. W. Buckland, *Geology and Mineralogy*, 7–8.

53. O'Connor, *Earth on Show*, 87.

54. Ibid., 175–176, 181; Zimmerman, *Excavating Victorians*, 28, 41–42.

55. Zimmerman, *Excavating Victorians*, 42.

56. Ibid., 41–42; Klaver, *Geology*, 45.

57. Lyell, *Principles of Geology*, I: 140, I: 146, III: 384, III: 385.

58. Ibid., I: 139–140. Emphasis in original.

59. Ibid., I: 85.

60. A. Buckland, *Novel Science*, 129; Secord, "Introduction," xviii.

61. A. Buckland, *Novel Science*, 110. She develops this argument at greater length in 95–130.

62. Rudwick, *Worlds Before Adam*, 82; Secord, "Introduction," xxix.

63. Lyell, *Principles of Geology*, I: 35.

64. See A. Buckland, *Novel Science*, 109.

65. W. Buckland, *Reliquiae Diluvianae*, 193.

66. Ibid., 224, 228. For a more extended treatment of his argument, see Rudwick, *Bursting the Limits*, 612–615.

67. Lyell, *Principles of Geology*, I, chs. 2, 3, 4, and 11.

68. A. Buckland, *Novel Science*, 113.

69. J. Smith, *Fact and Feeling*, 97–98.

70. W. Buckland, *Reliquiae Diluvianae*, 78.

71. Lyell, *Principles of Geology*, III: 274.

72. Ibid., I: 89.

73. Ibid., I: 182.

74. J. Smith, *Fact and Feeling*, 102.

75. Lyell, *Principles of Geology*, I: 116–117.

76. O'Connor cites these lines as examples of Lyell's authoritative rhetoric throughout; O'Connor, *Earth on Show*, 177, 248. Klaver, too, mentions Lyell's adoption of "the phraseology of Genesis"; Klaver, *Geology*, 45.

77. Lyell, *Principles of Geology*, II: 130.

78. Secord, "Introduction," xviii.

79. Lyell, *Principles of Geology*, I: 2.

80. Thackeray, *Vanity Fair*, 328.

81. Gallagher, "What Would Napoleon Do?" 322.

82. Gallagher, *Telling It*, 10–14.

83. Lyell, *Principles of Geology*, I: 374–375.

84. Gallagher, "What Would Napoleon Do?" 321.

85. Quoted by Zimmerman, who discusses Huxley's use of this term in his 1880 "On the Method of Zadig"; Zimmerman, *Excavating Victorians*, 11.

86. Eliot, *Adam Bede*, 221. Though the narrator's gender is a matter of debate, a number of critics have convincingly argued for identifying this voice as male. Kreisel, "Incognito"; Sedgwick, *Between Men*, 140.

87. Discussing the historicity of *Adam Bede* at some length, Sedgwick argues that Hetty's transfer from Arthur to Adam signifies the political shift from a land-based aristocracy to a society of skilled workers and professionals. Sedgwick, *Between Men*, 138–146.

88. Bowen contests Lukács's exclusion of Eliot's novels, noting that they are "saturated in historical understanding and a sense of period." Bowen, "Historical Novel," 247.

89. Trumpener, *Bardic Nationalism*, 151.

90. Duncan, "Authenticity Effects," 109.

91. Steedman, *Dust*, 90–91.

92. Eliot, *Adam Bede*, 476.

93. On the ways in which Eliot drew on popular accounts of seduction and infanticide in the period's journalism and literature in shaping Hetty Sorrel's narrative, see Jones, "Usual Sad Catastrophe," and McDonagh, "Child-Murder Narratives."

94. Duncan, "Authenticity Effects," 109.

95. Indeed, as Li argues, that "communal memory" is already scripted in the "archetypal rituals" described in the novel, in Hayslope's "language of seasonal movement" and "age-old conventions"; Li, *Memory and History*, 30.

96. Eliot's commitment to realism has been the focus of much critical work on *Adam Bede*; see, for example, Adam, "Structure of Realisms"; R. Gould, "*Adam Bede's* Dutch Realism"; and Nord, "George Eliot."

97. Eliot, *Adam Bede*, 223, 221.

98. Ibid., 223.

99. Ibid., 170.

100. Ibid., 170–171.

101. Ibid., 174, 175.

102. Dannenberg, *Coincidence and Counterfactuality*, 67. See also the narrative "maps" Dannenberg generates for Jane Austen's *Persuasion* (68) and *Mansfield Park* (69), for example. Her key literary example, of a character taking one path rather than another, is from Scott's *The Bride of Lammermoor* (71).

103. Eliot, *Adam Bede*, 184.

104. Adam remarks on the novel's flexible temporalities, where the first four chapters depict a single day, while a single paragraph in ch. 36 covers five days. Adam, "Structure of Realisms," 142–143.

105. Eliot, *Adam Bede*, 173.

106. Ibid., 179.

107. Zemka, *Time and the Moment*, 135.

108. Eliot, *Adam Bede*, 181.

109. Trumpener, *Bardic Nationalism*, 150. Gallagher makes a similar point in her analysis of counterfactual histories and fictions; *Telling It*, 7–14.

110. Eliot, *Adam Bede*, 182.

111. Ibid., 174.

112. Beer, *Darwin's Plots*, 151.

113. Gallagher, "What Would Napoleon Do?" 330.

114. Zemka, *Time and the Moment*, 122. Zemka's analysis focuses primarily on the effect of immediacy and historicity conveyed in ch. 47, "The Last Moment," in which Arthur saves Hetty from the gallows.

115. Doane, *Emergence of Cinematic Time*, 23.

116. Wordsworth, "Lines," lines 138, 155–156.

117. Wordsworth, *Prelude*, book XII, line 215.

118. Zemka, *Time and the Moment*, 135–136.

119. Eliot, *Adam Bede*, 335.

120. Ibid., 225.

121. Doane, *Emergence of Cinematic Time*, 11; Dannenberg, *Contingency and Counterfactuality*, 194.

122. Kern, *Cultural History*, 11.

123. Gettelman, "Reading Ahead," 26.

124. Gettelman, "Imagined 'Otherwise.'" Emphasis in original. See also Gettelman, "Reading Ahead," 31.

125. Eliot, *Adam Bede*, 181.

126. Darwin, *Origin of Species*, 125.

127. Darwin had read Paley's *Natural Theology* during his student years at Cambridge; see Topham, "Biology," 94. G. Levine traces some of the ways, in both form and argument, that Darwin's work is indebted to the natural theologians who preceded him. G. Levine, *Darwin and the Novelists*, 27–29.

128. G. Levine, *Darwin and the Novelists*, 90. See also Shuttleworth's account of Darwin's contemporaries, many of whom regarded *Origin* as affirming not the role of chance, but rather the uniformity and order of earlier theories; Shuttleworth, *George Eliot*, 15–16.

129. Darwin, *Origin of Species*, 210, 325, 318, 318–319.

130. Darwin makes an analogous point in his 1838 notebook when he remarks: "It is less wonderful that childs nervous system should build up its body like its parent than that it should be provided with many contingencies how to act.—So with the mind the simplest transmission is direct instinct & afterwards enlarged powers to meet with contingency" [sic]. Here, the predictable laws of inheritance and the expansive potential of contingency function as dynamic counterpoints to each other. Darwin, "Darwin's Notebooks," 142.

131. Allen, "Abyss," 382.

132. Beer, *Darwin's Plots*, 74; Doane, *Emergence of Cinematic Time*, 16.

133. G. Levine, *Darwin and the Novelists*, 85.

134. Dannenberg, *Coincidence and Counterfactuality*, 137.

135. For a fuller account of the ways Darwin acknowledged his debt to Lyell's work, see J. Smith, *Fact and Feeling*, 94–95.

136. Beer, "Reader," n. p.

137. See G. Levine, *Darwin the Writer*, 21–22, for a discussion of this aspect of Darwin's authorly persona.

138. Darwin, *Origin of Species*, 95.

139. Ibid., 377.

140. Ibid., 416.

141. Ibid., 119, 142.

142. Ibid., 128–129.

143. Beer, *Darwin's Plots*, 36.

144. Quoted in ibid., 36.

145. Darwin, *Origin of Species*, 79.

146. Ibid., 316.

147. Ibid., 456.

148. Rudwick, "Minerals, Strata and Fossils," 279.

149. Brink-Roby, "Natural Representation," 251, 254; Brink-Roby focuses here on the diagrams of Darwin's contemporary and fellow naturalist Hugh Edwin Strickland. As she notes, Darwin also seemed to recognize that language, by alluding to other kinds of "affinity" not representable in graphic form, might supply "the diagram's needed third dimension" (256).

150. Ibid., 247; Darwin, *Origin of Species*, 159.

151. Darwin, *Origin of Species*, 162.

152. Gallagher, "What Would Napoleon Do?" 324; see also her discussion of Clausewitz's work in *Telling It*, 39–44.

153. Darwin, *Origin of Species*, 459.

Chapter 3

1. L. Carroll, *Through the Looking-Glass*, 160. For the sake of consistency, I refer to Charles Dodgson throughout this chapter by his pseudonym, Lewis Carroll.

2. Ryan, Foote, and Azaryahu, *Narrating Space*, 103, 110.

3. Kaiser, *World in Play*, 8.

4. See, for example, Ryan, *Possible Worlds*, 38.

5. [advertisement], *Times* [London] (15 May 1839): 8a; [advertisement] *Times* [London] (18 December 1838): 8a; [advertisement], *Times* [London] (3 December 1846): 10e.

6. [advertisement], *Times* [London] (21 December 1847): 10e; [advertisement] *Times* [London] (5 December 1845): 12a; [advertisement], *Times* [London] (23 December 1846): 12e.

7. This history has been capably and comprehensively recounted elsewhere through the tracing of other genres of popular writing and performance. See for example, Altick, *English Common Reader*; Brantlinger, *Reading Lesson*; A. Fyfe, *Steam-Powered Knowledge*; "Steam Reading" in Secord, *Victorian Sensation*.

8. Nadel, "'Mansion of Bliss'"; Norcia, "Playing Empire"; Ray, "Beast in a Box"; S. Carroll, "Romantic Board Games," 155–156; Zimmerman, "Natural History." Helpful historical surveys of the board game appear in Goodfellow, *Collector's Guide*, and Parlett, *Oxford History*.

9. S. Carroll, "'Play You Must,'" 40.

10. The 1822 version was a reissue of an 1810 game with the same design and name.

11. Goodfellow, *Collector's Guide*, 55.

12. Kolb, "Plot Circles," 617.

13. Thrower, *Maps & Civilization*, 125.

14. Cain, "Maps."

15. Hyde, "Panoramas."

16. Indeed, as S. Carroll explains, in a number of such cases publishers reused the

plates they had created for maps to print geographical games, thus gaining two sets of products out of a single plate. S. Carroll, "Romantic Board Games," 153, 158.

17. To judge by their catalogues of publications and advertisements, these were moderately to very successful London-based businesses, with steady rosters of offerings over a period of at least a decade and sometimes longer: Sallis, c. 1850–60; E. Wallis, c. 1810s–40s; Spooner, c. 1830–50s.

18. John Wallis issued a very similar game in 1794, as *Tour Through England and Wales, a New Geographical Pastime*. Some of these retained the moral lessons of their nongeographical counterparts; for an overview of this early genre of geographical games and puzzles, see Dove, "Geographical Board Game."

19. On the publicity given to triangulation in 1783 by William Roy's ordnance maps, see Dorling and Fairbairn, *Mapping*, 97.

20. In this respect, the 1787 *A New Royal Geographical Pastime* also resembles the maps developed by John Adams in the late seventeenth century and marketed well into the middle of the eighteenth century, which displayed distance lines between towns and cities, even in the absence of direct routes linking them. Delano-Smith and Kain, *English Maps*, 162–163. Dove points to the difficulties that would have been encountered in trying to use these games as actual travel maps; Dove, "Geographical Board Game," 7–8; see also S. Carroll, "Romantic Board Games," 160.

21. "Review of *A Physical*," 99; Norcia, "Playing Empire." This emphasis on facts and memorization was much criticized, in this review and in many others; for one contemporaneous with the *New Royal Geographical Pastime*, see "Hints."

22. These examples, however, seem designed for the viewer's general edification, rather than for active play. Penner cites even earlier examples of such allegorical "maps"; she notes that while there may be "some movement between the paths and a few connecting roads" on occasion, all of them emphasize that in marriage as in moral life, "decisions are hard to undo." Penner, *Newlyweds*, 63–64, 61.

23. As she puts it, it was not so much geography that shaped British imperialism, but British imperial influence that shaped "a geography of the sea." Martins, "Mapping Tropical Waters," 148–149.

24. S. Carroll, "'Play You Must,'" 39, 40.

25. *The Pirate and Traders* did, however, allow players a limited measure of choice on some spins. The instructions, for example, note that, "Some sides of the totum have two letters, the player has the choice of moving in a direction according to either one of these letters. For instance, if it turn up N.W., he can move either to the north or to the west, but only in one of these directions."

26. The Victoria and Albert Museum gives a broader date range for this: 1837–46, but an 1845 advertisement in the *Times* describes it as a "New Game."

27. Interestingly, the branching, looped diagrams that narratologists like Dannenberg have relied on often resemble the surfaces of these boards; Dannenberg,

Coincidence and Counterfactuality, 2, 68–70. See also Rescher's diagram of conditional statements; Rescher, *Conditionals*, 180–181.

28. With the exception of "adult" games like chess, popular board games that allowed players to make judgments or decisions about direction of movement would appear only later, in the twentieth century.

29. S. Carroll, "Play You Must," 39.

30. Although Spooner commissioned work from a number of different artists and designers, including lithographer W. Clerk, artist G. F. Bragg, and printer L. M. Lefevre, he appears to have exercised considerable control over the production process, as most of his publications share a consistent, signature style from piece to piece.

31. The pagination restarts from "1" with the illustrations.

32. *Wanderings*, text page 2.

33. Ibid., image page 1.

34. Ibid., image page 3.

35. See Grossman, *Charles Dickens's Networks*, 104–115.

36. Spooner's illustrated "Comic Game of the Great Exhibition of 1851," issued in the same year, adhered to the traditional race-game model, with a single, circular path leading to the Crystal Palace at the board's center.

37. Grossman, *Charles Dickens's Networks*, 115.

38. "Sir Richard Whittington" (1845), 117.

39. "Whittington and His Cat" (1834), 202; "Review of *Tentamen*," 595.

40. The London publisher E. C. Bennett produced a board game and accompanying booklet based on Whittington's story, which Oxford University's Bodleian Library dates to c. 1860–70; Whittincton [sic].

41. Fisher, *Lays of Ancient Babyland*, 11; Pardon, "Dick Whittington," 345.

42. Fisher, *Lays of Ancient Babyland*, 25; Pardon, "Dick Whittington," 345.

43. *Merry Rhymes*, 2–4; "Sir Richard Whittington" (1880), n. p.

44. "Sir Richard Whittington" (1845), 118.

45. Cook, "Turn Again," 352.

46. Baker, *Holiday Album*, 254.

47. "Whittington and His Cat" (c. 1840).

48. Mitchell, however, does complicate this timeline by tracing a history that remains largely unexplored by scholars of graphic novels and comics; her reading of the visual conventions of Victorian print culture, especially in the second half of the nineteenth century, points suggestively to continuities with more recent forms of graphic narrative. See Mitchell, "Before and After."

49. McCloud, *Understanding Comics*, 106, 105.

50. Dittmer, "Comic Book Visualities," 224.

51. Bredehoft, "Comics Architecture," 872.

52. Ibid.; Dittmer, "Comic Book Visualities," 222.

53. *Merry Rhymes*; "Sir Richard Whittington" (1880).

54. "Dick Whittington and His Cat" (1859); *Nursery Tales*.

55. See, for example, Beckman, "Becoming Pawn"; and Henkle, "Carroll's Narratives."

56. These include psychoanalytic, Wittgensteinian, and postmodern approaches, such as those found in Cixous, "Introduction"; Deleuze, *Logic of Sense*; Guyer, "Girl"; Lopez, "Deleuze with Carroll"; May, "Wittgenstein's Reflection."

57. Groth, "Projections of Alice," 668; Hollingsworth, "Improvising Spaces," 86. Hollingsworth suggests that, as a photographer, Carroll would have been familiar with these aspects of photographic practice and display.

58. See especially Beer's *Alice in Space* on the role of contemporaneous science and math in Carroll's work (45–68), and on the influence of *Punch*'s satirical style (75–101). Abeles, "Mathemetical-Political Papers"; N. Armstrong, "Occidental Alice"; Bayley, "Alice's Adventures"; Bivona, "Alice the Child-Imperialist"; Henderson, "Symbolic Algebra"; Lovell-Smith, "Animals of Wonderland"; Puckett, "Caucus-Racing"; Pycior, "At the Intersection"; Rackin, "Blessed Rage"; Siemann, "Curiouser and Curiouser"; Throesch, "Nonsense."

59. *History of the House*, n. p.

60. See, for example, Downey, "Truth About Pawn Promotion."

61. Beer, *Alice in Space*, 33–34, 46.

62. Deleuze, *Logic of Sense*, 61.

63. Ibid., 60, 32.

64. Linking nineteenth-century board games to Thomas Hardy's novels, Kolb points out that both offer binary choices between "two apparently equivalent options"; at the same time, these operations also constitute the basis for the patterns of uninformed decision and regret common to his work—something decidedly absent from the examples this chapter discusses. Kolb, "Plot Circles," 597, 597–598.

65. Beer, *Alice in Space*, 30; see also Lovett, *Lewis Carroll*, for information about railway guides in Carroll's personal collection.

66. L. Carroll, *Sylvie and Bruno*, 169. Emphasis in original.

67. L. Carroll, *Alice's Adventures*, 37, 46.

68. L. Carroll, *Through the Looking-Glass*, 225. Emphasis in original.

69. Statements like, "Gwendolyn Harleth could have said no" or that "Pip could have been a blacksmith," enforce a recognition that characters are "bound" to the lives they lead. A. Miller, "Lives Unled," 124.

70. A. Miller, "Lives Unled," 124.

71. L. Carroll, *Alice's Adventures*, 68.

72. Though he travels by a different critical route, Kincaid makes a similar point about play in his reading of James Barrie's *Peter Pan* and Carroll's *Alice* books— though significantly, he reads Alice as a character less comfortable with play than

"with logic, accounts, work, death, and sentimentality: the rewards that come to those willing to grow up." Kincaid, *Child-Loving*, 276, 288–289.

73. L. Carroll, *Through the Looking-Glass*, 159.

74. L. Carroll, *Alice's Adventures*, 57. Emphasis in original.

75. Ibid.

76. Ibid., 32. Emphasis in original.

77. Beer, "Reader as Author."

78. L. Carroll, *Alice's Adventures*, 28, 29, 92, 24–25.

79. Deleuze, *Logic of Sense*, 9.

80. Williams, "Lewis Carroll," 661. Beer describes Carroll as "eagerly aware of the conversations around him in Oxford, conversations that included the recent publication of the *Origin* in 1859 and Müller's essays, based on his lectures at the Royal Institution in 1861"; Beer, *Alice in Space*, 141.

81. Thus Müller wrote, "the amateur derived fiend and foul and filth from faugh! and fie!—the instinctive verbal defense against bad smells—the professional traced fiend to Gothic fijan 'to hate' and fijan back to Sanskrit pìy 'to hate.'" Originally published in his *Lectures on the Science of Language*, and quoted in Williams, "Lewis Carroll."

82. Henderson, "Symbolic Logic," 97.

83. L. Carroll, "Word-Links." Dodgson published the instructions for this game in 1878 under the name Lewis Carroll, and reverted to that pen name again with later variations of the game, such as "Doublets" in the 1879 *Vanity Fair* (see Madden, "Orthographic Transformations," 68), and the more complex versions in *Syzygies and Lanrick: A Word Puzzle and a Game for Two Players* in 1893; as he notes in the preface to the latter, "the first version of the Rules was written on Dec. 26, 1878."

84. L. Carroll, "Word-Links," 4.

85. Ibid., 1. Italics in the original.

86. Ibid.

87. Quoted in Gardner, "Word-Ladders," 196. Interpreting this with relation to twentieth-century computational biology, Searls suggests that these games anticipated the logic of genomic evolution by means of base-pair changes; Searls, "From Jabberwocky."

88. Darwin, *Origin of Species*, 413.

89. Henderson, "Symbolic Logic," 97.

90. Madden, "Orthographic Transformations," 71.

91. L. Carroll, *Alice's Adventures*, 41, 33.

92. Gould, "Dodo"; Puckett, "Caucus-Racing," 21. Gardner notes that the Oxford University Museum, visited by Carroll and the Liddells, had a taxidermied dodo on display; the dodo had already been extinct for centuries, with the last known specimen dead in 1681. L. Carroll, *Annotated Alice*, 27, note 10.

93. Beer, *Alice in Space*, 137; L. Carroll, *Alice's Adventures*, 26. Emphasis in the original.

94. Darwin, *Origin of Species*, 215. The passage was roundly ridiculed by critics in 1859, and he later revised it to the more moderate, "the black bear was seen . . . swimming for hours with widely open mouth, thus catching, almost like a whale, insects in the water."

95. Ibid., 459.

96. See Daly, *Demographic Imagination*; Flint, *Victorians*; Meisel, *Realizations*; and Nead, *Victorian Babylon*.

97. Among the works discussing the extraordinary early Victorian culture of spectacle around Leicester Square are Altick, *Shows of London*; Lightman, "Spectacle"; and O'Connor, *Earth on Show*, 263–323. For a discussion of map makers and distributors in the area, see Howgego, *Printed Maps*, 25, 180–182, 263.

98. Spooner employed Graf and Soret as printers for both versions of his "The Destruction by Fire of the Houses of Parliament on Thursday night, Octr. 16th, 1834."

99. Mitchell, "Before and After," 241–242.

100. Wall, *Grammars of Approach*, 30, 76–77.

101. O'Connor, *Earth on Show*, 302.

102. Flint, *Victorians*, 144, 139. See also O'Connor, *Earth on Show*, 300–303, and Rudwick, *Bursting the Limits*, 191–193. Mitchell argues that the "before-and-after trope" in visual representations "largely coincides with the history of photography" and was used in philanthropic publications and in advertising; Mitchell, "Before and After," 243.

103. See Gunning, "Animating the Nineteenth Century," 466–467; and I. Armstrong, *Victorian Glassworlds*, 258–259, for a further discussion of these technologies and techniques.

104. Rickards, *Encyclopedia*, 339. It is worth noting that some nineteenth-century protean views maintained this older tradition of featuring atmospheric transformations; see, for example, *Quick's Diorama Transparent View*, which displayed Osborne House in both summer and winter.

105. O'Connor, *Earth on Show*, 283, 286–287; pages 263–323 provide an excellent, more general survey of the variety and range of these spectacles.

106. Altick, *Shows of London*, 136, 176.

107. Ibid., 96, 201–202.

108. Ibid., 95; O'Connor, *Earth on Show*, 267.

109. See Altick, *Shows of London*, 217–220, and O'Connor, *Earth on Show*, 265–266, for descriptions of some of these.

110. Kern, *Cultural History*, 10.

111. Altick, *Shows of London*, 96, 320.

112. I. Armstrong, *Victorian Glassworlds*, 262. On the period's many and varied

works (including spectacles and reenactments) depicting Vesuvius and Pompeii, see also A. Buckland, *Novel Science*, 255–261; Daly, *Demographic Imagination*, 17–45; and Zimmerman, *Excavating Victorians*, ch. 4.

113. Rudwick, *Bursting the Limits*, 193; Daly, *Demographic Imagination*, 37.

114. I. Armstrong, *Victorian Glassworlds*, 264–266.

115. Gunning, "Hand and Eye," 496; Crary, *Techniques of the Observer*, 97–110.

116. Gunning, "Hand and Eye," 503.

117. I. Armstrong, *Victorian Glassworlds*, 259.

118. Ibid., 259, 266.

119. Ibid., 259, 297.

120. These may refer to an avalanche near the Simplon Pass in March 1837, though the effects of an avalanche were also the subject of at least one diorama in 1836. See "The Federal of Geneva," *Times* [London] (1 April 1837): 7e and "The Diorama," *Times* [London] (2 April 1836): 5f.

121. See McCloud, *Understanding Comics*, and Pratt, "Narrative in Comics," 107–117, for their analyses of how readers comprehend temporal sequence and transitions in conventional comic narratives.

122. Meisel, *Realizations*, 201–228.

123. Davies, "Through the Proscenium Arch," 147; "Model of the Battle," 249.

124. The Battle of Waterloo, in particular, was regarded as an epochal event, one that would be contemplated even in the "unrecognizably distant future"; Semmel, "Reading the Tangible Past," 17.

125. Gallagher, "What Would Napoleon Do?" 329; Thackeray, *Vanity Fair*, 328.

126. Palmer, "Projecting the Gaze," 26.

127. Thackeray, *Vanity Fair*, 328.

128. Groensteen, *System of Comics*, 110.

129. Bredehoft, "Comics Architecture," 871.

130. Dittmer, "Comic Book Visualities," 230.

131. Deleuze and Guattari, *Thousand Plateaus*, 6, 5.

132. See Everett, "'Relative State' Formulation"; DeWitt, "Quantum Mechanics."

Chapter 4

1. Blackwood, "Letter," 183. Emphasis in original.

2. Indeed, Eliot's usage here is one of the first cited by the *Oxford English Dictionary* of "dynamic" in a figurative sense; see *OED* online, meaning 3a, which refers to an earlier occurrence in Ralph Waldo Emerson's 1856 *English Traits*. Prior to and even after the 1870s, its usage was limited almost exclusively to scientific contexts. The word does not appear in Eliot's published correspondence, but interestingly it does appear, albeit less prominently, in her description of Will Ladislaw in her 1871–72 *Middlemarch*: "he had found that humdrum world in a terribly dynamic condition,

in which even badinage and lyrism had turned explosive"; Eliot, *Middlemarch*, 860. Eliot's companion, George H. Lewes, also used the term "Dynamism" around this time, in his 1875 *Problems of Life and Mind*.

3. Maxwell, "Dynamical Theory of Gases," 49. This was a transcription of the lecture Maxwell delivered to the Royal Society in May 1866.

4. Ibid.

5. Maxwell, "Presidential Address."

6. *George Eliot's* Daniel Deronda *Notebooks*, 21, 22. As Tondre explains, Eliot had also been reading deeply in thermodynamic research before the publication of *Middlemarch*; Tondre, *Physics of Possibility*, 132.

7. Eliot, *Daniel Deronda*, 7. For Shuttleworth, this quality in Gwendolen's portrayal, her "conflicting impulses and self-division," reflects Eliot's interest in contemporaneous psychological accounts of the self; Shuttleworth, *George Eliot*, 184.

8. Pater, *Renaissance*, 151. See Knoepflmacher for a discussion of some of the alignments that emerged in the 1870s between Pater and Eliot, especially in their treatment of empiricism and belief; Knoepflmacher, "Religious Humanism," 209–210.

9. Herbert, *Victorian Relativity*, xiv; Garratt, *Victorian Empiricism*, 17, 18, 21. Garratt helpfully distinguishes here between empiricism and a term with which it is often conflated, "objectivity," as an abstract ideal defined precisely by the absence of a relational element; Garratt, *Victorian Empiricism*, 27–30.

10. See, for example, Grener, *Improbability*; Rosenthal, "Large Novel"; and Tondre, *Physics of Possibility*.

11. G. Levine, "*Daniel Deronda*," 62–63, 69.

12. Maxwell, "Molecules," 437.

13. Ibid.

14. Ibid., 440.

15. Ibid. Maxwell participated in a broader turn, starting in the 1860s, toward taking Lucretius's science more seriously; Brown, *Poetry of Victorian Scientists*, 168.

16. Maxwell's interest in Lucretius predated the publication of Tennyson's poem; Tondre, *Physics of Possibility*, 141. See also Maxwell's 1866 letter to Munro, in which he reflects on how best to discuss Lucretius; he writes, "Will you tell me if you think it unjust to Lucretius"? Maxwell, "Letter to Hugh Andrew Johnstone Munro," 250–251. He further extends these reflections on Lucretius in his article, "On the Dynamical Theory of Gases," published in 1867. Indeed, as Brown and Gold remind us, Maxwell was deeply interested in the ways in which poetic and scientific endeavors might converge; in poems like "Report on Tait's Lecture on Force," he articulated in verse form the concerns and questions driving the period's energy physics. Brown, *Poetry of Victorian Scientists*; Gold, *Thermopoetics*, 114–121.

17. Maxwell, "Molecules," 440.

18. Ibid., 438.

19. Ibid., 439.

20. Dear, *Intelligibility of Nature*, 115–119; J. Smith, *Fact and Feeling*, 233–235.

21. See Weber, "Elective Affinities," for a fuller account of the language of the German Romantic physical sciences.

22. Quoted in J. Smith, *Fact and Feeling*, 221.

23. Maxwell's disagreement with his German counterparts is evident here, too: "According to a theory of electricity which is making great progress in Germany, two electrical particles act on one another directly at a distance. . . . Another theory of electricity, which I prefer, denies action at a distance and attributes electric action to tensions and pressures in an all-pervading medium"; Maxwell, "Presidential Address," 228. See also Dear, *Intelligibility of Nature*, 13, 116; and J. Smith, *Fact and Feeling*, 211, 219.

24. Faraday, for example, posited the existence of "lines of force," while Maxwell, citing the plausibility of Faraday's explanation for the "intervening medium" between particles, speculated that something like intricate cogwheels could be thought of as the responsible intermediaries, though he intended this as a hypothetical explanation for electromagnetic phenomena, rather than as a claim about a physical reality. See Maxwell, *Treatise on Electricity and Magnetism*, x, 36; see also Dear, *Intelligibility of Nature*, 132–135; and J. Smith, *Fact and Feeling*, 220, 225–227.

25. Tyndall, "On the Scientific Use," 63. This was originally delivered as an address to the British Association for the Advancement of Science, 16 September 1870.

26. Ibid., 36.

27. Maxwell, "Presidential Address," 419. Maxwell's address was originally delivered as an address to the British Association for the Advancement of Science, 15 September 1870, and reprinted as a Sectional Proceeding report in *Nature* the following week. Elsewhere and at great length, Maxwell ridiculed what he saw as Tyndall's pretensions to a form of Romantic imagination; Brown, *Poetry of Victorian Scientists*, 145–163. The two scientists had also been involved in a bitter dispute over the direction of the energy sciences and their relationship to theology; see J. Smith, *Fact and Feeling*, 170–172, 249, and Tondre, *Physics of Possibility*, 142. Porter points as well to Maxwell's disagreement with Tyndall's "deterministic" interpretation of statistics; Porter, "Statistical Survey," 79.

28. Maxwell, "Presidential Address," 419.

29. Ibid.

30. Ibid., 421, 422. In his poetry, Maxwell applied a sexualized language to these molecular movements and collisions; Brown, *Poetry of Victorian Scientists*, 173–175.

31. Maxwell, "Letter to John William Strutt (1871)," 615.

32. Maxwell, *Theory of Heat*, 329.

33. Lightman, *Origins of Agnosticism*, 169.

34. Maxwell, "Drafts of Lecture," 930. Porter's account traces Maxwell's gradual

turn to probability through his interactions with other scientists, starting from the late 1850s; Porter, *Rise of Statistical Thinking*, 194–208.

35. Lightman, *Origins of Agnosticism*, 168.

36. Porter, *Rise of Statistical Thinking*, 31–33.

37. Noteworthy examples of critical work examining the normative aspects of population statistics include Gilbert, *Mapping*; Jaffe, *Affective Life*; Poovey, *Making a Social Body*; Rosenthal, "Large Novel."

38. L. Carroll, *Curiosa Mathematica*, xv. Emphasis in original.

39. "Registration of Sickness," 228.

40. Dickens, *Hard Times*, 97.

41. For a more extensive discussion of how Maxwell's turn to statistics might be contextualized with relation to contemporaneous study of populations, see Lightman, *Origins of Agnosticism*, 168–170; and Porter, "Statistical Survey," 77–116.

42. Maxwell, "Molecules," 440. In one of her epigraphs for *Daniel Deronda*, Eliot uses a quote from La Rochefoucauld to make a similar claim: "Il est plus aisé de connoître l'homme en général que de connoître un homme en particulier" (309); i.e., "It is easier to know mankind in general than to know one man in particular."

43. Maxwell, "Letter to Herbert Spencer," 959–960. Emphasis in original. Spencer seems to have struggled with Maxwell's argument, a result perhaps of his own belief in the achievability of epistemological clarity; in an ideal society, Spencer wrote, "emotions . . . will visibly exhibit themselves," and a "simultaneous increase in the power of interpreting . . . signs of feeling" will take place; Spencer, *Data of Ethics*, 286, 287. I am grateful to Kathy Psomiades for alerting me to this element in Spencer's work.

44. Maxwell was among the leading Cambridge intellectuals who attended meetings of the Eranus Society, where the implications of new methodologies were often debated. See Lubenow, *"Only Connect,"* 44–48, for an extended discussion of its history.

45. Maxwell, "Essay for the Eranus Club," 818.

46. Maxwell, "Drafts of Lecture," 932.

47. In this sense, Maxwell's work anticipated twentieth-century quantum mechanics by describing a probabilistically rather than empirically known world of energies, movements, and collisions; Dyson, "Maxwell's Theory," 5.

48. Porter, *Rise of Statistical Thinking*, 116.

49. Clausius only acknowledged the mathematical significance of the distribution once, in an 1874 paper; see Whitaker, "Maxwell's Famous (or Infamous) Demon," 167–169.

50. Porter, *Rise of Statistical Thinking*, 125.

51. Maxwell, "On the Dynamical Evidence," 374.

52. Maxwell, "Manuscript," 657.

53. Maxwell, *Theory of Heat*, 308–309.

54. Maxwell, "Letter to John William Strutt (1870)," 582, 583. "Demon" was Kelvin's coinage, and the term I will continue to use throughout this chapter for the sake of continuity. See Harman's introduction to *The Scientific Letters* for a longer discussion of the demon's origins, especially p. 17.

55. In his letter, Maxwell went further, speculating that perhaps "even intelligence might . . . be dispensed with and the thing . . . made self-acting"; Maxwell, "Letter to John William Strutt (1870)," 583.

56. Ibid., 585.

57. For a discussion of Ludwig Boltzmann's contribution to reinterpreting the second law as a probabilistic one, see Porter, *Rise of Statistical Thinking*, 125–128.

58. Maxwell, "Letter to John William Strutt (1870)," 585. Maxwell repeats this same language in *Theory of Heat*, 308.

59. According to the late-Victorian statistician and eugenicist Karl Pearson, Maxwell's "demon" demonstrated that scientific law "owes its existence to the creative power of [human] intellect" (quoted in Herbert, *Victorian Relativity*, 160). For other interpretations, see Daub, "Maxwell's Demon"; Smith and Wise, *Energy and Empire*, 624–625; Rosenthal, "Large Novel"; Stanley, "Pointsman." A discussion of how a wider range of scientific works adopted the demon appears in Whitaker, "Maxwell's Famous (or Infamous) Demon." The conceit of the demon persists in contemporary science; see, for example, Merali, "Demonic Device."

60. Brown, *Poetry of Victorian Scientists*, 253.

61. Gold, *Thermopoetics*, 226. Emphasis in original. Tondre, *Physics of Possibility*, 143. Brown links Maxwell's tendency to assign atoms an "anthropomorphic character" to William Thomson's and others' use of the term "demon" to describe this experiment; Brown, *Poetry of Victorian Scientists*, 173.

62. Heimann, "Molecular Forces," 204. See also the effort by recent physicists to retrace the mathematics of Maxwell's physics; for them, too, the demon is no more than an abstraction demonstrating that "anti-thermodynamic evolutions are possible, but improbable"; Hemmo and Shenker, *Road to Maxwell's Demon*, 271.

63. Canales, taking the popularity of the demon as her starting point, traces some of the cultural and scientific contexts that shaped its reception by Thomson, Peter G. Tait, and others. Canales, *Bedeviled*, 151–175.

64. Maxwell, *Theory of Heat*, 309; Maxwell, "Molecules," 440.

65. Maxwell, "Note to Tait," 186. Maxwell's ambivalence over how best to describe the sorting mechanism echoes Darwin's grappling with metaphors to describe the process of natural selection; as G. Levine points out, the agent of selection in his 1844 draft is a "Being," but becomes a personified "nature" in published editions of *Origin*. G. Levine, *Darwin and the Novelists*, 99–100.

66. Daston, *Classical Probability*, 108; Porter, *Rise of Statistical Thinking*, 72.

67. Porter, *Rise of Statistical Thinking*, 72; De Morgan quoted in ibid., 75.

68. Daston, *Classical Probability*, 183.

69. For a more extended discussion of the main figures espousing frequentism during this period, see Porter, *Rise of Statistical Thinking*, 78–85.

70. Daston, *Classical Probability*, 285.

71. Porter, *Rise of Statistical Thinking*, 73. Daston traces the slow separation of "objective" and "subjective" forms of probability in French philosophical thought through the nuances of Condorcet's account of probability in the eighteenth century, to Cournot's nineteenth century "objective frequencies"; Daston, *Classical Probability*, 210–225.

72. Porter, *Rise of Statistical Thinking*, 86.

73. Maxwell, "Letter to John William Strutt (1870)," 583.

74. Maxwell, "Letter to Lewis Campbell," 198.

75. Herschel, "Review of *Lettres*." On the influence of this article on Maxwell, see Hacking, *Taming of Chance*, 234 n. 12; Porter, *Rise of Statistical Thinking*, 118–119; and P. M. Harman's footnote in Maxwell's "Letter to Lewis Campbell," 197 n. 11.

76. Herschel, "Review of *Lettres*," 1, 20.

77. Ibid., 25, 26, 32.

78. Ibid., 3.

79. Stanley, *Huxley's Church*, 17–18, 47, 180.

80. Maxwell, "Draft Letter," 194. Maxwell wrote to Francis W. H. Petrie, the secretary of the Victoria Institute, to turn down an offer of membership.

81. Maxwell, "Letter to John William Strutt (1870)," 582.

82. For examples of these readings, see Cat, "On Understanding," 400; Daub, "Maxwell's Demon"; Heimann, "Molecular Forces," 203; Stanley, *Huxley's Church*, 287–288; Stanley, "Pointsman."

83. Porter contends that "It would be an anachronism to treat his sorting demon . . . as implicit in the ideas he espoused" before the 1860s; Porter, "Statistical Survey," 94. However, I suggest that there are continuities joining Herschel's ideas in 1850, Maxwell's work on distributions, and his thought experiment of 1867.

84. Maxwell, "Essay for the Eranus Club," 815.

85. Ibid., 822.

86. For a fuller discussion of the ways in which Eliot's work engaged the period's sciences, see, for example, Beer, *Darwin's Plots*; G. Levine, *Darwin and the Novelists*; G. Levine, "George Eliot's Hypothesis"; and Rothfield, *Vital Signs*.

87. Shuttleworth, *George Eliot*, ix.

88. *George Eliot's* Daniel Deronda *Notebooks*, 16–23. Describing Eliot's reading in the years leading up to *Middlemarch*, Tondre recounts this history of mutual influence between literary and scientific endeavors with admirable clarity and nuance; Tondre, *Physics of Possibility*, 137–142.

89. Shuttleworth, *George Eliot*, 179, xii.

90. Ibid., 175.

91. See, for example, Beer, *Darwin's Plots*, 169–195; G. Levine, *Dying to Know* 172–185; G. Levine, "George Eliot's Hypothesis"; Rosenthal, "Large Novel"; and Shuttleworth, *George Eliot*.

92. Griffiths analyzes Eliot's use of failed analogies as a way of pointing to these distinctions; her narrators move "from formal model to a particular instance that does not fit"; Griffiths, *Age of Analogy*, 180. See also Gallagher, who identifies in Eliot's narratorial interventions, which move from generality to particular, one of the signatures of her mode of realism; Gallagher, "Immanent Victorians."

93. Eliot, *Adam Bede*, 180, 128.

94. Eliot, *Daniel Deronda*, 111.

95. Ibid.

96. Ibid.

97. See Ablow, "Tortured Sympathies"; Albrecht, "Sympathy and Telepathy"; and Ermarth, "George Eliot's Conception."

98. Greiner, "Sympathy Time"; and Greiner, "Thinking of Me," 418.

99. Pyle, "A Novel Sympathy," 6.

100. G. Levine, "*Daniel Deronda*," 57.

101. Eliot, *Daniel Deronda*, 42.

102. Eliot, *Middlemarch*, 297.

103. Eliot, *Daniel Deronda*, 281–282.

104. For an extensive discussion of intersubjectivity in the British literary tradition, see Butte, *I Know*.

105. Beer, *Darwin's Plots*, 175.

106. G. Levine makes this observation as well; see G. Levine, "George Eliot's Hypothesis," 18–19.

107. Beer, *Darwin's Plots*, 175.

108. Greiner quotes from Smith's *Theory of Moral Sentiments*. Greiner, "Sympathy Time," 296. Emphasis in original.

109. See "iridescence" in the *Oxford English Dictionary*, online edition, meanings a and b. Eliot's use of "iridescence" in *Daniel Deronda* is one of two examples given for the then-less-common figurative usage.

110. Eliot, *Daniel Deronda*, 298.

111. Anderson, *Predicting the Weather*, 7.

112. Eliot, *Daniel Deronda*, 678.

113. Ibid., 729–730.

114. Ibid., 515.

115. Ibid., 433.

116. Ibid., 188.

117. Ibid., 205.

118. Ibid., 607.

119. Ibid., 179.

120. Ibid., 689.

121. Eliot, *Middlemarch*, 896. Tracking the characters' lost energies, Tondre offers a persuasive reading of this phrase with relation to the period's theories of entropy; *Physics of Possibility*, 158–161.

122. Maxwell, "Presidential Address," 421.

123. Ryan, "Cheap Plot," 58.

124. Eliot, *Daniel Deronda*, 32, 259, 810, 259.

125. Ibid., 238.

126. Ibid., 370.

127. Ibid., 10.

128. Ibid., 164.

129. Ibid., 186.

130. Ibid., 509. Eliot's own translation.

131. In the novel, which we might suspect of being too ordered, the absence of intervention is a useful fiction, whereas in a vessel full of molecules, which we might expect to be always disordered, the intervening demon is the useful fiction.

132. Eliot, *Daniel Deronda*, 765.

133. Ibid., 136.

134. One notable exception occurs in Dickens's last completed novel, *Our Mutual Friend*, when John Harmon, who has been evading another, Mortimer Lightwood, comments upon the occasion of their meeting: "chance has brought us face to face at last—which is not to be wondered at, for the wonder is, that, in spite of all my pains to the contrary, chance has not confronted us together sooner"; Dickens, *Our Mutual Friend*, 827.

135. Eliot, *Daniel Deronda*, 378.

136. Ibid., 382.

137. Rosenthal, "Large Novel," 783.

138. Eliot, *Daniel Deronda*, 391.

139. Ibid., 387.

140. Ibid., 382.

141. Ibid., 510.

142. Ibid., 510.

143. While Maxwell's work on distributions and averages seemed to allude, implicitly, to the principle of a standard deviation from the mean, the term and the calculable entity were introduced later, by Karl Pearson.

144. Eliot, *Daniel Deronda*, 511.

145. Ibid., 513.

146. Ibid., 512.

147. Ibid., 167.

148. Ibid., 606.

149. Ibid., 681, 685.

150. Ibid., 690.

151. Ibid., 691, 695. Although Raffles in *Middlemarch* dies under similar circumstances, where his sudden demise serves the convenience of the man he had been blackmailing, Eliot frames that episode within what is more clearly a providential subplot about hypocrisy and moral comeuppance.

152. Gettelman, "Reading Ahead," 42, 44; Beer, *Darwin's Plots*, 194. See New's contrasting reading of the role of "Destiny" in Eliot's novel; New, "Chance, Providence and Destiny."

153. Eliot, *Daniel Deronda*, 17.

154. G. Levine, "*Daniel Deronda*," 71.

155. Maxwell, "Letter to Lewis Campbell," 197. Emphasis in original. The phrase "Calculus of Probabilities" alludes to Herschel's use of the same in his *Edinburgh Review* article: "the delicate and refined system of mathematical reasoning, now generally known as the 'Calculus of Probabilities'"; [Herschel], "Review of *Lettres*," 4.

Epilogue

1. Trollope, *Barchester Towers*, 126, 127.

2. Dever, "Trollope," 863. Emphasis in original.

3. See, for example, Daston, *Classical Probability*; Freedgood, *Victorian Writing*; Hacking, *Taming of Chance*.

4. "Royal Surrey."

Bibliography

Games, Protean Views, and Broadsides

The Cottage of Content or Right Roads and Wrong Ways. London: William Spooner, 1848.

Geographical Recreation; or a Voyage Round the Habitable World. London: John Harris at the Juvenile Library, 1809.

The Journey, or Crossroads to Conqueror's Castle. London: William Spooner, 1845.

"Little Red Riding Hood." London: William Spooner, n. d.

The Mansion of Bliss. London: William Darton, 1822.

The Mirror of Truth. London: John Wallis, 1811.

"Mount Vesuvius." *Spooner's Protean Views.* London: William Spooner [c. 1840].

"Napoleon at the Battle of Wagram, Changing to the Conflagration of Moscow." *Spooner's Protean Views.* London: William Spooner [c. 1840].

"Napoleon Powerful and Napoleon Powerless." *Spooner's Protean Views.* London: William Spooner [c. 1840].

New Game of Wanderers in the Wilderness. London: Edward Wallis, 1844.

"The New Houses of Parliament." *Spooner's Protean Views.* London: William Spooner [1839].

A New Royal Geographical Pastime for England and Wales. London: Robert Sayer, 1787.

"Perspective View of the Great Exhibition." London: William Spooner, 1851.

The Pirate and Traders of the West Indies. London: William Spooner, 1847.

"The Royal Exchange, London, with a View of Its Destruction by Fire." London: William Spooner, 1838.

Royal Geographical Pastime: Exhibiting a Complete Tour Round the World. London: Thomas Jefferys, 1770.

"Temple Bar, London, Changing to the Queen's Visit to Guildhall and Her Reception on Entering the City." London: William Spooner, 1837.

"Tomb of Napoleon at St. Helena." *Spooner's Protean Views.* London: William Spooner [c. 1840].

Tour Through England and Wales, a New Geographical Pastime. London: John Wallis, 1794.

The Travellers of Europe. London: William Spooner, 1849.

A Voyage of Discovery; or, The Five Navigators. London: William Spooner, 1836.

Wallis's Locomotive Game of Railroad Adventures. London: Edward Wallis, 1838.

Whittincton [sic] and His Cat: A New Comical Game. London: E. C. Bennett, c. 1860–70.

"Whittington and His Cat." London: William Spooner [c. 1840].

Works Cited

Abeles, Francine. "The Mathematical-Political Papers of C. L. Dodgson." In *Lewis Carroll: A Celebration, Essays on the Occasion of the 150th Anniversary of the Birth of Charles Lutwidge Dodgson.* Ed. Edward Guiliano. New York: Clarkson N. Potter, Inc., 1982, 195–210.

Ablow, Rachel. "Tortured Sympathies: Victorian Literature and the Ticking Time-Bomb Scenario," *ELH* 80.4 (2013): 1145–1171.

Achinstein, Peter. *Particles and Waves: Historical Essays in the Philosophy of Science.* Oxford: Oxford University Press, 1991.

Adam, Ian. "The Structure of Realisms in *Adam Bede*." *Nineteenth-Century Fiction* 30.2 (1975): 127–149.

Aegis Life Assurance Company. Almanack [London, 1851].

Albert Life Assurance Company. Prospectus. London, 1851.

Alborn, Timothy. *Regulated Lives: Life Insurance and British Society, 1800–1914.* Toronto: University of Toronto Press, 2009.

Albrecht, Thomas. "Sympathy and Telepathy: The Problem of Ethics in George Eliot's *The Lifted Veil*." *ELH* 73 (2006): 437–463.

Alfred Life Assurance Company. Pamphlet. London: F. Lothbury, 1851.

Allen, Barry. "The Abyss of Contingency: Contingency and Purposiveness in Darwin and Kant." *History of Philosophy Quarterly* 20 (2003): 373–391.

Altick, Richard D. *The English Common Reader: A Social History of the Mass Reading Public, 1800–1900.* Chicago: University of Chicago Press, 1957.

——. *The Shows of London.* Cambridge, MA: Belknap Press of Harvard University Press, 1978.

Anderson, Katharine. *Predicting the Weather: Victorians and the Science of Meteorology.* Chicago: University of Chicago Press, 2005.

Armstrong, Isobel. *Victorian Glassworlds: Glass Culture and the Imagination 1830–1880.* Oxford: Oxford University Press, 2008.

Armstrong, Nancy. "The Occidental Alice." *Differences: A Journal of Feminist Cultural Studies* 2.2 (1990): 3–40.

Ashworth, William J. "Memory, Efficiency, and Symbolic Analysis: Charles Babbage, John Herschel, and the Industrial Mind." *Isis* 87 (1996): 629–653.

Athenaeum Life Assurance Society. Prospectus. London, c. 1851.

[Babbage, Charles]. "Addition to the Memoir of M. Menabrea on the Analytical Engine." In *The Works of Charles Babbage.* Vol. 3. Ed. Martin Campbell-Kelly. London: William Pickering, 1989, 83–88.

Babbage, Charles. *A Comparative View of the Various Institutions for the Assurance of Lives. The Works of Charles Babbage.* Vol. 6. Ed. Martin Campbell-Kelly. London: William Pickering, 1989.

——. "A Letter to Sir Humphry Davy, Bart., President of the Royal Society, on the Application of Machinery to the Purpose of Calculating and Printing Mathematical Tables." In *The Works of Charles Babbage.* Vol. 2. Ed. Martin Campbell-Kelly. London: William Pickering, 1989, 6–14.

——. *The Ninth Bridgewater Treatise. A Fragment. The Works of Charles Babbage.* Vol. 9. Ed. Martin Campbell-Kelly. London: William Pickering, 1989.

——. "On the Mathematical Powers of the Calculating Engine." In *The Works of Charles Babbage.* Vol. 3. Ed. Martin Campbell-Kelly. London: William Pickering, 1989, 15–61.

——. "On the Theoretical Principles of the Machinery for Calculating Tables." In *The Works of Charles Babbage.* Vol. 2. Ed. Martin Campbell-Kelly. London: William Pickering, 1989, 38–43.

——. *Passages from the Life of a Philosopher.* Ed. Martin Campbell-Kelly. 1864. New Brunswick, NJ: Rutgers University Press, 1994.

——. "Rates of the Protector Life Assurance Society." In *The Works of Charles Babbage.* Vol. 4. Ed. Martin Campbell-Kelly. London: William Pickering, 1989, 16–19.

——. [Scrapbook of clippings put together by Charles Babbage from 1847? to 1851?]. *The Making of the Modern World.* Gale Primary Sources.

——. "Statement Addressed to the Duke of Wellington Respecting the Calculating Engine." In *The Works of Charles Babbage.* Vol. 3. Ed. Martin Campbell-Kelly. London: William Pickering, 1989, 2–8.

Baily, Francis. "On Mr Babbage's New Machine for Calculating and Printing Mathematical and Astronomical Tables." In *The Works of Charles Babbage.* Vol. 2. Ed. Martin Campbell-Kelly. London: William Pickering, 1989, 44–56.

Baker, Sarah Schoonmaker. *The Holiday Album: A Book of Easy Reading for Children: By Aunt Friendly*. London: Frederick Warne and Co.; Scribner, Welford, and Co. [c. 1870].

[Barrow, John]. "Review of *A Comparative View of the Various Institutions for the Assurance of Lives*, by Charles Babbage." *Quarterly Review* 35 (1827): 1–31.

Bayley, Melanie. "Alice's Adventures in Algebra: Wonderland Solved." *New Scientist* 2739 (16 December 2009).

Beckman, Frida. "Becoming Pawn: Alice, Arendt and the New in Narrative." *Journal of Narrative Theory* 44.1 (2014): 1–28.

Beer, Gillian. *Alice in Space: The Sideways Victorian World of Lewis Carroll*. Chicago: University of Chicago Press, 2016.

——. *Darwin's Plots: Evolutionary Narrative in Darwin, George Eliot and Nineteenth-Century Fiction*. Cambridge: Cambridge University Press, 2000.

——. "The Reader as Author." *Authorship* 3.1 (2014). http://dx.doi.org/10.21825/aj.v3i1.1066

Bivona, Daniel. "Alice the Child-Imperialist and the Games of Wonderland." *Nineteenth-Century Literature* 41 (1986): 143–171.

Blackwood, John. "Letter to George Eliot (10 November 1875)." In *The George Eliot Letters*. Vol. 6. Ed. Gordon S. Haight. New Haven: Yale University Press, 1954, 182–184.

Bowen, John. "The Historical Novel." *A Companion to the Victorian Novel* 85 (2002): 244–259.

Brink-Roby, Heather. "Natural Representation: Diagram and Text in Darwin's *On the Origin of Species*." *Victorian Studies* 51.2 (2009): 247–273.

Brantlinger, Patrick. *The Reading Lesson: The Threat of Mass Literacy in Nineteenth-Century British Fiction*. Bloomington: Indiana University Press, 1998.

Bredehoft, Thomas A. "Comics Architecture, Multidimensionality, and Time: Chris Ware's *Jimmy Corrigan: The Smartest Kid on Earth*." *Modern Fiction Studies* 52.4 (2006): 869–890.

Bromley, Allan G. "Charles Babbage's Analytical Engine, 1838." *Annals of the History of Computing* 4.3 (1982): 196–217.

——. "The Evolution of Babbage's Calculating Engines." *Annals of the History of Computing* 9.2 (1987): 113–136.

Brown, Daniel. *The Poetry of Victorian Scientists: Style, Science and Nonsense*. Cambridge: Cambridge University Press, 2013.

Buckland, Adelene. *Novel Science: Fiction and the Invention of Nineteenth-Century Geology*. Chicago: University of Chicago Press, 2013.

Buckland, William. *Geology and Mineralogy Considered with Reference to Natural Theology*. Vol. 1. London: William Pickering, 1836.

——. *Reliquiae Diluvianae; Or, Observations on the Organic Remains Contained in Caves, Fissures, and Diluvial Gravel, and on Other Geological Phenomena, Attesting the Action of a Universal Deluge*, 2nd ed. London: John Murray, 1824.

Bullock, Seth. "Charles Babbage and the Emergence of Automated Reason." In *The Mechanical Mind in History*. Eds. Philip Husbands, Owen Holland, and Michael Wheeler. Cambridge, MA: MIT Press, 2008, 19–40.

Butte, George. *I Know That You Know That I Know: Narrating Subjects from* Moll Flanders *to* Marnie. Columbus: Ohio State University Press, 2004.

Cain, Mead T. "The Maps of the Society for the Diffusion of Useful Knowledge: A Publishing History." *Imago Mundi* 46 (1994): 151–167.

Campbell-Kelly, Martin. "Charles Babbage and the Assurance of Lives." *IEEE Annals of the History of Computing* 16.3 (1994): 5–14.

——. "Introduction to *Passages from the Life of a Philosopher*, by Charles Babbage. 1864." New Brunswick, NJ: Rutgers University Press, 1994, 7–36.

——. "Introduction to *The Ninth Bridgewater Treatise. A Fragment*." In *The Works of Charles Babbage*. Vol. 9. Ed. Martin Campbell-Kelly. London: William Pickering, 1989, 5–7.

Canales, Jimena. *Bedeviled: A Shadow History of Demons in Science*. Princeton: Princeton University Press, 2020.

——. *A Tenth of a Second: A History*. Chicago: University of Chicago Press, 2009.

Cannon, Walter. "The Problem of Miracles in the 1830s." *Victorian Studies* 4 (1960): 5–32.

Cardinal, Roger. "Collecting and Collage-Making: The Case of Kurt Schwitters." In *The Cultures of Collecting*. Eds. John Elsner and Roger Cardinal. London: Reaktion Books, 1994, 68–96.

Carey, Henry C. *Scrapbook Containing Newspaper Clippings, Magazine Articles and Sundry Biographical Essays*. 1859. *The Making of the Modern World*. Gale Primary Sources.

Carroll, Lewis [Charles Lutwidge Dodgson]. *Alice's Adventures in Wonderland*. In *Alice's Adventures in Wonderland and Through the Looking-Glass and What Alice Found There*. Ed. Peter Hunt. Oxford: Oxford University Press, 2009, 1–111.

——. *The Annotated Alice: Alice's Adventures in Wonderland and Through the Looking Glass*. Ed. Martin Gardner. Harmondsworth: Penguin Books, 1972.

——. *Curiosa Mathematica*. London: Macmillan & Co. [1888–93].

——. *Sylvie and Bruno Concluded*. London: Macmillan and Co., 1893.

——. *Syzygies and Lanrick: A Word Puzzle and a Game for Two Players*, 2nd ed. [London, 1893].

——. *Through the Looking-Glass*. In *Alice's Adventures in Wonderland and Through the Looking-Glass and What Alice Found There*. Ed. Peter Hunt. Oxford: Oxford University Press, 2009, 112–245.

——. "Word-Links: A Game for Two Players, or a Round Game." [England, c. 1878].

Carroll, Siobhan. "'Play You Must': *Villette* and the Nineteenth-Century Board Game." *Nineteenth Century Contexts* 39.1 (2016): 33–47.

——. "Romantic Board Games and the 'World in Play.'" In *Romantic Cartographies: Mapping, Literature, Culture, 1789–1832*. Eds. Sally Bushell, Julia S. Carlson, and Damian Walford Davies. Cambridge: Cambridge University Press, 2020, 151–170.

Cat, Jordi. "On Understanding: Maxwell on the Methods of Illustration and Scientific Metaphor." *Studies in the History and Philosophy of Modern Physics* 32.3 (2001): 395–441.

Catholic, Law, and General Life Assurance Company. Prospectus. n. d.

Chambers, Robert. "*Vestiges of the Natural History of Creation.*" *1844*. In *Vestiges of the Natural History of Creation and Other Evolutionary Writings*. Ed. James A. Secord. Chicago: University of Chicago Press, 1994, 1–390.

Choi, Tina Young. "Writing the Victorian City: Discourses of Risk, Connection, and Inevitability." *Victorian Studies* 43 (2001): 561–589.

Cixous, Hélène. "Introduction to Lewis Carroll's *Through the Looking Glass* and *The Hunting of the Snark*." Trans. Marie Maclean. *New Literary History: A Journal of Theory and Interpretation* 13.2 (1982): 231–251.

Clark, Geoffrey. "Embracing Fatality Through Life Insurance in Eighteenth-Century England." In *Embracing Risk: The Changing Culture of Insurance and Responsibility*. Eds. Tom Baker and Jonathan Simon. Chicago: University of Chicago Press, 2002, 80–96.

Collins, Bruce. *The Little Engines That Could've: The Calculating Machines of Charles Babbage*. New York: Garland Publishing, 1990.

The Colonial Life Assurance Company. Prospectus. c. 1850.

Cook, Eliza. "Turn Again Whittington." *Eliza Cook's Journal* 48 (30 March 1850): 352.

Cooter, Roger, and Bill Luckin. "Accidents in History: An Introduction." In *Accidents in History: Injuries, Fatalities and Social Relations*. Eds. Roger Cooter and Bill Luckin. Amsterdam and Atlanta: Rodopi, 1997, 1–16.

Corporation of the London Assurance. *Agent's Instructions for Fire and Life Assurance*. London: H. Teape and Son, 1843.

——. *Agent's Instructions for Fire and Life Assurance*. London: H. Teape and Son, 1846.

——. *Agent's Instructions for Fire and Life Assurance*. London: H. Teape and Son, 1853.

Crary, Jonathan. *Techniques of the Observer: On Vision and Modernity in the Nineteenth Century*. Cambridge: MIT Press, 1990.

Cullen, Michael. *The Statistical Movement in Early Victorian Britain: The Foundations of Empirical Social Research*. New York: Harvester Press Limited, 1975.

Daly, Nicholas. *The Demographic Imagination and the Nineteenth-Century City: Paris, London, New York*. Cambridge: Cambridge University Press, 2015.

Dannenberg, Hilary P. *Coincidence and Counterfactuality: Plotting Time and Space in Narrative Fiction*. Lincoln: University of Nebraska Press, 2008.

Darwin, Charles. "Darwin's Notebooks on Transmutation of Species, Part III. Third Notebook, July 15th 1838—October 2nd 1838." Ed. Gavin de Beer. *Bulletin of the British Museum (Natural History)* 2.4 (1960).

——. *The Origin of Species by Means of Natural Selection, or the Preservation of Favoured Races in the Struggle for Life*. 1859. Harmondsworth: Penguin Books, 1968.

Daston, Lorraine. *Classical Probability in the Enlightenment*. Princeton: Princeton University Press, 1988.

——. "Enlightenment Calculations." *Critical Inquiry* 21 (1994): 182–202.

——. "Historical Epistemology." *Questions of Evidence: Proof, Practice, and Persuasion Across the Disciplines*. Eds. James Chandler, Arnold I. Davidson, and Harry Harootunian. Chicago: University of Chicago Press, 1993, 282–289.

Daub, Edward E. "Maxwell's Demon." *Studies in History and Philosophy of Science* 1.3 (1970): 213–227.

Davies, Rachel Bryant. "Through the Proscenium Arch." In *Time Travelers: Victorian Encounters with Time & History*. Eds. Adelene Buckland and Sadiah Qureshi. Chicago: University of Chicago Press, 2020, 126–151.

Dawson, Gowan. "Literary Megatheriums and Loose Baggy Monsters. Paleontology and the Victorian Novel." *Victorian Studies* 53.2 (2011): 203–230.

Dear, Peter. *The Intelligibility of Nature: How Science Makes Sense of the World*. Chicago: University of Chicago Press, 2006.

Delano-Smith, Catherine, and Roger J. P. Kain. *English Maps: A History*. Toronto: University of Toronto Press, 1999.

Deleuze, Gilles. *The Logic of Sense*. Trans. Mark Lester with Charles Stivale. Ed. Constantin V. Boundas. New York: Columbia University Press, 1990.

Deleuze, Gilles, and Félix Guattari. *A Thousand Plateaus: Capitalism and Schizophrenia*. Trans. Brian Massumi. London: Athlone Press, 1988.

Dever, Carolyn. "Trollope, Seriality, and the 'Dullness' of Form." *Literature Compass* 7/9 (2010): 861–866.

DeWitt, Bryce S. "Quantum Mechanics and Reality." In *The Many Worlds Interpretation of Quantum Mechanics: A Fundamental Exposition by Hugh Everett, III, with Papers by J. A. Wheeler, B. S. DeWitt, L. N. Cooper and D. Van Vechten, and N. Graham*. Eds. Bryce S. DeWitt and Neill Graham. Princeton: Princeton University Press, 1973, 155–166.

"Dick Whittington and His Cat." In *The Home Treasury of Old Story Books: Illustrated with Fifty Engravings by Eminent Artists*. Eds. Henry Cole and William John Thoms. London: Sampson Low, Son, and Co., 1859, 67–77.

Dickens, Charles. *Bleak House*. Ed. Nicola Bradbury. 1852–53. London: Penguin Books, 1996.

——. *Hard Times*. 1853. London: Penguin Books, 1969.

——. *Our Mutual Friend*. 1864–65. London: Penguin Books, 1985.

Dittmer, Jason. "Comic Book Visualities: A Methodological Manifesto on Geography, Montage, and Narration." *Transactions of the Institute of British Geographers* 35.2 (2010): 222–236.

Doane, Mary Ann. *The Emergence of Cinematic Time: Modernity, Contingency, the Archive*. Cambridge, MA: Harvard University Press, 2002.

Dorling, Daniel, and Daniel Fairbairn. *Mapping: Ways of Representing the World*. London: Longman, 1997.

Dove, Jane. "Geographical Board Game: Promoting Tourism and Travel in Georgian England and Wales." *Journal of Tourism History* 8.1 (2016): 1–18.

Downey, Glen Robert. "The Truth About Pawn Promotion: The Development of the Chess Motif in Victorian Fiction." PhD dissertation, University of Victoria, 1998.

Duncan, Ian. "Authenticity Effects: The Work of Fiction in Romantic Scotland." *South Atlantic Quarterly* 102.1 (2003): 93–116.

Dyson, Freeman. "Why Is Maxwell's Theory So Hard to Understand?" *The Second European Conference on Antennas and Propagation*. 11–16 November 2007, Edinburgh. London: Institution of Engineering and Technology, 2007, 1–6.

Edinburgh Life Assurance Company. *Prospectus and Rates*. Edinburgh,1849.

Eliot, George. *Adam Bede*. Ed. Stephen Gill. 1859. London: Penguin Books, 1985.

——. *Daniel Deronda*. 1876. London: Penguin Books, 2003.

——. *Middlemarch*. 1871–72. London: Penguin Books, 1965.

Elliott, Mary. *The Wax-Taper, or, Effects of Bad Habits*. London: William Darton, 1819.

Ermarth, Elizabeth D. "George Eliot's Conception of Sympathy." *Nineteenth-Century Fiction* 40.1 (1985): 23–42.

Everett, Hugh. "'Relative State' Formulation of Quantum Mechanics." *Reviews of Modern Physics* 29.3 (1957): 434–462.

Ewald, François. "Insurance and Risk." In *The Foucault Effect: Studies in Governmentality*. Eds. Graham Burchell, Colin Gordon, and Peter Miller. Chicago: University of Chicago Press, 1991, 197–210.

Fildes, John. "Campaign Builds to Construct Babbage Analytical Engine." *BBC News* (14 October 2010). http://www.bbc.co.uk/news/technology-11530905

Fisher, Richard Trott. *Lays of Ancient Babyland: To Which Are Added Divers Small Histories Not Known to the Ancients*. London: Basil M. Pickering, 1857.

Flint, Kate. *The Victorians and the Visual Imagination*. Cambridge: Cambridge University Press, 2000.

Francis, John. *Annals, Anecdotes and Legends: A Chronicle of Life Assurance*. London: Longman, Brown, Green, and Longmans, 1853.

Freedgood, Elaine. *Victorian Writing About Risk: Imagining a Safe England in a Dangerous World*. Cambridge: Cambridge University Press, 2000.

Fyfe, Aileen. *Steam-Powered Knowledge: William Chambers and the Business of Publishing, 1820–1860*. Chicago: University of Chicago Press, 2012.

Fyfe, Paul. *By Accident or Design: Writing the Victorian Metropolis*. Oxford: Oxford University Press, 2015.

Gallagher, Catherine. "The Formalism of Military History." *Representations* 104.1 (2008): 23–33.

——. "George Eliot: Immanent Victorian." *Representations* 90.1 (2005): 61–74.

——. *Telling It Like It Wasn't: The Counterfactual Imagination in History and Fiction*. Chicago: University of Chicago Press, 2018.

——. "What Would Napoleon Do? Historical, Fictional, and Counterfactual Characters." *New Literary History* 42.2 (2011): 315–336.

Gardner, Martin. "Word Ladders: Lewis Carroll's Doublets." *The Mathematical Gazette* 80.487 (1996): 195–198.

Garratt, Peter. *Victorian Empiricism: Self, Knowledge, and Reality in Ruskin, Bain, Lewes, Spencer, and George Eliot*. Madison, NJ: Fairleigh Dickinson University Press, 2010.

Genette, Gérard. *Narrative Discourse: An Essay in Method*. Trans. Jane E. Lewin. Ithaca: Cornell University Press, 1980.

George, Alexander. *The Everlasting Check: Hume on Miracles*. Cambridge, MA: Harvard University Press, 2016.

George Eliot's Daniel Deronda Notebooks. Ed. Jane Irwin. Cambridge: Cambridge University Press, 1996.

Gettelman, Debra. "That Imagined 'Otherwise': *Middlemarch*'s Counterfictions." North American Victorian Studies Association Conference. 13 November 2014, London, Ontario.

——. "Reading Ahead in George Eliot." *Novel: A Forum on Fiction* 39.1 (2005): 25–47.

Gilbert, Pamela. *Mapping the Victorian Social Body*. Albany: State University of New York Press, 2004.

Gold, Barri J. *Thermopoetics: Energy in Victorian Literature and Science*. Cambridge, MA: MIT Press, 2010.

Goodfellow, Caroline. *A Collector's Guide to Games and Puzzles*. London: Chartwell House, 1992.

Gould, Rebecca. "*Adam Bede*'s Dutch Realism and the Novelist's Point of View." *Philosophy and Literature* 36.2 (2012): 404–423.

Gould, Stephen Jay. "The Dodo in the Caucus Race." *Natural History* 105.11 (November 1996): 22–33.

——. *The Structure of Evolutionary Theory*. Cambridge, MA: Harvard University Press, 2002.

Grant, Maurice. *The People's Guide to Life Insurance*. London, c. 1870.

Grattan-Guinness, Ivor. "Charles Babbage as an Algorithmic Thinker." *IEEE Annals of the History of Computing* 14.3 (1992): 34–48.

Green, Christopher D. "Was Babbage's Analytical Engine Intended to Be a Mechanical Model of the Mind?" *History of Psychology* 8.1 (2005): 35–45.

Greiner, Rae. "Sympathy Time: Adam Smith, George Eliot, and the Realist Novel." *Narrative* 17.3 (2009): 291–311.

——. "Thinking of Me Thinking of You: Sympathy Versus Empathy in the Realist Novel." *Victorian Studies* 53.3 (2011): 417–426.

Grener, Adam. *Improbability, Chance, and the Nineteenth-Century Realist Novel*. Columbus: Ohio State University Press, 2020.

Griffiths, Devin. *The Age of Analogy: Science and Literature Between the Darwins*. Baltimore: Johns Hopkins University Press, 2016.

Grishakova, Marina. "Narrative Causality Denaturalized." In *Unnatural Narratives— Unnatural Narratology*. Eds. Jan Alber and Rüdiger Heinze. Berlin: DeGruyter, 2011, 127–144.

Groensteen, Thierry. *The System of Comics*. Trans. Bart Beaty and Nick Nguyen. Jackson: University Press of Mississippi, 2007.

Grossman, Jonathan H. *Charles Dickens's Networks: Public Transport and the Novel*. Oxford: Oxford University Press, 2012.

Groth, Helen. "Projections of Alice: Anachronistic Reading and the Temporality of Mediation." *Textual Practice* 26.4 (2012): 667–686.

Gunning, Tom. "Animating the Nineteenth Century: Bringing Pictures to Life (or Life to Pictures?)." *Nineteenth-Century Contexts* 36.5 (2014): 459–472.

——. "Hand and Eye: Excavating a New Technology of the Image in the Victorian Era." *Victorian Studies* 54.3 (2012): 495–516.

Guyer, Sara. "Girl with the Open Mouth: Through the Looking Glass." *Angelaki* 9.1 (2004): 159–163.

Hacking, Ian. *The Taming of Chance*. Cambridge: Cambridge University Press, 1990.

Hahn, Roger. *Pierre Simon Laplace, 1749–1827: A Determined Scientist*. Cambridge, MA: Harvard University Press, 2005.

Harman, P. M. "Introduction." In *The Scientific Letters and Papers of James Clerk Maxwell*. Vol. 2. Ed. P. M. Harman. Cambridge: Cambridge University Press, 1990, 1–37.

Heimann, P. M. "Molecular Forces, Statistical Representation and Maxwell's Demon." *Studies in History and Philosophy of Science, Part A* 1.3 (1970): 189–211.

Helfand, Jessica. *Scrapbooks: An American History*. New Haven: Yale University Press, 2008.

Hemmo, Meir, and Orly R. Shenker. *The Road to Maxwell's Demon: Conceptual*

Foundations of Statistical Mechanics. Cambridge: Cambridge University Press, 2012.

Henderson, Andrea. "Symbolic Logic and the Logic of Symbolism." *Critical Inquiry* 41.1 (2014): 78–101.

Henkle, Roger B. "Carroll's Narratives Underground: 'Modernism' and Form." In *Lewis Carroll: A Celebration, Essays on the Occasion of the 150th Anniversary of the Birth of Charles Lutwidge Dodgson*. Ed. Edward Guiliano. New York: Clarkson N. Potter, 1982, 89–100.

Herbert, Christopher. *Victorian Relativity: Radical Thought and Scientific Discovery*. Chicago: University of Chicago Press, 2001.

Heringman, Noah. *Romantic Rocks, Aesthetic Geology*. Ithaca: Cornell University Press, 2004.

[Herschel, John]. "Review of *Lettres à S. A. R. le Duc Règnant de Saxe-Cobourg et Gotha sur la Théorie des Probabilités Appliquée aux Sciences Morales et Politiques* [Letters Addressed to H. R. H. the Grand Duke of Saxe-Cobourg and Gotha on the Theory of Probabilities as Applied to the Moral and Political Sciences], by M. A. Quetelet." *Edinburgh Review* 92.185 (July 1850): 1–57.

Hesketh, Ian. *The Science of History in Victorian Britain: Making the Past Speak*. London: Pickering and Chatto, 2011.

"Hints Respecting the Study of Geography." *The Bee* 6 (14 December 1791): 208–214.

The History of Dick Whittington, Lord Mayor of London. Banbury: J. G. Rusher [1820].

The History of the House That Jack Built. Wellington: F. Houlston & Son [c. 1820].

Hollingsworth, Cristopher. "Improvising Spaces: Victorian Photography, Carrollian Narrative, and Modern Collage." In *Alice Beyond Wonderland: Essays for the Twenty-First Century*. Ed. Cristopher Hollingsworth. Iowa City: University of Iowa Press, 2009, 85–100.

Howgego, James. *Printed Maps of London Circa 1553–1850*, 2nd ed. Folkestone, Kent: Dawson, 1984.

Hume, David. *An Enquiry Concerning Human Understanding: A Critical Edition*. Ed. Tom L. Beauchamp. Oxford: Oxford University Press, 2000.

Hyde, Ralph. "Panoramas and the Illustrated Weeklies." *The Map Collector* 31 (June 1985): 2–7.

"Introduction." *Saturday Magazine* 1 (7 July 1832): 1.

Jaffe, Audrey. *The Affective Life of the Average Man: The Victorian Novel and the Stock-Market Graph*. Columbus: Ohio State University Press, 2010.

Jones, Miriam. "'The Usual Sad Catastrophe': From the Street to the Parlor in *Adam Bede*." *Victorian Literature and Culture* 32.2 (2004): 305–326.

Kahneman, Daniel. "Varieties of Counterfactual Thinking." *What Might Have Been: The Social Psychology of Counterfactual Thinking*. Eds. Neal J. Roese and James M. Olson. New York: Psychology Press, 1995, 375–396.

Kaiser, Matthew. *The World in Play: Portraits of a Victorian Concept*. Stanford: Stanford University Press, 2012.

Kafalenos, Emma. *Narrative Causalities*. Columbus: Ohio State University Press, 2006.

Kern, Stephen. *A Cultural History of Causality: Science, Murder Novels, and Systems of Thought*. Princeton: Princeton University Press, 2004.

Ketabgian, Tamara. *The Lives of Machines: The Industrial Imaginary in Victorian Literature and Culture*. Ann Arbor: University of Michigan Press, 2011.

———. "Prosthetic Divinity: Babbage's Engine, Spiritual Intelligence, and the Senses." *Victorian Review* 35.2 (2009): 33–36.

Kincaid, James. *Child-Loving: The Erotic Child and Victorian Culture*. New York: Routledge, 1992.

Klaver, J. M. I. *Geology and Religious Sentiment: The Effect of Geological Discoveries on English Society and Literature Between 1829 and 1859*. Leiden: Brill, 1997.

Knoepflmacher, U. C. "Religious Humanism and the Victorian Novel: A Postscript." In *British Victorian Literature: Critical Assessments*. Ed. Shiv K. Kumar. New Delhi: Atlantic Publishers, 2002, 202–214.

Kolb, Margaret. "Plot Circles: Hardy's Drunkards and Their Walks." *Victorian Studies* 56.4 (2014): 595–623.

Kreisel, Deanna. "Incognito, Intervention, and Dismemberment in *Adam Bede*." *ELH* 70.2 (2003): 541–574.

Lardner, Dionysius. "Babbage's Calculating Engine." In *The Works of Charles Babbage*. Vol. 2. Ed. Martin Campbell-Kelly. London: William Pickering, 1989, 118–186.

Legal and Commercial Life Assurance Society. [Prospectus]. n. d.

Leibniz, Gottfried Wilhelm. *Theodicy: Essays on the Goodness of God, the Freedom of Man, and the Origin of Evil*. Ed. Austin Farrer. Trans. E. M. Huggard. La Salle, IL: Open Court, 1985.

Levine, Caroline. *Forms: Whole, Rhythm, Hierarchy, Network*. Princeton: Princeton University Press, 2017.

Levine, George. *Darwin and the Novelists: Patterns of Science in Victorian Fiction*. Chicago: University of Chicago Press, 1988.

———. *Darwin the Writer*. Oxford: Oxford University Press, 2011.

———. "*Daniel Deronda*: A New Epistemology." In *Knowing the Past: Victorian Literature and Culture*. Ed. Suzy Anger. Ithaca: Cornell University Press, 2001, 52–73.

———. *Dying to Know: Scientific Epistemology and Narrative in Victorian England*. Chicago: University of Chicago Press, 2002.

———. "George Eliot's Hypothesis of Reality." *Nineteenth-Century Literature* 35.1 (1980): 1–28.

Li, Hao. *Memory and History in George Eliot: Transfiguring the Past*. London: Macmillan, 2000.

Lightman, Bernard. *Evolutionary Naturalism in Victorian Britain: The "Darwinians" and Their Critics*. Burlington, VT: Ashgate/Variorum, 2009.

———. *The Origins of Agnosticism: Victorian Unbelief and the Limits of Knowledge*. Baltimore: Johns Hopkins University Press, 1987.

———. "Spectacle in Leicester Square: James Wyld's Great Globe, 1851–61." In *Popular Exhibitions: Science and Showmanship, 1840–1910*. Eds. Joe Kember, John Plunkett, and Jill A. Sullivan. London: Pickering and Chatto, 2014, 19–40.

———. *Victorian Popularizers of Science: Designing Nature for New Audiences*. Chicago: University of Chicago Press, 2007.

Liu, Alan. *Local Transcendence: Essays on Postmodern Historicism and the Database*. Chicago: University of Chicago Press, 2008.

London and Lancashire Life Assurance Company. Advertisement. *Indian Spectator* [Bombay, India] (17 March 1895): 216.

Lopez, Alan. "Deleuze with Carroll: Schizophrenia and Simulacrum and the Philosophy of Lewis Carroll's Nonsense." *Angelaki* 9.3 (2004): 101–120.

Lovelace, Ada. "Sketch of the Analytical Engine." In *The Works of Charles Babbage*. Vol. 3. Ed. Martin Campbell-Kelly. London: William Pickering, 1989, 89–170.

Lovell-Smith, Rose. "The Animals of Wonderland: Tenniel as Carroll's Reader." *Criticism* 45.4 (2003): 383–415.

Lovett, Charlie. *Lewis Carroll Among His Books: A Descriptive Catalogue of the Private Library of Charles L. Dodgson*. Jefferson, NC: McFarland, 2005.

Lubenow, William C. *"Only Connect": Learned Societies in Nineteenth-Century Britain*. Woodbridge: Boydell & Brewer, 2015.

Luhmann, Niklas. *Observations on Modernity*. Trans. William Whobrey. Stanford: Stanford University Press, 1998.

Lutz, Deborah. "A Portrait of the Writer as a Young Woman, by Emily and Charlotte Brontë." Lecture. 2018 Victorian Studies Association of Ontario. 28 April 2018, Toronto.

Lynch, Deidre. "Recycled Paper: Readers' Scrapbooks in Late Georgian Literary Culture." 2012 Jackman Humanities Institute, University of Toronto, 22 March 2012.

Lyell, Charles. *Principles of Geology*. 3 vols. London: John Murray, 1830–33.

Madden, Fred. "Orthographic Transformations in *Through the Looking Glass*." *Jabberwocky* 64 (1985): 67–76.

Martins, Luciana de Lima. "Mapping Tropical Waters: British Views and Visions of Rio de Janeiro." In *Mappings*. Ed. Denis Cosgrove. London: Reaktion Books, 1999, 148–168.

Matz, Jesse. *Modernist Time Ecology*. Baltimore: Johns Hopkins University Press, 2019.

Maxwell, James Clerk. "Draft Letter to Francis W. H. Petrie (c. 15 March 1875)." In *The Scientific Letters and Papers of James Clerk Maxwell*. Vol. 3. Ed. P. M. Harman. Cambridge: Cambridge University Press, 1990, 194.

——. "Drafts of Lecture on 'Molecules' (c. August/September 1873)." In *The Scientific Letters and Papers of James Clerk Maxwell*. Vol. 2. Ed. P. M. Harman. Cambridge: Cambridge University Press, 1990, 922–933.

——. "Essay for the Eranus Club on Science and Free Will (11 February 1873)." In *The Scientific Letters and Papers of James Clerk Maxwell*. Vol. 2. Ed. P. M. Harman. Cambridge: Cambridge University Press, 1990, 814–823.

——. "Letter to Herbert Spencer (5 December 1873)." In *The Scientific Letters and Papers of James Clerk Maxwell*. Vol. 2. Ed. P. M. Harman. Cambridge: Cambridge University Press, 1990, 956–961.

——. "Letter to Hugh Andrew Johnstone Munro (7 February 1866)." In *The Scientific Letters and Papers of James Clerk Maxwell*. Vol. 2. Ed. P. M. Harman. Cambridge: Cambridge University Press, 1990, 250–252.

——. "Letter to John William Strutt (6 December 1870)." In *The Scientific Letters and Papers of James Clerk Maxwell*. Vol. 2. Ed. P. M. Harman. Cambridge: Cambridge University Press, 1990, 582–588.

——. "Letter to John William Strutt (15 March 1871)." In *The Scientific Letters and Papers of James Clerk Maxwell*. Vol. 2. Ed. P. M. Harman. Cambridge: Cambridge University Press, 1990, 614–616.

——. "Letter to Lewis Campbell (c. July 1850)." In *The Scientific Letters and Papers of James Clerk Maxwell*. Vol. 1. Ed. P. M. Harman. Cambridge: Cambridge University Press, 1990, 193–198.

——. "Manuscript on the History of the Kinetic Theory of Gases: Notes for William Thomson (c. summer 1871)." In *The Scientific Letters and Papers of James Clerk Maxwell*. Vol. 2. Ed. P. M. Harman. Cambridge: Cambridge University Press, 1990, 654–660.

——. "Molecules." *Nature* 8 (25 Sept 1873): 437–441.

——. "Note to Tait 'Concerning Demons' (c. 1875)." In *The Scientific Letters and Papers of James Clerk Maxwell*. Vol. 3. Ed. P. M. Harman. Cambridge: Cambridge University Press, 1990, 185–187.

——. "On the Dynamical Evidence of the Molecular Constitution of Bodies." *Nature* 11 (11 March 1875): 374–77.

——. "On the Dynamical Theory of Gases." *Philosophical Transactions of the Royal Society of London* 157 (1867): 49–88.

——. "Presidential Address, Section A.—Mathematical and Physical Science." *Nature* (22 September 1870): 419–422.

——. *Theory of Heat*. London: Longmans, Green, and Co., 1871.

——. *A Treatise on Electricity and Magnetism*. Vol. 1. Oxford: Clarendon Press, 1873.

May, Leila S. "Wittgenstein's Reflection in Lewis Carroll's *Looking-Glass*." *Philosophy and Literature* 31.1 (2007): 79–94.

McCloud, Scott. *Understanding Comics: The Invisible Art*. New York: Harper Perennial, 1994.

McDonagh, Josephine. "Child-Murder Narratives in George Eliot's *Adam Bede*: Embedded Histories and Fictional Representation." *Nineteenth-Century Literature* 56.2 (2001): 228–259.

Meisel, Martin. *Realizations: Narrative, Pictorial, and Theatrical Arts in Nineteenth-Century England*. Princeton: Princeton University Press, 1983.

Menabrea, L. F. "Notions sur la Machine Analytique de M. Charles Babbage." In *The Works of Charles Babbage*. Vol. 3. Ed. Martin Campbell-Kelly. London: William Pickering, 1989, 62–82.

Merali, Zeeya. "Demonic Device Converts Information to Energy." *Nature News* (14 November 2010). https://www.nature.com/news/2010/101114/full/news.2010.606.html

Merry Rhymes and Stories for Merry Little Learners: With Numerous Laughable Pictures. Illus. Charles Henry Bennett. London: Ward, Lock and Tyler [c. 1865–72].

Metropolitan Counties and General Life Assurance, Annuity, Loan, and Investment Society. [Prospectus]. London, c. 1850.

Miller, Andrew. "Lives Unled in Realist Fiction." *Representations* 98.1 (2007): 118–134.

Miller, Gordon. "Charles Babbage and the Design of Intelligence: Computers and Society in 19th-Century England." *Bulletin of Science, Technology & Society* 10.2 (1990): 68–76.

Minerva Life Assurance. Prospectus. 1850.

Mitchell, Rebecca N. "Before and After: *Punch*, Steampunk, and Victorian Graphic Narrativity." In *Drawing on the Victorians: The Palimpsest of Victorian and Neo-Victorian Graphic Texts*. Eds. Anna Maria Jones and Rebecca N. Mitchell. Athens: Ohio University Press, 2017, 237–266.

"Model of the Battle of Waterloo." *The Mirror* 32.916 (13 October 1838): 249.

Monk, Leland. *Standard Deviations: Chance and the Modern British Novel*. Stanford: Stanford University Press, 1993.

Nadel, Ira. "'The Mansion of Bliss,' or the Place of Play in Victorian Life and Literature." *Children's Literature* 10 (1982): 18–36.

Nead, Lynda. *Victorian Babylon: People, Streets and Images in Nineteenth-Century London*. New Haven: Yale University Press, 2000.

New, Peter. "Chance, Providence and Destiny in George Eliot's Fiction." *English* 34.150 (1985): 191–208.

Norcia, Megan. "Playing Empire: Children's Parlor Games, Home Theatricals, and Improvisational Play." *Children's Literature Association Quarterly* 29.4 (2004): 294–314.

Nord, Deborah Epstein. "George Eliot and John Everett Millais: The Ethics and Aesthetics of Realism." *Victorian Studies* 60.3 (2018): 361–389.

Nursery Tales for Good Little Boys: Containing Hop O' My Thumb, the Butterfly's Ball, Little Dog Trusty, the Cherry Orchard, Dick Whittington & His Cat, Punch and Judy; with Coloured Illustrations. London: Routledge, Warne, and Routledge, 1860.

O'Connor, Ralph. *The Earth on Show: Fossils and the Poetics of Popular Science, 1802–1856.* Chicago: University of Chicago Press, 2007.

Oriental Life Company. Advertisement. *Indian Spectator* [Bombay, India] (17 March 1895): 202.

Paley, William. *Natural Theology, or Evidence of the Existence and Attributes of the Deity, Collected from the Appearances of Nature.* Eds. Matthew D. Eddy and David Knight. 1802. Oxford: Oxford University Press, 2006.

Palmer, Sally B. "Projecting the Gaze: The Magic Lantern, Cultural Discipline, and *Villette.*" *Victorian Review* 32.1 (2006): 18–40.

Pardon, George Frederick. "Dick Whittington." *Reynold's Miscellany of Romance, General Literature, Science, and Art* 13.337 (23 December 1854): 345.

Parlett, David. *The Oxford History of Board Games.* Oxford: Oxford University Press, 1999.

Pater, Walter. *The Renaissance: Studies in Art and Poetry.* Ed. Adam Phillips. 1873. Oxford: Oxford University Press, 1996.

Penner, Barbara. *Newlyweds on Tour: Honeymooning in Nineteenth-Century America.* Durham: University of New Hampshire Press, 2009.

Pocock, Lewis. *A Familiar Explanation of the Nature, Advantages and Importance of Assurances upon Lives.* London: Smith, Elder and Co., 1842.

Poovey, Mary. *A History of the Modern Fact: Problems of Knowledge in the Sciences of Wealth and Society.* Chicago: University of Chicago Press, 1998.

——. *Making a Social Body: British Cultural Formation, 1830–1864.* Chicago: University of Chicago Press, 1995.

"Popular Illustrations of Life Assurance." *Saturday Magazine* 11 (1 July 1837): 5–7.

Porter, Theodore M. *The Rise of Statistical Thinking: 1820–1900.* Princeton: Princeton University Press, 1986.

——. "A Statistical Survey of Gases: Maxwell's Social Physics." *Historical Studies in the Physical Sciences* 12 (1981): 77–116.

Pratt, Henry John. "Narrative in Comics." *Journal of Art and Aesthetics* 67.1 (2009): 107–117.

Prudential Insurance. Prospectus. c. 1849.

Prudential Mutual Assurance, Investment, and Loan Association. Prospectus [c. 1849–50].

Puckett, Kent. "Caucus-Racing." *Novel: A Forum on Fiction* 47.1 (2014): 11–23.

Pycior, Helena M. "At the Intersection of Mathematics and Humor: Lewis Carroll's 'Alices' and Symbolical Algebra." *Victorian Studies* 28 (1984): 149–170.

Pyle, Forest. "A Novel Sympathy: The Imagination of Community in George Eliot." *Novel: A Forum on Fiction* 27.1 (1993): 5–23.

Rackin, Donald. "Blessed Rage: Lewis Carroll and the Modern Quest for Order." In *Lewis Carroll: A Celebration, Essays on the Occasion of the 150th Anniversary of the Birth of Charles Lutwidge Dodgson.* Ed. Edward Guiliano. New York: Clarkson N. Potter, 1982, 15–25.

Railway Passengers' Assurance Company. Prospectus. London, c. 1866.

Ray, Romita. "The Beast in a Box: Playing with Empire in Early Nineteenth-century Britain." *Visual Resources* 22.1 (2006): 7–31.

"Registration of Sickness." *All the Year Round* 4 (1860): 227–228.

Rescher, Nicholas. *Conditionals.* Cambridge, MA: MIT Press, 2007.

"Review of *A Comparative View of the Various Institutions for the Assurance of Lives,* by Charles Babbage." *Edinburgh Review* 45 (1827): 482–513.

"Review of *A Physical and Political School Geography.*" *The Critic* 9.213 (15 February 1850): 99.

"Review of *Tentamen; or an Essay Towards the History of Whittington, Some Time Lord Mayor of London.*" *The Literary Gazette* 4.191 (16 September 1820): 594–596.

Richardson, Brian. *Unlikely Stories: Causality and the Nature of Modern Narrative.* Newark: University of Delaware Press, 1997.

Rickards, Maurice. *Encyclopedia of Ephemera: A Guide to the Fragmentary Documents of Everyday Life for the Collector, Curator and Historian.* Ed. Michael Twyman. London: British Library, 2000.

Roese, Neal J., and James M. Olson. "Counterfactual Thinking: A Critical Overview." In *What Might Have Been: The Social Psychology of Counterfactual Thinking.* Eds. Neal J. Roese and James M. Olson. New York: Psychology Press, 1995, 1–55.

Romano, Richard M. "The Economic Ideas of Charles Babbage." *History of Political Economy* 14 (1982): 385–405.

Rosenthal, Jesse. "The Large Novel and the Law of Large Numbers; or, Why George Eliot Hates Gambling." *ELH* 77.3 (2010): 777–811.

Rothfield, Lawrence. *Vital Signs: Medical Realism in Nineteenth-Century Fiction.* Princeton: Princeton University Press, 1992.

"Royal Surrey Zoological Gardens." Advertisement. *The Examiner* 2007 (18 July 1846): 462.

Rudwick, Martin. *Bursting the Limits of Time: The Reconstruction of Geohistory in the Age of Revolution.* Chicago: University of Chicago Press, 2005.

——. "Lyell, Sir Charles, First Baronet (1797–1875), Geologist." *Oxford Dictionary of National Biography.*

——. "Minerals, Strata and Fossils." In *Cultures of Natural History.* Eds. N. Jardine, J. A. Secord, and E. C. Spary. Cambridge: Cambridge University Press, 1996, 266–286.

——. *Worlds Before Adam: The Reconstruction of Geohistory in the Age of Reform.* Chicago: University of Chicago Press, 2008.

Ryan, Marie-Laure. "Cheap Plot Tricks, Plot Holes, and Narrative Design." *Narrative* 17.1 (2009): 56–75.

——. *Possible Worlds, Artificial Intelligence, and Narrative Theory.* Bloomington: Indiana University Press, 1991.

——. "Toward a Definition of Narrative." In *The Cambridge Companion to Narrative.* Ed. David Herman. Cambridge: Cambridge University Press, 2007, 22–36.

Ryan, Marie-Laure, Kenneth Foote, and Maoz Azaryahu. *Narrating Space/Spatializing Narrative: Where Narrative Theory and Geography Meet.* Columbus: Ohio State University Press, 2016.

Schaffer, Simon. "Babbage's Intelligence: Calculating Engines and the Factory System." *Critical Inquiry* 21 (1994): 203–227.

Searls, David B. "From *Jabberwocky* to Genome: Lewis Carroll and Computational Biology." *Journal of Comparative Biology* 8.3 (2001): 339–348.

The Second Chapter of Accidents and Remarkable Events: Containing Caution and Instruction for Children. London: Darton and Harvey, 1801.

Secord, James A. *Victorian Sensation: The Extraordinary Publication, Reception, and Secret Authorship of* Vestiges of the Natural History of Creation. Chicago: University of Chicago Press, 2000.

——. "Introduction." In Charles Lyell, *Principles of Geology.* 1830–33. London: Penguin Books, 1997.

——. *Visions of Science: Books and Readers at the Dawn of the Victorian Age.* Chicago: University of Chicago Press, 2014.

——. "Scrapbook Science: Composite Caricatures in Late Georgian England." In *Figuring It Out: Science, Gender, and Visual Culture.* Eds. Ann B. Shteir and Bernard Lightman. Hanover, NH: Dartmouth College Press, 2006, 164–191.

Sedgwick, Eve Kosofsky. *Between Men: English Literature and Male Homosocial Desire.* New York: Columbia University Press, 1985.

Semmel, Stuart. "Reading the Tangible Past: British Tourism, Collecting, and Memory After Waterloo." *Representations* 69 (2000): 9–37.

Sharman, H. Riseborough. "Have You Insured Your Life? If Not—Why Not?" London: G. J. Stevenson, c. 1850.

Shuttleworth, Sally. *George Eliot and Nineteenth-Century Science: The Make-Believe of a Beginning*. Cambridge: Cambridge University Press, 1984.

Siemann, Catherine. "Curiouser and Curiouser: Law in the Alice Books." *Law and Literature* 24.3 (2012): 430–455.

"Sir Richard Whittington." In *The Merry Ballads of the Olden Time: Illustrated in Pictures & Rhyme*. London: Frederick Warne & Co., c. 1880.

"Sir Richard Whittington, Knt." *Sharpe's London Magazine* 1.8 (20 December 1845): 117–120.

Smith, Crosbie, and M. Norton Wise. *Energy and Empire: A Biographical Study of Lord Kelvin*. Cambridge: Cambridge University Press, 1989.

Smith, Jonathan. *Fact and Feeling: Baconian Science and the Nineteenth-Century Literary Imagination*. Madison: University of Wisconsin Press, 1994.

Smith, William. *Advertise: How? When? Where?* London: Routledge, Warne, and Routledge, 1863.

Spencer, Herbert. *The Data of Ethics*. 1879. New Brunswick, NJ: Transaction Publishers, 2011.

Spufford, Francis, and Jennifer S. Uglow, eds. *Cultural Babbage: Technology, Time and Invention*. London: Faber & Faber, 1996.

Spurr, Geoffrey. "The Contested Identity of the Victorian and Edwardian Clerk." Conference Presentation. 2004 North American Conference on British Studies. 29 October 2004, Philadelphia.

Stanley, Matthew. *Huxley's Church and Maxwell's Demon: From Theistic Science to Naturalistic Science*. Chicago: University of Chicago Press, 2016.

——. "The Pointsman: Maxwell's Demon, Victorian Free Will, and the Boundaries of Science." *Journal of the History of Ideas* 69.3 (2008): 467–491.

Steedman, Carolyn. *Dust: The Archive and Cultural History*. New Brunswick, NJ: Rutgers University Press, 2002.

Stern, Rebecca. "Time Passes: An Introduction to Temporalities." *Narrative* 7.3 (2009): 235–241.

Sussman, Herbert. *Victorian Technology: Invention, Innovation, and the Rise of the Machine*. Santa Barbara: Praeger, 2009.

Swade, Doron. "Charles Babbage (1791–1871)." In *Oxford Dictionary of National Biography*. Oxford University Press, 2018.

——. "'It Will Not Slice a Pineapple': Babbage, Miracles and Machines." In *Cultural Babbage: Technology, Time and Invention*. Eds. Francis Spufford and Jennifer S. Uglow. London: Faber & Faber, 1996, 53–80.

——. "The Construction of Charles Babbage's Difference Engine No. 2." *IEEE Annals of the History of Computing* 27.3 (2005): 70–88.

Thackeray, William Makepeace. *Vanity Fair*. 1848. Penguin Books, 1985.

Throesch, Elizabeth. "Nonsense in the Fourth Dimension of Literature: Hyperspace Philosophy, the 'New' Mathematics, and the Alice Books." In *Alice Beyond Wonderland: Essays for the Twenty-First Century*. Ed. Cristopher Hollingsworth. Iowa City: University of Iowa Press, 2009, 37–52.

Thrower, Norman J. W. *Maps & Civilization: Cartography in Culture and Society*. Chicago: University of Chicago Press, 2007.

Tondre, Michael. *The Physics of Possibility: Victorian Fiction, Science, and Gender*. Charlottesville: University of Virginia Press, 2018.

Topham, Jonathan. "Biology in the Service of Natural Theology: Paley, Darwin, and the *Bridgewater Treatises*." In *Biology and Ideology from Descartes to Dawkins*. Eds. Denis Alexander and Ronald L. Numbers. Chicago: University of Chicago Press, 2010, 88–113.

——. "Science and Popular Education in the 1830s: The Role of the *Bridgewater Treatises*." *British Journal for the History of Science* 25 (1992): 397–430.

Trollope, Anthony. *Barchester Towers*. 1857. London: Penguin Books, 1983.

Trumpener, Katie. *Bardic Nationalism: The Romantic Novel and British Empire*. Princeton: Princeton University Press, 1997.

Tyndall, John. "On the Scientific Use of the Imagination." In *Scientific Addresses*. New Haven: Charles Chatfield & Co., 1870, 33–74.

Uglow, Jennifer S. "Introduction: 'Possibility.'" In *Cultural Babbage: Technology, Time and Invention*. Eds. Francis Spufford and Jennifer S. Uglow. London: Faber & Faber, 1996, 1–23.

Vargish, Thomas. *The Providential Aesthetic in Victorian Fiction*. Charlottesville: University Press of Virginia, 1985.

Wall, Cynthia. *Grammars of Approach: Landscape, Narrative, and the Linguistic Picturesque*. Chicago: University of Chicago Press, 2019.

The Wanderings of Mrs. Pipe & Family to View the Crystal Palace. Illustrated by Percy Cruikshank. London: William Spooner, 1851.

Weber, Christian. "Elective Affinities/Wahlverwandtschaften: The Career of a Metaphor." In *Fact and Fiction: Literary and Scientific Cultures in Germany and Britain*. Ed. Christine Lehleiter. Toronto: University of Toronto Press, 2016, 97–129.

Whewell, William. *Astronomy and General Physics Considered with Reference to Natural Theology*. London, 1833.

——. *History of the Inductive Sciences: From the Earliest to the Present Time*. London: John W. Parker, 1837.

——. ["When any one acknowledges a moral governor"]. *Saturday Magazine* 10 (17 June 1837): 228.

Whitaker, Andrew. "Maxwell's Famous (or Infamous) Demon." In *James Clerk Maxwell: Perspectives on His Life and Work*. Eds. Raymond Flood, Mark McCartney, and Andrew Whitaker. Oxford: Oxford University Press, 2014, 163–186.

"Whittington and His Cat." *Saturday Magazine* 4.122 (31 May 1834): 201–202.

Williams, James A. "Lewis Carroll and the Private Life of Words." *Review of English Studies* 64 (2013): 651–671.

Wordsworth, William. "Lines Composed a Few Miles Above Tintern Abbey, on Revisiting the Banks of the Wye During a Tour. July 13, 1798." In *William Wordsworth: Selected Poems*. Ed. John O. Hayden. London: Penguin Books, 1994, 66–70.

——. *The Prelude, 1799, 1805, 1850*. Eds. Jonathan Wordsworth, M. H. Abrams, and Stephen Gill. New York: W. W. Norton, 1979.

Zemka, Sue. *Time and the Moment in Victorian Literature and Society*. Cambridge: Cambridge University Press, 2012.

Zimmerman, Virginia. *Excavating Victorians*. Buffalo: State University of New York Press, 2008.

——. "Natural History on Blocks, in Bodies, and on the Hearth: Juvenile Science Literature and Games, 1850–1875." *Configurations: A Journal of Literature, Science, and Technology* 19.3 (2011): 407–430.

Index